Combat Ready

Lessons Learned in the Journey to Fighter Pilot

Captain Taylor Fox

Combat Ready: The Journey from Civilian to Fighter Pilot.

Copyright 2016 by S. Taylor Fox. No part of this book may be used or reproduced in any manner whatsoever without written permission except in the case of brief quotations embodied in critical articles and reviews.

For more information visit at www.combatreadypilot.com.

Printed by CreateSpace

Approved under U.S Air Force Security and Policy Review,
Case #2016-11-14-001

Printed in the United States of America

SBN-13: 978-1540527684

ISBN-10: 1540527689

COMBAT READY

To my grandparents, Dobbie and Pop.

There is no journey without your support.

PREFACE

This is an unparalleled look at what it takes to go from being a kid in college with no plans of a military career to a fighter pilot flying the F-16 and F-22 in the U.S. Air Force. From doing pushups in the mud while getting yelled at to flying Mach 1 through the mountains at night wearing night vision goggles and dropping live bombs with 100 other aircraft in the fight, the journey is an amazing one and I hope you enjoy.

I had just been hired for the job and was traveling to my flight medical screening at Brooks Air Force Base in San Antonio. At the end of the trip, my grandparents, parents and friends all wanted to hear what the experience was like. It was then I knew I couldn't repeat the stories to each of them every week. Instead, I chose to write. Every week I would send the weeks' description and interesting stories to my closest family and friends. The result is this book as a summation of all of these posts. It is my real-time authentic voice as I experienced the stress and successes of pilot training. Only the beginning, the stories of my civilian flying, were not written as I was going through the experience.

As I reread the posts, some of them embarrass me, some I now disagree with, but most I am proud of. It will have undoubtedly been the greatest journey of my life. I hope it gives insight into the lives of a small but privileged community.

I should also mention this is the experience of just one pilot going through the journey and I am sure others have had far different experiences, even within my classes. I have left out some names but others gave me permission to include them in the story. I also left out most of the tactical discussion after I began flying the F-16 and F-22 for obvious reasons. Other than that, I don't hold back.

At the end of some of the posts I have included a lesson learned, not necessarily about flying, but about business and life. The Air Force has taught me how to fly these jets but it has also taught me a lot about myself and those around me. I expect you will find many of these applicable in your life, no matter what your profession.

You may also find the glossary at the end of the book helpful.

CONTENTS

INTRODUCTION 6

PART 1: LIFE AS A CIVILIAN 9

PART 2: PRE-PILOT TRAINING 26

PART 3: UNDERGRADUTE PILOT TRAINING (UPT) 40

PART 4: INTRODUCTION TO FIGHTER FUNDAMENTALS (IFF) ... 135

PART 5: THE VIPER B-COURSE 158

PART 6: MISSION QUALIFICATION TRAINING 242

AFTERWORD 247

INTRODUCTION

It's a clear January night in 2015 and I am walking out to my F-16 with the Las Vegas strip providing a jarring contrast to the F-15s, F-15Es, F-22s and Eurofighters I am about to fight with and against. There is a loud high-pitched whistle from adjacent idling jets as I inspect the missiles and six live 500 lb bombs I will be dropping tonight. This mission is a part of Red Flag, the world's largest advanced aerial combat exercise. Tonight there will be over one hundred and forty jets fighting in one airspace and the job of my four ship (formation of four F-16s) is to put bombs on a surface-to-air missile site.

After deeming the jet airworthy and starting the engine, I go through a variety of checks to make sure all of the sensors, cameras, flight controls and weapons are ready for the mission. I organize my target photos and stow my NVGs (night vision goggles) to the side, waiting for my flight lead to taxi our four ship out to the runway.

Over the radio I hear the other pilots say, "Lobo check," "2," "3," and I respond with "4."

"Nellis ground, Lobo 1, taxi four Vipers from the Red Flag ramp, information Juliet." With that, our mission begins. We have a precise takeoff time as we only have a five-minute window to drop our bombs, about forty-five minutes from now. We have been preparing this mission to get those bombs on target within that window of time for twenty-four hours. After being cleared for takeoff, I watch three 30' flames roar down the runway in twenty second intervals, before I follow in my F-16. I push the power up, checking the engine gauges before throwing the throttle full forward into max afterburner. A second or two later, I feel a kick and the rapid acceleration begins. The big flame has lit and 29,000 lbs of thrust is hurtling me down the runway. At 155 knots I pull back on the stick and the rumble of the imperfect runway gives way to the perfect calm air of the night sky. After raising the gear, I am accelerating through 350 knots and locking #3 up with my radar to follow them to the fight airspace.

COMBAT READY

There is complete darkness over the uninhabited desert so I throw on my night vision goggles. I now see the world, the mountains and desert landscape, through a fuzzy green filter. I am setting up the infrared camera, ensuring the bombs are ready, flying in the proper formation and listening to updates of the war over the radio and via text messages sent to the jet.

Tonight our four ship is staying low, hugging mountains to hide from SAMs (surface-to-air missiles) and keeping out of the chaotic air-to-air war that will undoubtedly unfold above. Other jets should be providing an escort cover so we can focus on our bombing but we have heat-seeking and radar-guided missiles to attack enemy aircraft as well.

As we change to the fight radio frequency, the war is well underway. There isn't a second of quiet time as guys are shooting and getting shot, and the air battle manager is trying to help everyone understand what's going on. Through my NVGs, I see hundreds of lights flashing and airplanes expending fireballs, called flares, all across the sky. It is chaos. About that time my flight lead signals us all to drop it down to the floor and push west toward the enemy targets. It now feels like a surreal dream as I am screaming through mountains at 600 mph while keeping track of three other jets in my formation, at times upside down to stay as close to the mountain peaks as we legally can through these NVGs. Without them on, I can't see anything.

As we cross into enemy territory, I get a terrible beeping in my headset and despite my best efforts to go unnoticed by enemy SAMs, they are tracking me. I push the throttle forward to light the afterburner and begin a maneuver I hope will defeat the radar tracking me and if he shoots, defeat the missile as well. I let the entire war know of my situation, "Lobo 4, Mud 2 bearing 260, Bullseye 080 for 60!" Hopefully someone will kill it before it kills me. This is a high G-force maneuver with a lot of turning and I need to make sure I don't smack into the side of a mountain. Instead I use the mountain to hide from where I think the SAM is and the warning goes away. I am safe, for now.

We continue to press west with everyone in my flight getting tracked by different SAMs but no aircraft have targeted us. We have been aggressively flying low for almost fifteen minutes and are just 15 miles from the target when we hear two enemy aircraft are headed our way. We pop up to gain a few thousand feet to put our cameras on the target. I am supposed to put all six of my bombs on one missile-launching site and I am frantically searching in the 4x4-inch camera screen to find it in this complex of structures. If I can't, we will have to start circling the target area to find it, making ourselves an easy target for the enemy and tonight, that almost certainly means death. I am now four miles from dropping, making sure I don't run into my wingman, when I get another warning of a SAM tracking me. I don't care. I need to find this damn target and I am struggling. The entire success of the mission rests on finding this tiny missile silo and because we are low, it is hard to see with other structures blocking the view. With fifteen seconds to release, the sweat pouring down my face, I am blinded and my NVGs go white temporarily before quickly recovering. I look to the right and see four mushroom clouds of explosions from the flight of four F-15Es next to us, lighting up the entire sky. Holy shit, that was awesome, but I have no time to enjoy the view.

At ten seconds to release, I think I see the target. Unfortunately, "I think" is not good enough. I am about to consent to 3,000 lbs of explosives coming off my jet. I am about to choose who lives or dies with the red button under my right thumb and I have to be 100% confident before I hit it. Based on the target picture on my lap, the concrete slab under the launcher looks like a T but I can't see it yet. I start lining my jet up with that object, hoping I will see this confirming feature at the last second as mission success rests on it. At three seconds to release, the concrete T in the camera pod emerges and I hear Lobo 1 and 2 release their weapons. I let out a sigh of relief, continue to refine the steering to the target and hit the red button. I feel the six bombs ripple off my wings and then aggressively maneuver back east. I briefly lift the NVGs and roll up to 90 degrees of bank so I can watch the six, near instantaneous explosions create a fireball where the target once was right below my jet. The adrenaline is pumping now. The mission is a success and I can't help but smile. This is awesome.

PART 1: LIFE AS A CIVILIAN

"No yoops, papa." This was the deal I made at the age of three, unable to properly say "loops," with my grandfather before I would board any flight he was piloting until age eleven. I loved flying and sitting in the cockpit but the fear of going upside down was overwhelming. Everyone else in my family had performed numerous "yoops" with my grandfather, including my sister, who at fifteen months younger, I had written off as reckless and irresponsible. On trips to Disney World, I was the kid refusing to go on any of the rides. I preferred going to the various countries at Epcot to get my passport book stamped. For each decision at that age I looked at every risk and this generally led me to not pursue the more dangerous course of action—clearly not the expected mindset of someone willing to go to war in a fighter jet.

My grandfather, Jack Fox, but known to the family as "Pop," went to the University of Missouri to play football in the early 1950s but also joined the Air Force ROTC, having never flown in an airplane. After going through pilot training in a T-6 Texan, he ultimately flew the F-86D fighter jet, becoming an early member of the Mach Busters Club. To break the sound barrier in those days required a straight down nosedive at full power and then maybe, just maybe, you'd have enough speed to break through. He remained a pilot the rest of his life, flying corporately in his retirement. My grandparents had a couple planes so any time I was with them, we were inevitably near an airport.

Fortunately, at age eleven, my attitude changed. I looked up to my cousin Mike who was spending the summer learning to fly. This envy in what Mike was doing, along with the magic of flight, sparked a desire to be a pilot and within an hour, my grandpa had me in the air and upside down. The feeling of twists and turns was amazing and from that point on, I could not get enough. I started taking lessons immediately, propped up by my grandmother's couch pillows so I could see over the instrument panel and touch the rudder pedals.

I continued to fly off and on until I was sixteen, an age where you can actually start flying alone and work on getting licenses. I would drive the hour to my grandparents almost every weekend during the school year and spent the majority of the summer at their house, jumping into every airplane I could find. I got my private license on the day of my seventeenth birthday, my instrument license a few months later and my commercial and multi-engine license as soon as I turned eighteen.

The taste of military flying began with the 1942 Boeing Stearman my grandfather had rebuilt in the 1970s. A perfect yellow Navy paint scheme, the Stearman is an open cockpit bi-plane. I would argue it is one of the best planes in which to learn the basics of flying, just as they did during World War II. Planes of this era taught the basic stick and rudder skills far better than the planes of today. Starting my training in this plane with my grandfather's guidance gave me an advantage, a natural feel for flying that I could fall back on, even in an F-16.

Being a pilot at age 17 and competing in aerobatic contests tends to create a few interesting life dynamics. Putting it mildly, I had some confidence. I would like to think it was moderated to a decent degree but every day I would drive to the airport jamming to the Top Gun favorite, "Highway to the Danger Zone." I am almost embarrassed to write that but as I remember how pumped-up it made me feel, I wouldn't have done it any other way. Aviation is inherently exciting and when I reflect on my civilian flying days, a few stories always come to mind.

Six years after my final declaration of "no yoops, papa," I was competing in an aerobatics competition at the National Stearman

Fly-In in Galesburg, Illinois. Not exactly a huge, nationally recognized event, it is a judged competition with generally 6-8 pilots participating. The evening before the event, my friend JR Mitchell and I were practicing and got an idea to spice it up a little. Generally, aerobatics have a 1,500 feet above-the-ground or higher restriction for a margin of safety. The lowest I had probably ever been above the ground while doing aerobatics was 1,000 feet and since I had been practicing a lot, there wasn't much adrenaline rush anymore. "What about those air show pilots? They do their maneuvers just off the ground," I thought. If they can do it, we can do it.

So we decide to practice the loop five times in a row, documenting the precise amount of altitude we lost each time and then added 100 feet for buffer. Assuming we performed the maneuver exactly the same way as every time we'd done it in practice, we would finish with one hundred feet to spare, or 1/3 the length of a football field. Not only was this well below the 1,500-foot legal limit, we were doing it just for excitement.

If you fly a perfect loop, after you have gone over the top and are pointing straight down, you can hit the wake turbulence you made when starting the loop maneuver. This shudders the airplane and momentarily cripples your control over the plane, generally for less than a second. While that doesn't sound like much time, when you are 250 feet over the earth pointing straight down and doing 100+ mph, it feels like an eternity. Because it isn't a big deal 1,000+ feet above the ground, I didn't consider this in my buffer or nerve calculation.

So we finally decide to execute after both of us were sure we wanted to try. However, true to form, as we were pointing straight down just above the earth, the stick became uncontrollable and my heart sank to the floor. The surge of adrenaline roared through my body and I perceived time to dramatically slow. Again, it probably lasted half a second or so but it felt like five. I pulled back on the stick as much as

I could allow after regaining control and we both exhaled yells of excitement over the experience we had just shared.

Fighter pilots should never take unnecessary risks, but there is a certain attitude needed to fly the dangerous missions the profession requires. Looking back, this appears to be an example of that attitude emerging. Civilian flying is generally very tame and safe so I would assume this was my teenage self trying to push the envelope a little.

My time at Galesburg also gave me a taste of formation flying. I had flown formation a few years before with my grandpa at the controls and had been convinced we were seconds away from death the entire time. My second experience, now as an actual pilot receiving instruction on how to fly just feet away from another plane, went immeasurably better. Sure there were nerves, but I loved it. There is something about engaging in an activity requiring 100% of your focus that is refreshing. Most activities, no matter how demanding, allow for your mind to escape from them by daydreaming or worrying about other problems. Close formation, especially at first, requires complete attention and constant corrections as you are almost never in the perfect position. Every subtle movement by the lead airplane requires an adjustment from you. A slight bump of the throttle or stick to correct the new imperfection. Your eyes are locked on to that airplane. I was also amazed at the idea of communicating between airplanes using hand signals. I remember flying for a few minutes and I was so tense that I stood on the rudder pedal, subconsciously trying to guide my plane away from the other. It is a natural response for a newcomer to formation flying, as your proximity to the other plane is intimidating. Skidding through the air, it was actually making the plane more difficult to control in relation to lead. My grandpa had to remind me for the tenth time to just 'relax.'

Being a pilot in high school and college also created an opportunity with members of the opposite sex, which I took advantage of as often as I could. Instead of driving around town looking for something to do, we could fly around town or fly to places for dinner. For prom, I flew my date to a grass strip with a restaurant in northern Arkansas overlooking a beautiful river. After dinner, we flew the 30 minutes back to Missouri, landed, and drove to the dance. I normally took dates up in a Cessna 172, a small four-seat plane my grandpa had purchased for my training but if they were a little more special, they got a ride in the Stearman. As a running joke in the family, if a girl wanted acceptance from the family, she had to go for a ride in the Stearman and be put through a solid aerobatic routine. If she could handle it, she was approved. If she complained, she would not get my grandfather's blessing—a death sentence on the relationship.

One late spring day, I was flying the Stearman around my grandparent's small town of Monett, Missouri and decided to buzz my old flight instructor's house. I made two or three passes as low as I could stand and he came out and waved, so I climbed up and performed a few aerobatic maneuvers for him. All was well and I was having a great time back in the airplane for the first time in months. But someone at the airport came over the radio asking for "the person flying the yellow biplane," saying the sheriff was at the airport and would like to talk with me. The fun quickly subsided as I nervously turned back toward the airport, landed, and pulled up to the hangar. Not exactly sure what this was concerning, I started rehearsing excuses the entire flight back for any violations he might bring up.

After I landed the sheriff approached the plane, chest puffed, as I was climbing out of the cockpit and said, "You were flying pretty low over by the high school weren't you?"

I replied, "I was in that area, yes sir."

"What is the legal limit for aircraft altitude?"

I confidently replied, "500 feet."

With a tone knowing he had me, he said, "Well you were not 500 feet!"

I paused, reflecting on my flight instructor's advice to never actually admit fault unless they could prove it. "Sir, I don't know how much experience you have judging aircraft height, but my instruments said I was at 500 feet." Considering I'd been maybe 50 feet over my instructor's house, I had no idea what his reaction would be but I was damn proud of the answer I'd improvised.

He skeptically said, "Well, I guess I am just a little nervous with it being graduation week that someone is going to pull a prank at the high school." I reassured him I was not doing anything of the sort and we both moved on. I am to this day the only pilot I know who has been pulled over by a sheriff from the ground.

MY GRANDFATHER'S 1942 BOEING STEARMAN

A lot of flying can be learned from textbooks but experiencing things in the plane is always the best teacher. It is the screw-ups that really stick with you and I will share one of them.

This event occurred during one of my first instrument flights—a type of flight where you rely entirely on the instruments in the plane without looking outside. This allows a pilot to safely fly in clouds. My grandpa, having been an instructor in the Air Force and throughout his civilian career, knew tricks to confuse and test students. One afternoon, while I was under goggles that block out the windows of the plane, simulating being in a cloud, he asked me to climb to 2,800 feet at a very hectic time during the flight just after takeoff. Unfortunately, when the airplane reaches 1,800 feet, the thousand-foot pointer is basically pointing at the two on the altimeter. (An altimeter looks similar to a round clock.) Under the stressful environment, I make a rookie mistake and read this as 2,800, even though I was 1,000 feet short.

Fortunately for me, we were in Missouri where there is nothing to hit at 1,800 feet, until we started a simulated instrument approach to land. In the real world, the air traffic controller would have probably said something to me because he can see my altitude on radar most of the time. Still wearing my vision-limiting goggles, I couldn't see anything and was expecting to descend to 1,700 feet, but I was unknowingly beginning a descent to 700 feet. This is a real problem when the ground elevation is 1,300 feet. We were at about 1,400 feet above sea level, just 100 feet above the ground and descending, when my grandpa asked me to take the goggles off and have a look. We were seconds away from crashing into a forest.

As I corrected my descent, a rush of confused adrenaline raced through my body. This moment, which was the only time in my training I would have killed myself and everyone involved, definitely had an impact on me. After we landed, my grandpa explained how he was able to confuse me but didn't say anything further, allowing me to deal with the mistake on my own terms. I remember being very down on myself right after the flight but not much past that. Whether that is good or not is debatable but I have always been good at putting negative events behind me. You need to learn from the mistakes you make but not dwell on them as they can detract from your confidence, and ultimately performance, on future flights.

I also had a fair share of minor emergencies but nothing ever ended with serious consequences. I had my alternator and battery fail while flying in clouds and rain with my dad one afternoon. This means I lost all ability to communicate and navigate except for the old magnetic compass. Had this occurred in a mountainous area, it would have been far more serious as determining the location of mountains while in the clouds would have been nearly impossible. Fortunately, in Missouri there isn't much to hit except cell phone towers, as long as you have a decent idea of how low the clouds go. I just cautiously descended through the clouds, and once below, simply looked around for an airport to land.

The closest I was to ever having a serious problem was when my carburetor was icing over. I was flying a little Cessna through heavy rain in the clouds and noticed the RPM slowly wind back. This decline in power without any inputs from the pilot is not normal and I couldn't explain it. I kept pushing the throttle forward until it was all the way forward, yet the RPM continued to slowly roll back. Furthermore, there was weather all the way down to the ground, including fog, making a forced landing in a field very difficult. I never thought carburetor icing was possible at full power and when I added carburetor heat as one of the last things I could think of doing, for a moment the engine continued to decrease power output even further. My heart skipped a couple beats until the engine roared back to life—after melting the ice that was choking it.

I think the importance of my civilian experience was the lack of any formal courses. I was very fortunate to have access to a range of planes, instructors and a variety of experiences but I never attended a flight school—something I feel very fortunate to not have gone through. It allowed me to progress at my own pace and learn without large bureaucratic constraints and rules inherent within any larger training organization. I would go on to experience these limitations and rules in military training but learning without them gave me a different attitude from most, which would help me throughout my future military training.

The Application

Growing up and hearing fighter pilot stories from my grandpa and his friends captured my attention from an early age. As I was learning to fly and get my various licenses during high school, the idea of the Air Force Academy was tossed around. I spoke to a recruiter a few times and he informed me the Academy was the best route if I wanted to fly a fighter jet. However, I had noticed one of my eyes becoming slightly worse and he said without perfect vision, I had no chance. I didn't even go to the optometrist, I just assumed this was accurate and moved on with my life. Being intimidated by the military culture also kept me from pursuing it further. So

I quit trying and attended Arizona State University in Tempe, AZ. It was one recruiter, who didn't know much about the Air Force Academy and the process of becoming a pilot, who changed my entire future. He had no clue that perfect vision was not a prerequisite. It was my immaturity and lack of investigating further that ironically allowed me to stumble upon a coveted fighter slot.

Moving forward three years, I was a senior at the University of Missouri, majoring in Finance and Real Estate. Flying sporadically when I went home for various vacations, aviation had taken a backseat in my life and I was in the process of applying to various schools to get my Master's degree in Business. One evening, Eli Bozeman, one of my best friends from Missouri and a fellow aviation enthusiast, called and asked if I had heard of the Air National Guard. Negative. He had just moved to Tulsa, Oklahoma where an F-16 guard unit was stationed and had come across something seemingly too good to be true. The F-16 is a multirole fighter jet, meaning it can accomplish a variety of missions from attacking other airplanes to supporting troops on the ground with bombs. It is an awesome machine with a huge afterburner, creating enormous amounts of power. Fighter jets had always been the pinnacle of aviation in my mind. It was a job of honor and it seemed like an amazing experience. Fight for your country in one of the most powerful, most advanced machines man has ever built, all while dancing through the sky. Damn.

Eli said something to the effect of, "Man, I may be wrong but it sounds like if you apply to a certain Guard unit and they accept you, you get to fly their plane. Further, you might get to have a real job and just fly on the weekends or something." Full of excited skepticism, we both had hundreds of questions. To be able to join a part of the Air Force and ensure I would fly a fighter jet sounded like heaven on earth.

The alternative was to go through flying school via the active duty Air Force, but the fear of doing this and then getting stuck with an unmanned aerial vehicle (UAV) assignment or, as they say in Top Gun, "fly a cargo plane full of rubber dog shit out of Hong Kong" was too much for me. The military was intimidating and I had heard too many bad stories about promises gone awry. Let me point out there is absolutely nothing wrong with either of those jobs, cargo or UAV. They are essential to the US Air

Force mission and some things about those careers are arguably better than of a fighter pilot. However, we all have various personalities and mine doesn't seem to fit anything but a fighter.

The next few months became a quest to find out as much as we could about the validity of what we'd heard. I kept thinking this concept of being a part-time fighter pilot flying an F-16 couldn't be real. But we interviewed a few people, tried to call units and I made sure the eye situation was fine. As an aside, most people believe Air Force fighter pilots must have perfect vision. False. 20/70 correctable to 20/20, or LASIK and various other surgeries are acceptable, just requiring more extensive testing for those candidates.

Through all of our research, it appeared this 'too good to be true' option was legitimate. One day I was able to call a couple former Air Guard pilots who flew F-15s (the F-16 counterpart focused only on shooting down other airplanes) to learn about the process of getting selected.

I learned it is easier to get a pilot spot in the active duty Air Force, but you don't know what plane you will fly. There is a "drop" night during pilot training where the "needs of the Air Force" (which planes are available) are put on a board and the top of the class gets first choice and down the list they go. Depending on the needs of the Air Force, there may not even be a fighter available. In the Air Guard however, it is harder to get a pilot spot, but once you do, you know what you will fly. I didn't want to join the Air Force to fly a tanker or cargo plane. I wanted to fly fighters.

Unfortunately, the Guard spots are tough to get. I summarized the process for Eli: "We have to drive to these units, buy them beer, spend the weekend there and do this numerous times all while there are 150 other people trying to do the same thing to get that one spot. Even if I am the best of the 150 candidates, odds are still not in my favor. The guard is essentially joining a fraternity."

This revelation took a lot of the wind out of my sails. The closest unit to me was six hours away. Not only would this mean a significant amount of time spent "schmoozing" these guys, but also a significant amount of money for a very small chance.

Accepting a position with the Guard can also put guys in a tough spot. While you will have a full time job for three to four years during training, after that you might essentially be thrown on the street. There might be a full time job at the end but if none were available, you'd have to fly about one week per month with the Guard and then figure out another career willing to accommodate that difficult schedule.

Further, I was in line to start my MBA so I was anticipating having other promising options in life. It was at this point, early 2009, my senior year of college, I quit pursuing the fighter pilot dream for a while. I hate to use the word quit, but the demands to get a spot appeared too difficult at the time. Life is about calculated risks and in my logical business mind, a lot of luck was required for something that would command a lot of time and resources, things I didn't have much of.

We were nervous about many factors which now just seem ridiculous but at the time limited our motivation to continue. I remember being at various bars in college covering my "better" eye, trying to read signs and being depressed because I could only read them with my good eye. I also thought about not applying because my right elbow clicks when I do pushups. Clearly there could be no way I'd even get through boot camp.

These minor concerns almost kept me from doing the coolest job in the world. In hindsight, they are all absurd and embarrassing to even consider but that was my mentality at the time.

But then came June of that same year. Ky Miller, a 16 year old aspiring pilot, called me up regarding flying to Dayton, OH for an airshow with The Thunderbirds and to visit the National Museum of the United States Air Force. We started with the Air Force Museum. From using pistols to duel another biplane in the sky, to stealth aircraft firing missiles from miles away and dropping bombs on targets through clouds to within a foot of the target, the rapid evolution of aviation is amazing. It made me want to be a part of it, to be an instrumental part of history, all while doing something exhilarating and badass. Then we met the F-16 pilots of The Thunderbirds and watched their demonstration. They sold me on something for which I shouldn't have needed selling. Seeing an afterburning engine at near-supersonic speeds and rolling inverted was more than enough. Leaving that airshow I was going to give the application process a shot. I would at least take the tests and see how I performed.

Each Guard unit has different application requirements, but they all require a candidate to take the Air Force Officer Qualifying Test (AFOQT), a standardized test similar to the SAT and ACT. It has verbal and mathematical sections but also a pilot and navigator section. In a decision made from ignorance, I only studied for the pilot section for fear I would end up looking like a better candidate for a navigator position. Complete ignorance. While I scored pretty well on the other sections, I scored a 99 on the pilot section and almost jumped through the roof when I received my score. Now it felt like I had a chance. A candidate must also get a Test of Basic Aviation Skills (TBAS) score. This combines your total number of flight hours with a score on a computerized test that measures a variety of skills using a control stick and rudders. After getting a 98 on this measure, I now had confidence and was ready to start applying.

Unfortunately, applying was not easy. They don't need pilots—they have hundreds apply for every spot so there is absolutely zero time spent on recruiting or providing material on what is necessary for an application. I generated a spreadsheet of every Guard fighter unit in the country flying F-15s and F-16s. It took me weeks to even get phone numbers for these places. I had no clue how the military worked or what the proper etiquette was. The first couple of units I called reestablished my discouragement. They would say things like, "oh, we aren't hiring for 10 months," "we don't accept people off the street," "we don't accept people out of our state," or even, "we are switching airframes this year." Just as soon as I had gained momentum from my scores, I had tried to get ahold of every unit yet had no applications to even send in.

Finally, one day I got a call saying the 187th Fighter Wing in Montgomery, Alabama was accepting applications and they gave me a list of all the requirements. After submitting all of the necessary material, a variety of transcripts, letters of recommendation and medicals, I got a call a few weeks later saying I had earned an interview.

My grandpa, cousin and I hopped in our Bonanza and flew down for the three-day interview process. The candidates hung out in the pilot's bar, went out to eat, watched the jets take off, did a physical test and had a formal interview. 140 people applied for one spot and twelve of us even made the interview. They told us a few different times how difficult it is to get one of these spots. They said more people become football players in the NFL each year than fighter pilots. Not only that, but you must pay your way to each visit and interview. Go to one or two interviews and it is not that big of a deal—each trip is probably $5-600 if done cheaply—but I knew people who had made it to interviews 10+ times and never got a spot. Quite a significant expense when you are in your early twenties.

I scoured the Internet for any tips on what interview questions would be like. Here are a few examples from my research and how I prepared to answer them.

- *How do you feel about killing someone?*
    o It is not something I would look forward to but I also realize it could be a part of the mission. I would have no problem killing someone in order to defend the United States and carry out the mission objectives.
- *We know you want to fly but what other reasons brought you to making this commitment?*
    o They say to be happy and effective, do what you are passionate about. This often conjures up selfish images but with the Air National Guard, my profession will be my passion, with the best equipment and eventual peers in the world, all while serving my country. Doing the thing I love most while helping and protecting those around me seems to be the pinnacle.
- *How much flight time do you have?*
    o 880 hours or so. About 120 in a Boeing Stearman, 120 in Citation Encores, Beechcraft Bonanza and a few with a variety of other planes. I have a decent amount of aerobatics training and competed in a couple contests, and have eight hours or so of formation experience.
- *Give us an example of when your integrity was challenged?*
    o Every moment in golf. You enforce the rules on yourself leaving many opportunities to take advantage of the game. I saw instances when people cheated and were caught

cheating. There is something about that clean feeling of living a good life that is great.
- *What if this wing was told to fly C-5s, how would you react to that?*
    - I understand I am signing up to serve my country and would continue to do so. However, I feel based on my skill set I would be better served in a fighter role.
- *Why?*
    - Competitiveness, love for aerobatics and maneuverability.

In the actual interview they asked some similar questions but they also asked more personal questions such as my interest in hunting to see if I would be a good fit within the unit.

Throughout the weekend I learned a lot about the process and some great stories from guys who had flown in Desert Storm, Northern Watch, Enduring Freedom and Iraqi Freedom. One pilot mentioned a story where he was patrolling around Iraq and got the call to come take out a building with two guys on the roof. Through the targeting pod, he could see two men on this specific roof smoking. The bomb he was dropping didn't detonate on impact; it waits momentarily to make sure it reaches the bottom of the building before detonating so the entire building is brought down. So the pilot released the bomb, watching through the targeting pod as a hole in the roof of the building suddenly appeared. He saw the men's heads look over to the hole just long enough to realize what had happened before the building disappeared in a ball of flames. Another pilot told a story of marines on ATVs riding through the desert when terrorists in a suburban began chasing and shooting at them. They called in an F-16 and in one strafing pass, eliminated the threat. I hadn't really heard stories like these but they fired me up. They added a perspective past my afterburners-and-dogfighting image of being a Fighter Pilot.

Two weeks after leaving Alabama, I found out I did not get the spot. I heard one of their prior enlisted guys got it with little flying experience. My confidence in the process decreased tremendously. I had a few more applications coming up in the next few months but there was really nothing I could change about my application.

A couple months later I got the call from the 175th Fighter Squadron in Sioux Falls, South Dakota, informing me I had landed an interview. I had a typo on my resume and they had had to call one of my references to get my cell phone number. Not a great start, but they let it slide. I was told to be at a specific building in two weeks at 10:40 AM for an interview. Each Guard unit does things completely differently—Alabama had a complete weekend of activities while South Dakota had one 30-minute interview and that was it. I practiced my interview questions in the hotel room that morning but was not nearly as nervous as I was in Alabama. I think it was a perception that a lot of the outcome was out of my hands. Regardless, I showed up for my interview and in 20 minutes I was back on the road heading to Missouri to run a half marathon the next morning. I felt the interview went well but was not overly confident. They asked a lot of questions about what I would do for work after I went part time.

At one point in the drive I looked at my phone and saw I had missed a call from the Sioux Falls area code. There was a voicemail from the commander asking me to call him back. My heart jumped. I had no idea what to think. Was he calling to clarify something? It had taken Alabama two weeks to get back to me. Still naïve about the military, I didn't even know what to call him when he picked up the phone. He talked around the issue for a few minutes, asking how the drive was going and if I was really going to run a half marathon the next morning. Finally, he said he appreciated me coming up and would like to offer me a spot to fly the F-16 for their unit. I remember starting to shake and looking at my friend with huge eyes and a grin on my face. He gave me a couple small details and said someone from recruiting would be in touch in the next couple weeks to start paperwork.

It was the moment where you realize your dream just came true. I tried to soak it all in. I still remember my hand shaking and occasionally breaking down into laughter. I didn't know what to do. Who should be called first? Should I text everyone? Facebook post? No, this was bigger than that. I realized if possible, this was something I wanted tell people close to me in person. Even with a half marathon to run the next morning, I only slept about an hour, watching F-16 videos on my phone all night.

I had received the most exciting news of my life, but over the next couple weeks when my grandpa or dad would ask if I had heard anything, I would deflect the questions and act frustrated by the slow process. I wanted the moment where I revealed the news to be special. My mom was the first I told and as expected, she broke down in tears. Whether they were of happiness or fear, I shall never completely know but I have always assumed they were for both.

My grandfather, having a huge influence on my life and career as an aviator, had been wildly hopeful for me receiving the fighter pilot position. I had to wait two weeks to drive down to his home from school. It was a beautiful day and I suggested we take the Stearman out for a spin. There were a few people wanting to go for a ride so when I asked him to go with me first he dismissed the idea saying he didn't need to go. I made up an excuse that I wanted him to join me to practice a landing, as it had been a while since I had flown, so he reluctantly agreed.

We fired the radial engine up and just a minute or so after takeoff, as I was deciding how to tell him, he said, "this ole bird has taught you a lot about flying. She is a great machine."

I responded with, "Yeah she is, just like the F-16 I got hired to fly last week."

He was speechless, looking at me through the mirror allowing the pilots of the plane to see each other even with tandem seating. His eyes got big and began welling up as he started fist pumping out the side of the airplane, hooting and hollering through the microphone. It was a moment of elation where the only proper way to express how you feel is to do a barrel roll and loop and we were in the perfect position to celebrate. It is a moment and flight I will never forget.

Months later, I found out one of the key hiring factors from my interview was my commitment to flying fighters and nothing else. At one point they asked me, "we see you have essentially lived in Missouri your entire life. Do you want to live there?"

I replied with, "Missouri doesn't have a fighter wing so I am not interested in living there." I wanted to be a fighter pilot. Nothing else. That is the attitude they want.

The reactions from my MBA classmates were mixed. Most of the Americans thought it was badass. I had others ask me why in the hell I would want to do this. "You are getting an MBA, go make a lot of money." You always hear you should love what you do and when I think about various careers, I can't imagine myself loving too many things behind a desk. I responded to them saying that I couldn't imagine doing anything better than flying a jet and serving my country at the same time. It would allow me to combine my passion while serving others. Furthermore, the Air Force estimates it costs around $4 million to train an F-16 pilot. So another way to look at it was that I was about to make $4,090,000 over the next two years and blow $4 million of it on flying fighter jets. I was able to finish my MBA watching my classmates stress over jobs and salary negotiations while I sat back, not caring in the slightest how much money I was going to make.

PART 2: PRE-PILOT TRAINING

Medical Screening

Trips to the flight doctor are the single greatest fear of the pilot. With all of their confidence, fighter pilots feel doctors are the only thing capable of shooting them out of the sky. One bad eye exam, hearing test or chest scan could render a pilot wingless, stealing not only a job, but a way of life for those spirits who feel the need to fly upside down at Mach 1.

Eight months after getting hired, I was sent to Brooks Air Force Base in San Antonio, Texas for the most thorough medical examination I will ever experience. We were the last class of pilot selectees to ever be examined at Brooks, the base where every pilot had been examined for years. The base was closing and it felt like a ghost town.

I appeared to be in good health but was very nervous as the examinations approached. During our initial physical six months prior, my counterpart in the South Dakota Air Guard, Ryan Hawk, had passed out numerous times while giving his blood test, making my first military examination experience an ugly one. Hawk was an airline pilot from Minneapolis and had thousands of hours flying people around the country. We would eventually go through all of our training together. I had failed the EKG test three times before the doctor realized my pulse was too low due to running and made me do pushups before retaking the test to get my heart rate up. Funny looking back now—but not so funny at the time.

As a pilot, I have constantly worried about my eyes. While I was applying for fighter pilot positions, I sat in bars with my friends at college covering my left eye, trying to read football scores on the TV or bar signs at a distance and getting depressed because I couldn't. While getting my first flight physical for the FAA at age 16, I confided with my grandpa my concern so he pulled me aside and said, "Just remember DEFPOTEC" (pronounced "deaf-po-tek"). It is the 20/20 line on almost every basic eye chart—something he learned taking the Air Force eye tests back in the

1950s. He knows the 20/15 line as well but I never bothered learning that one. That might have got me through that test and every physical since then but it wasn't going to work with the military's extensive screening process.

My final anxiety was that while doing pushups, my right elbow clicks. I remember thinking I probably couldn't survive boot camp or endure military life with this painless, but annoying problem. Now, hundreds of pushups later, it scares me to think this was a deterrent to me applying—but it illustrates how concerned pilots can be about this physical.

Air Force Medical Checkout

You could sense the tension amongst all the pilot candidates in the room. We were all so close to our dream and this was arguably the last big hurdle we had no control over.

Along with numerous eye examinations, x-rays and hearing tests, the examiners had us take psychological, IQ and emotional stability tests, asking questions like, "Have you ever cheated in solitaire? Do you feel like demons are controlling your actions or thoughts? Do you feel like everyone is out to get you?" It was 500+ similar questions and IQ tests for almost five straight hours.

My worst moment of anxiety occurred toward the end of the final examination with the flight doc. He had gone through my medical history, tested my reflexes, had me drop my pants and cough, and bend over, before he started listening to my heart.

"Has anyone ever mentioned you having a heart murmur?" he asked.

"Uhhh no, what do you mean?" I choked out.

He listened further in silence while occasionally asking me to flex my abs or clench my fists. Having just completed my fourth marathon and being a healthy eater, I was near anger at this point. He left to find the cardiologist, only to return saying he couldn't find him so we would do more tests the next day.

I went to sit in the waiting room with the others, realizing I would have to attempt sleep knowing this could be the end. A fun eighteen hours of pondering my quickly disappearing future as a fighter pilot. I could care less about my heart having a problem, I just wanted to fly a fighter.

After going over me again with a cardiologist, they told me that because of my thin frame, my heart rests closer to the front of my chest, causing the blood to rush a little quicker through a smaller space, as opposed to air moving in and out of the heart. I passed.

The doctor later told me that he felt my heart racing the second he mentioned the word murmur. He laughed and said, "I can tell how much this means to you." I was beyond relieved.

In total, there were 20 or so in the last class of Brooks AFB physicals. Three didn't pass their medical and saw their dreams of flying in the United States Air Force disappear.

Anxiety

It was nine months from getting hired to starting officer training school in January 2011. The level and varieties of stress I experienced leading up to training were comical. When you want to do something so badly, you notice anything capable of getting in your way, no matter how trivial. Right after being accepted, I remember taking more care crossing the street on campus. Not that I didn't care about life and limb before, but now I just couldn't blow my chance to fly a fighter jet.

I quit playing basketball and all sports having higher probabilities of injury. Every disease or pain brought upon thoughts of the worst-case scenario. I took worrying to a whole new level but it shows how excited I was for this opportunity.

Reading the news about the wars winding down in the Middle East would also cause anxiety. Would they cut funding? I'd watch as they cut F-35 funding, wondering if this would be the difference in our unit getting them after the F-16.

I spent a lot of time before flight training started trying to work on my attitude. There were weeks I would feel down. I have a terrible fear of failure, of disappointing myself and those who are a part of my life. I also feared I would be miserable with concern about my effort and performance. It was the first time I had ever been truly excited about an opportunity and I didn't want to blow it. I felt like this opportunity had given my life purpose, to do what I love while serving others—not just for the United States but for humanity.

My Grandpa, without being prompted, said, "Try to enjoy every minute." Five years later, this quote still hangs over my desk.

Officer Training School

The journey down to Montgomery, Alabama marked the introduction to military life we see and fear in movies. I'll be honest—it had made me nervous. I had always been a pretty decent kid and never really got in trouble so I was not used to being reprimanded. I knew the shenanigans with yelling and pushups was part of the game but it still sucked worse than I expected. I kept a daily journal but wouldn't want to spoil all of the details for those lucky enough to experience it in the future. I will tell a few stories but leave the rest to your imagination.

The day before it started I wrote:

"I haven't even started and it's considerably more stressful than expected. As the lunch lady today put it, 'you guys are going to get jacked up tomorrow.' I have never really missed people terribly until today and everyone else here has prior military experience. I know absolutely nothing about the military and it sounds like that won't be an excuse tomorrow morning. I have spent half of yesterday and all of today preparing and am still not done setting up the dorm room. If it weren't for my roommate, there would be no way I could have made it through these setup days."

My roommate was prior enlisted in the guard and had received a job flying the KC-135, an air refueling jet, in a different state. He already knew the military customs but was also very sharp and patient with someone new like me.

The training was interesting, to say the least. At its core, it was not difficult—many classes on leadership and the Air Force throughout the day—but it was all of the bullshit in between and never being comfortable that made it difficult. For two weeks I was always hot or cold, hungry and being yelled at. I was miserable. The thought of walking away from it actually crossed my mind, but that same day an F-16 happened to do a low approach and fly over us, quickly erasing those negative thoughts. I never let the objective out of my mind again.

There were the cinematic moments of doing pushups in the cold rain and mud but overall, it was much more docile than expected. I think the reputation of the Air Force being a little softer than the other branches is probably true.

The second morning it was raining and cold when we set up in formations outside. I caused quite the scene when after room inspections I went downstairs without my hydration pack. Chris Young, a Michigan guy who would go on to be one of my best friends, was standing behind me in formation and told me he remembers thinking, "oh shit, that dude doesn't have a hydration pack. That sucks for him!" He then proceeded to realize he didn't either. As our flight was ready to leave we were sent back to our rooms and I messed up greetings to numerous officers, all causing pushups and delays. So I ran upstairs, grabbed it, sprinted downstairs, only to mess up greetings to the same officers again, and when I got outside I realized I didn't have my hat.

I went back looking for it, doing push-ups along the way as I continued messing up greetings. I had dropped it on the stairs. I ran back down the stairs, messed up the greetings once more, before returning to my flight. As I finally returned, out of breath, the Flight Commander told me "to get out of his flight" so I had to march with another. As I look back on my Air Force career, now five years in, I call this moment the low point.

It was the longest six weeks of my life but at the end I became a second lieutenant. My grandpa, a retired captain in the Air Force, was able to swear me in making for a special moment as a sixty-year gap in the Fox family military service was reconciled with one crisp salute. It was his dream to be a part of creating a fighter pilot in his family and the first step was behind us.

MY GRANDFATHER SWEARING ME IN AS A SECOND LIEUTENANT

MY FIRST MARCHING EXPERIENCE

A few days before I left for Initial Flight Screening (IFS), I was back home. My grandpa and I headed out to the airport for my final flight in our ole Stearman before I started flying for the Air Force. Generally, my grandpa doesn't fly with me anymore. He enjoys watching me give other people rides. After I gave a couple rides he asked to fly with me for just a few minutes. He made the comment, "I want to fly with you one last time when I know I am still a better aviator than you. I know how good the Air Force is at training people so you might start getting close." After almost every ride I have ever given, he has made this comment to the passenger: "too bad you couldn't fly with a real aviator."

Initial Flight Screening

The first stop in my military aviation career was Pueblo, Colorado for IFS. Created in 2006, IFS is contracted out to a civilian company and was designed to screen out pilot and navigator candidates early, before a significant amount of money was spent on training them at the next level. It conducts flight screening for 1,300 to 1,700 USAF officers annually, with 8-12% eliminated for a variety of reasons. They said the actual purpose was to determine if a student was capable of learning the military way.

While IFS is designed to be a stressful environment to weed out those who won't be able to handle military aviation, I actually enjoyed it. Since I had a significant amount of prior flying experience, I didn't have to worry about learning to fly. I just had to learn the airplane and military procedures. The course is also designed to take students without prior flight experience and solo them within 3 weeks. For those students, it was understandably more stressful.

The first week of IFS was academic lectures in an auditorium. Good presenters are always taught to start a presentation with a bang and they chose to show a 15-minute video of airplane crashes. This was some of these students' first taste of aviation—there's nothing like a warm welcome. These classes were relatively remedial for me so I chose to not pay attention and study the more difficult concepts, which paid off later on once we began flying. The instructors, however, were really good, always incorporating entertaining stories into the lessons. For example, during one class they were teaching us about go-arounds and when they can happen. Go-arounds are essentially an aborted landing and can be due to a variety of reasons such as a bad approach, gusty winds or a traffic conflict. The instructor, full of energy, said something to the effect of, "So there we were, in the Mighty Katana, rapidly approaching the field at a blistering 60 knots on short final and there was a group of antelope near the runway. I love animals and they know it so I knew they wouldn't do anything stupid like run in front of the airplane. We continued on the approach and all of the antelope heard the mighty roar of our engine and moved away—except for one. And then it hit me: antelope lie! So what do you do? A Go-Around!" If all instructors, in elementary school or the Air Force had as much energy as these did, the world would be a smarter place.

IN FRONT OF THE DA-20

The airplane of choice for this class was the "Mighty" DA-20. The Diamond Katana is essentially a glider with a lawnmower engine strapped to the front. The instructors would joke relentlessly about the power and performance of this bird. They would tell us to check the trailing edges of the wings for bird strikes because we'd get rear-ended all of the time. It had 125 horsepower and 2 seats. Stalling at 34 knots in the landing configuration, when the wind was blowing 25-30 knots, it damn near became a hovercraft approaching touchdown.

I worked really hard the first week and weekend, studying all day until it was time to go to bed. Our first ride, the "Dollar Ride," was Friday and I really wanted to impress my instructor and get ahead of the curve. I have no idea where the name "Dollar Ride" comes from but it is a tradition to pay your instructor for the risk of this first flight. It is customary to decorate your dollar in any way you choose. I decided to tie in my South Dakota, University of Missouri and F-16 affiliations. I accurately predicted that once I could fully understand the military system of flying, I would be set and the rest of the course would become significantly easier. Just like in sports, if you can master the fundamentals, military radio calls, procedures, checklist use, etc., you can excel by focusing on the details that separate you from the competition.

I really enjoyed the flying while we were there. I had studied and prepared the first week so each flight went well and I was able to get an 'Excellent' overall grade on each flight throughout the program. All flights are graded Excellent, Good, Fair or Unsatisfactory. I believe we got three chances to pass a ride before being eliminated from the program. It dawned on me halfway through the program that I was getting paid to go for a flight each day. I reflected on where I would have been had I taken a business job right out of the MBA program I graduated, and it instantly reaffirmed my decision, even though I was flying a plane not worth bragging about.

IFS was also my first exchange, or lack thereof, with aviation medicine. Halfway through the first week, I got relatively sick. Friday was our first day of flying and while I am not exactly sure what medications you can take and still fly, I know they are very limited. They had a full time medical person there to help with any concerns you might have—however, there is a problem with seeing him. If you seek any medical help, you run the risk of them saying you cannot fly. If you cannot fly, you cannot graduate IFS. So while a fighter pilot may need to be in top physical shape and has medical teams at their disposal, no one ever wants to go see them unless they absolutely have to.

Flying is famous for having interesting stories and while this class was designed to consist of only very boring flying, two of my flights were more interesting than the rest.

With ten flights in the program, I flew with five different instructors. I had a new instructor for my pre-check ride. A check ride is essentially a test and is weighted far more heavily than normal flights. On the pre-check ride, you fly the same profile as the check ride, allowing you to practice everything for the final ride. While I had flown with retired military instructors, I had yet to fly with an active military pilot until this ride. He had all of the negative stereotypes I heard can appear in military flying. He started or concluded every sentence with "man" or "dude." I could tell early on in my military adventure "dude" would become a larger part of my vocabulary in the fighter world—but every sentence was a bit much. He never smiled or seemed like he wanted to be there and our pre-flight brief, which normally lasts 30 minutes, lasted about seven so he could go eat. We walked out to the plane and he continued the silent treatment, except for the occasional comment. Compare this to my prior flights which were generally constant, friendly conversations.

We were checking the engine immediately before takeoff. I put the flaps into the takeoff position and confirmed this on the before takeoff checklist. However, as soon as I advanced the throttle, he noticed they were back in the cruise position, something I could ultimately fail the check ride for the next day. He confirmed he saw me put them in the right position and had no idea why it had changed. Regardless, I was now pissed as I had given him some fuel for his continually deteriorating attitude. The whole flight was silent except for an occasional comment from him about something minor. Finally on the ride back toward the airport he started asking about my flight experience. I reciprocated the questions and found out he was an F-15 and F-117 Nighthawk (Stealth Fighter) pilot. I immediately understood his "I hate life flying the Diamond Katana" attitude. Not many people would be happy about that career change. Regardless, his misery wasn't helping either one of us.

We were coming into land and all of a sudden, in an unfriendly tone, he exclaimed, "I have the aircraft" and shook the stick. This is the standard protocol to change authority of the airplane but generally only happens when the student is screwing up so bad that safety is an issue. It had yet to happen to me so I was caught off guard and, quite frankly, offended. So the approach continued, me with my hands in my lap, my mind racing to figure out the cause of this debacle when I noticed he was high, really high above glide slope. He began slipping, a maneuver to lose altitude while not increasing speed, all the way down to about ten feet above the ground and we were already halfway down a 3,700-foot runway. It was policy to go around if less than half a runway remained but he was determined to get it on the ground ASAP and failed to flare at all. We hit the nose wheel and bounced so hard I brought my hands onto the controls out of reflex and fear of safety. We literally bounced 30 feet in the air but since we impacted in a dive, we weren't even close to stalling yet, so I let him clean up his mess and get us back on the ground. However, as soon as the nose wheel touched again, the plane started shaking violently.

The Pueblo control tower immediately radioed and said, "Tiger 20, looks like you have a flat front nose gear tire, depart the runway at your discretion."

Inside, I was now leaping for joy. I thought to myself, "this is going to be hilarious. He is going to have to write a report about why the plane broke and everyone will be dumbfounded when it was completely an instructor's fault. This is karma for his attitude."

He taxied to the end of the runway and told tower he was heading all the way back to the IFS ramp. I asked, "sir, I have no problem hopping out and checking the tire really quick."

He said no and spent the rest of the time taxiing back saying, "That was awesome. Awesome landing. Freakin' awesome landing." I kept silent and held back a smile. Tower even deployed maintenance crews to meet us out on the ramp, which he also called off. It turned out the landing dislodged a pin in the nose gear causing a tremendous shimmy.

His attitude changed slightly after all this and once he found out I was on a fighter pilot track, he began to engage in a little conversation. Apparently I was now worthy of a little extra attention and he was probably trying to appease me after the controlled crash we just experienced. As we sat down to debrief, he pulled out the grade sheet for the flight. It outlined every aspect of the flight and you got a grade for each item. Expecting to get humbled here, he started with the first item. "Takeoffs, got nothing for you, excellent. Situational awareness, got nothing, excellent. Landings, got nothing, excellent." This continued for essentially the whole flight except for the flap debacle at the onset of the flight. He ended up giving me the best grades I had received the whole class. He also gave me tips about pilot training and becoming a fighter pilot, all of which I wrote down and will undoubtedly remember through the upcoming two years:

- *Don't get behind the power curve.*
- *Ask the stupid questions.*
- *If it's going well, don't pat yourself on the back.*
- *Never pass up an opportunity to shut the f$%# up.*
- *As a corollary, the only time you really need to say anything is when:*
  - *You are Bingo Fuel, on fire or lead is on fire. [Bingo fuel essentially means you have reached the minimum fuel to get home from the airspace.]*
- *Act as though you are the sole manipulator of controls throughout training. Pretend no one is in the back seat.*

A lot of the instructors gave me advice, but this seemed like a straightforward, honest opinion of flight school, which was appreciated. Unexpected considering how the entire flight had gone and then ultimately concluded.

The actual check ride the next day had its interesting quirks. First impressions are important, so when I pre-flighted the wrong airplane, the start wasn't exactly what I had in mind. In my defense, the clipboard had the wrong parking spot written down from the previous flight and I was lucky to even catch it. I spent ten minutes checking the oil, fuel, instruments and had untied the airplane when I realized the error and started putting it all back together. This was also, conveniently, the same time the check pilot came out and asked why I was retying down the airplane. He laughed and actually helped me with the correct airplane since I was now behind schedule.

Once we had reached our airspace, I was in a ten degree bank turn flying toward the middle of our area when something flashed off to our right.

Odd—not many things shine and glisten up at 8,000 feet. Maybe the occasional pond that meets the angle of the sun just right, but unusual enough to merit a glance for confirmation, which is what I did.

Our planes had traffic avoidance equipment on them but it failed to pick up the Bonanza I had just seen. The instructor was looking elsewhere so when I jerked the stick full left, pulled back and added an "oh shit," he obviously snapped his head toward me in a confused manner. All I had to do was point at the V-tail Bonanza flying within 300 feet of us.

I am not sure if we would have collided had I not taken evasive action but the fact that I am "not sure" should be evidence enough of the proximity. After the adrenaline settled down I jokingly asked the important check ride question of, "sir, does this mean I will get an 'Excellent' or an 'Unsatisfactory' on the Collision Avoidance portion of the check ride?"

He quickly replied, "That was the most excellent example of collision avoidance I have seen."

This ride was the culmination of IFS and my final blessing to move on to the next phase of training. I had graduated IFS. Cue another sweet exhale.

Lesson Learned: The Power Curve

IFS was a great example of strong preparation paying off. Not only did I have experience flying before the class as a civilian, I also worked harder than any of my peers the first week, not taking any time off. Having as much experience flying as I did, this course could have been a class I coasted through. I would see this theme reappear numerous times throughout my training as working hard early and separating yourself from your peers pays significant dividends down the road. Essentially an extended first impression, this early work ethic puts you in a favorable light with instructors, leadership or bosses for the remainder of the course or job. You are the guy who has his act together and has answers early when everyone else is flailing or as we say in this business, barely hanging on to the tail of the rudder. You are always assumed to be motivated and trustworthy so when a mistake is made, you get the benefit of the doubt.

You can afford to take a little time off because you have established a solid reputation for yourself.

Furthermore, working hard early also made my training so much more enjoyable. Being ahead of the power curve, or ahead of where others think you should be, is a position breeding success. You know more than is required for the flight or meeting so the stress diminishes significantly. Not only do you perform better for knowing your shit, you perform better because you are confident. From the Diamond Katana to the F-16, this principle made the entire training a relatively stress-free pleasure in comparison to some of my peers.

PART 3: UNDERGRADUTE PILOT TRAINING (UPT)

Undergraduate Pilot training is a 54-week crash course learning to fly, and more specifically, fly military aircraft. While it is a lot of work, it is a phenomenal experience and many lessons are learned in the skies and in life. It is an experience millions dream of, thousands apply for and a few hundred per year get to enjoy. It is, however, a stressful experience as you are always one week away from failing and going home.

Attempting to get ahead like I had in IFS, I began studying flashcards I found online weeks before the class officially started. I was so excited and committed to flying the F-16 I wouldn't let anything, especially any form of laziness or procrastination, stand in my way. Even before driving down to Wichita Falls for the class, I knew details of the T-6 down to the number of static wicks on each control surface of the airplane.

Weeks 1-5: Fears

The highly anticipated first day was anything but exciting. It was a lot of introductions and paperwork as we continued to in-process to the base and course. There are a few different bases in the country to go through Undergraduate Pilot Training (UPT) but the training in Wichita Falls is unique due to the Euro Nato Joint Jet Pilot Training (ENJJPT) program. It is the only base like it in the world with many of NATO's countries sending students and instructor pilots. It is regarded as the best training program, due to the influence of all participating nations contributing to the syllabus. At ENJJPT, we get thirty more hours of flight time in a month shorter course than the other Air Force pilot training bases.

We had shown up with twenty-six students in our class and were told to expect an attrition rate of one per class. It was also mentioned that the

United States government could train an entire platoon of Navy Seals for the price of one of us to go through this training. Being in the guard, I knew I had a coveted fighter spot but I still had to graduate the program and get a "fighter qualified" designation on my final report. We'd heard rumors of guys not getting that distinction and it was enough to strike fear into my heart and provide more motivation. This designation became my sole focus for the next thirteen months. Anything getting between me and the F-16 was going to get a significant amount of my attention.

The active duty Air Force guys, however, had to compete for class rank in order to have a better chance of getting the jet they want. During the last two years, active duty guys had received the following aircraft: 27% fighters, 13% UAVs, 21% cargo and refueling jets, 12% FAIP and the rest, something else. FAIP stands for First Assignment Instructor Pilot. After graduation, those pilots who are assigned to be FAIPs generally stay at this base for another three years teaching the next waves of aspiring military aviators before getting their assignment to a combat aircraft.

The first day addressed other concerns many guys have. The G-forces were a significant concern of mine so I was less than thrilled when they mentioned, "the guys who generally struggle the most with Gs and centrifuge training are endurance runners who are tall and skinny." Having run two marathons in the last year, being 6'2" and 170 lbs put me in that category. Airsickness was addressed by informing us there was a spinning chair the doctor would put us through, ultimately correcting any airsickness problems should they arise. Apparently it sucks, but everyone who has ever made it through this airsickness training has found that it remedied all problems later in the airplane.

The twenty-six of us were separated into two flights with the lone captain in our group of 2nd lieutenants being the class leader. A flight is a sub-unit within a flying squadron under an organizational hierarchy and is essentially your close family for the duration of the course. Our class leader was Matt "CAIN" Olde. He was a former weapon systems officer in the F-15E Strike Eagle and came from a family full of fighter pilots. He had deployed to Afghanistan in that jet but always wanted to sit in the front seat of a fighter. He already had some grey hair so we often called him the old man.

As a class, we were responsible for coming up with a class patch idea, something we would wear on the right shoulder of our flight suit for the majority of the training. But the very day we started pilot training, the Air Force came down with a regulation barring many of the fighter traditions that had been in place for decades. No more special shirts on Friday, no more black boots, restrictions on the patches we could wear and many others. Personally, I hardly knew different as I had never experienced any of these traditions in the first place but the disappointment and frustration around the squadrons was palpable. In response, much of the debate regarding our class patch centered around this unfortunate development. We had designed a patch to look like a Friday T-shirt with another piece of Velcro allowing additional patches to be placed on the original. While difficult to explain, just know it was a rebellion against the new directive and we were damn proud of it. Most of us hadn't had much or any time in a flying unit, aside from CAIN, but just by reading books and immersing yourself in the "fighter pilot" culture, you can get a feel for the importance of carrying on traditions and customs, almost ALL of which were under attack.

The first week of training centered primarily on Aerospace Physiology. We learned about the ejection seat—when and how to launch ourselves from a crippled plane. Flying the T-6 would be the first time I could actually say "I get to fly something with a rocket strapped to my ass." I had heard rumors you can only eject from a jet twice due to the health problems the traumatic event can have on your spine—so now I could add a fear of ejection to my list of concerns that might keep me from flying the F-16. The number of ejections is so statistically insignificant this shouldn't have been a concern in the slightest. As one of the instructors described the decision to eject: "we would like to think you are worth more than the airplane...right now you aren't, but you will be."

We each got a turn in the spinning chair of sickness, not because we were assumed to be airsick candidates, but because...well, I have no idea, but it was not enjoyable. I'm someone who never gets airsick, but this machine did a number on most of us in just a couple minutes. It is a device I would imagine siblings putting each other through for a good laugh and to 'see what would happen.' I sure pitied the students who had to go back for 30-minute sessions, multiple times.

The introduction to the Anti-G straining maneuver was an interesting experience as well. It consists of a combination of flexing all of your muscles below your heart and taking short, crisp breaths every three seconds allows for increased G tolerance. Designed to maintain a level of blood pressure and air in your lungs, it is a relatively difficult action to master, especially under G.

We also had to go through an altitude chamber. The chamber created the atmospheric conditions of various altitudes, in which we would remove our oxygen masks to experience the effects and learn what signs our body exhibited when experiencing an oxygen deficiency. We experienced up to 25,000 feet and felt the effects of hypoxia before donning the mask again. We also experienced a rapid decompression. This is what the airlines brief you on should the masks fall. The Air Force used to take us up to 43,000 feet in the chamber but said the benefits were no longer worth the problems and health risks created as a result. Some of my classmates were pretty hilarious as hypoxia set in. One of the Italian students in our class passed out before putting his mask on. He started twitching and couldn't remember any of it. Other guys giggled the entire time at everything. It was actually rather disgusting for as you ascend, gas expands. Sixteen guys in one tiny chamber ascending to 25,000 feet. You do the math.

The Italians were becoming a very appreciated and entertaining part of our group. They were wonderful cooks and had been inviting us over to partake in the serious sport of pasta eating. You can disrespect a lot of things but their pasta is not one of them. The Europeans of ENJJPT were also notorious for buying very nice cars. While still expensive, Ferraris, BMWs and other sports cars are far cheaper in the States than in Europe, and combining that fact with a bonus the Europeans got for going to pilot training, many of them took advantage of this opportunity. One of the Italians, Ciccio "Cheech" Iadecola, the only red headed Italian I have ever met, was from Rome and had the finest foreign accent a woman could ever dream of. One afternoon he was telling me, "I have less than $18,000." After five minutes of trying to understand what he meant I derived, "I am in debt $18,000." It is always an interesting conversation with them but he insisted he needed that BMW.

The beginning of UPT also marked my first real introduction to the Air Force culture and most notably, the phrase "so to speak." Many may disagree with my perception and interpretation but I always have seen it as a classy way to say, "at least that's what she said." If any statement, said by you or anyone else around you, could possibly be construed as sexual, a "so to speak' needs to follow. It is unbelievable how many times each day this phrase is uttered around a squadron. Even some of the higher ranking instructors, making an announcement over the intercom across an entire building, are not exempt from the unwritten rule. An example could be, "Lt. Fox needs to go down, so to speak, to Colonel Meyer's office immediately." Then, due to the sexual connotations in the words "box" and "head," they could never be spoken and were to be replaced with words like "container" and "cranium." It would not be surprising to hear someone say they are going to "cranium over to someone's house" as opposed to "head over."

While I have been describing a few of the cultural aspects of the Air Force, the first five weeks of training were mostly about academics. Essentially, assuming we had little-to-no knowledge about flying, the classes ranged from aerodynamics and weather to aircraft systems and military flying procedures. A few weeks into the program we started simulator rides. From learning to start the T-6 to the basics of flying it, the simulators were a good stepping stone for guys with no flying experience.

I was genuinely excited about flying the T-6. As a civilian I had flown private jets but nothing had compared with the performance capability of this plane. I thought of it as a modern day P-51 and I would imagine she has some similar characteristics. The T-6 is a single-engine turboprop aircraft built by the Raytheon Aircraft Company. With over 600 built, it is a 7G-capable 1,100 horsepower machine of fun. It comes in at around $6 million+ to produce. I heard the ejection seat accounted for half of the price tag.

Lesson Learned: Tradition and Heritage

Just as many of us have family traditions relating to the holidays, the military is notorious for having a significant amount of heritage and tradition. It is a wonderful feeling to be a part of something special and have these traditions to bond over. Their importance is highlighted when they are taken away. Throughout my first week and the next couple years, I saw many of these fighter pilot traditions get taken away and it was painful, especially for the older guys. In an effort to be more politically correct and not offend anyone, the Air Force was looking to manage every aspect of our lives. I can understand this direction in the 21st century but it felt like a corporate office. Our business is a unique one. A profession of arms has a significant amount of stress with actual lives at stake and I think this culture of brotherhood is a critical factor in boosting morale and ultimately, mission success.

Week 6: Today is, No Kidding, Today

Week six was quite a week. A couple simulator rides Monday and Tuesday before the highly anticipated first flight or "Dollar Ride" on Wednesday. We were finally transitioning from all academics, tests and simulators to the real airplane. The simulator instructors were all retired pilots, now in a civilian contract role. Many of these guys had flown in Vietnam or Desert Storm. This transition also meant moving into our flight room with the active duty Air Force instructors. The flight room would be home for the next six months as all of the flight briefs, debriefs and general studying took place here. There were eight or nine desks for the instructors, a table in the middle for the students to corral around and a bar in the corner for snacks and drinks after a long day of flying.

Tuesday, the squadron commander walked into our flight room to give us a little pep talk the day before flying began. Saying things to the effect of, "some of you have been waiting your whole life for this. It starts now," and "today is, no kidding, today."

So the Dollar Rides began. An ungraded welcome to the airplane, the Dollar Ride is entirely about enjoying the flight and doing what you want. All fun except they don't really let you fly much because you probably suck. Captain Butch Baumann, my instructor pilot (IP), was a former B-52 pilot and my assigned instructor for the T-6 program. He would be in charge of my training and I would fly with him more than any other IP.

I persuaded Capt. Baumann into letting me do about six Cuban Eights, a few aileron rolls and a couple cloverleaves. While they are all fun aerobatics, I mainly wanted to feel some Gs. We only pulled about 4 Gs but they were more significant than expected. However, just three flights in, I could already feel my G tolerance going up. When the instructor flew a 5 G turn to demonstrate something, I had a grand ole time trying to pick my hands up and move them around. It is a wild feeling not being able to simply raise your hand and touch your face.

I tried to make the dollar I paid Capt. Baumann personal. My grandpa flew the original T-6 in 1956 and I flew the T-6 II this week, 55 years later. I found a picture of those two airplanes flying formation and pasted it on the front side. We did a lot of Cuban 8's so I put a Cuban flag with an 8 written in. Our callsign for the day was BLADE 54, which I wrote in toward the bottom of the dollar. The back side is generally reserved for a little less G-rated material. One of my nicknames in the flight was Megan, in reference to the actress Megan Fox (no relation). I included a couple of pictures of her, fully dressed of course, to make it more interesting.

Things had started off well and this was an email sent by CAIN, our class leader, on Friday,

"Gentlemen,

Great start. Any time your Flight Commander, during the FIRST WEEK of your UPT career, says you are a SHIT HOT group --- that is a GOOD thing. 'Nough said (don't get a bloated nugget over it...)

I must say, we have a heck of a cadre of instructors. Keep up the level of professionalism you have and life will be GOOD. Not only will you get to fly for a living (and get paid!) you might actually enjoy the ride.

Remember, acting like a fighter pilot is not simply who gets the most trashed on a Friday... it's who you want to go to war with on your wing come Monday morning."

-CAIN

Lesson Learned: Enjoy the Ride

Pilot training is all about passing rides and getting to the next phase so you can graduate with a pair of wings on your chest. Then what? Then I get to the F-16 training where every flight will be the same. As humans, we want to be successful and look to the future but one must also live in the present and enjoy the journey. Bear with me as I quote Andy Bernard from the NBC show *The Office*: "I wish there was a way to know you're in the good old days before you've actually left them." It is a select few who get to fly these awesome machines and while there is a lot of pressure, this is a great group of guys getting to do something awesome. I am guessing this training will at some point be the 'good old days' in my life.

Week 7: Lady Luck

The first full week of flying began with a wakeup time of 0430 every morning. Over the week I had four flights, three simulators, a weather test and we had our first instruments test.

As CAIN said in another email Sunday night:

"Get ready for another week of doing what you DREAMED of, and what most people DREAM of. Take a moment during the hectic flights to breath, and realize how awesome your "job" is (if you want to call it a "job"). Realize people want to BE YOU. Then check your altimeter because you're probably not on altitude."

We had a checklist for emergencies that was supposed to be attached to your lap somewhere for easy access. It was rather large and annoying so Sean Schiess, an Embry-Riddle ROTC graduate from Jersey and one of the most selfless guys I have ever met, decided to just hide it on the circuit breakers next to him. It was also his first time doing aerobatics and while we always made a "loose items stowed?" callout before beginning, he overlooked his loose checklist. So they start the maneuver and while upside down, the checklist flew to the top of the canopy, straight backward into the lap of the instructor and then onto the ground.

Apparently he just calmly said, "is this your f$%&ing checklist?"

"Uhhh, yes sir."

"Alright, roll into a 60 degree bank and then push aggressively forward on the stick."

This allowed the checklist to float up from its final resting place on the floor so the IP could grab it. This story resulted in laughs back in the flight room but it was still a safety issue—accounting for everything loose in the cockpit is vital as it could be dangerous if an object were to jam a flight control.

Thursday, Capt. Baumann and I were flying in the practice airspace and finished all of the maneuvers we were required to perform. At this stage we were doing practice turns, stalls and a slight introduction to aerobatics. We had a little extra time so he asked what I wanted to do.

"Sir, I would like to pull 6 Gs."

He replied, "Sounds good, just make sure to be smooth and don't roll at all."

The structural G-limit on the airplane is 7 but if you roll at all, the limit becomes 4.7 Gs as the added rolling increases the chances of bending the airplane. So we rolled into 90 degrees of bank and pulled back on the stick, holding the 6Gs for about 10-15 seconds.

When we rolled out Capt. Baumann exclaimed, "Woooeeeee! Like a strong cup of coffee in the morning!"

The average flight was about 1.4 hours and we flew 40 or 50 miles to a designated airspace to practice our maneuvers. Civilian flying is often associated with lots of boredom and staring out the window, whilst almost every second of military flying is tasking with the machines being fast and the distances short. We tried to get valuable training out of every drop of gas. I was sure it would only get more challenging as I advanced through the programs.

We started instrument classes and as the instructor said, "instrument flying is all about brain overriding ass." Instrument flying is the ability to navigate and safely fly without any exterior cues, as though you are flying in clouds. Pilots can get in dangerous situations if they fly based on what it feels like the plane is doing rather than relying on what the instruments indicate the plane is doing. Our first instrument simulator rides are next week, the second week of flying.

A bit of sad news occurred this week as one of the other Guard guys in our class, from Louisiana going to F-15s, developed a back problem when he went to survival training a few months ago. Pulling Gs on his Dollar Ride in the T-6 left him almost unable to walk after the ride. He hadn't flown since and his future status was unknown. In the best-case scenario, he would wash back a few classes. He was expecting to have back surgery on a disk in his lower back, which could permanently eliminate him from the program.

As our Flight Commander dismissed us yesterday: "guys, you have a three day weekend ahead. Don't do anything stupid like barbeque inside."

Lesson Learned: Sometimes you just need to be on the right side of luck

Even with the best training and preparation, events can still not go according to plan. This undoubtedly bothered me more than anything throughout training. No matter how intensely I studied, worked out or how well I flew, there was still a chance I could not be a fighter pilot. It is a dangerous business in the air, just moments away from catastrophe, even in training. Even with the aerial risk, hundreds of factors on the ground can keep us from flying and achieving the ultimate goal of being a fighter pilot. My buddy, on the very first step in training, had his dream taken due to something completely out of his control with a health issue. He had done everything he could to fly a fighter and was on a great path but sometimes luck isn't on your side. No matter how many angles are analyzed for a presentation or meeting, factors outside of your control can still arise creating roadblocks, sometimes insurmountable.

Week 8: The Gang

One more week and four more flights down. We had a few class parties to celebrate another great week of flying and started a motorcycle gang within the class. Fortunately, I had missed the first ride on which five guys went out on their bikes and four crashed in some form. I was speechless and it could only be laughed at since no one was seriously injured. One of other the Italians got to America and immediately bought a Jeep Liberty, Harley Davidson motorcycle and got a tattoo that said "mama." Having hardly ridden motorcycles at all, his crash was the worst. Apparently he entered a turn with too much speed and instead of leaning further over to turn and possibly slide out, he says to himself, "Ahh, dis a nota luking berry guude." He stood the bike up and drove straight off into a field. Witness reports claim he did a full barrel roll before crashing but walked away. Regardless of the fortune, I chose to ride in the back of the pack to avoid our kamikaze riders.

All of my flights continued to go well as my prior flight time as a civilian really paid off. Most of my debriefs were pretty casual conversations and I really didn't experience much stress. Our flight did experience a "bloody Friday" with three guys hooking (failing) rides. One kid now had failed two rides and is on Commanders Awareness Program (CAP). Not a huge deal but it meant they would give him more attention now and he would only fly with certain instructors to ensure continuity of training.

The reason for one of the other failed rides was comical. In the traffic pattern around the airport, we flew 200 knots and the max speed with the gear down is 150 knots. Ryan Morrison, a horseshoeing, don't-tread-on-me flag-bearing, Irish kid from Massachusetts, took off while he and his IP were in conversation and he simply forgot to bring the gear up. They were on outside downwind when he said, "sir, I have max power in and I am only getting 180 knots."

The instructor replied, "Yeah, that's weird... (5 seconds later) Oh shit! The gear is down!"

They had a chase plane to fly next to them, looking over their gear to make sure everything appeared intact. The base also deployed fire trucks to be waiting along the runway during landing. As with almost every gear overspeed, everything was fine and they landed uneventfully but it was our class's first emergency, so it was fun to gather around the bar to hear this story unfold. Morrison has a great, optimistic attitude and while I am sure he was disappointed, he charismatically told the story with great enthusiasm and laughter.

There was also an assignment night on Friday for another class. This was the night, two weeks from graduation, where the active duty kids would find out what plane they'd graduate to fly. For 54 weeks everyone competed for class ranking to determine the order of picking the airplane you want to fly. Along with what planes were available from the Air Force, the active duty kids chose in order of class rank, selecting the plane they want from what was available. However, they did this a week prior in writing, ranking the planes available so they didn't know what they'd get until they were standing in front of an audience of around three hundred people as they were given the news. It is a fun night with kegs and food but a few guys were literally in tears as they got a Remotely Piloted Aircraft (RPA) and another got a cargo plane he really didn't want.

Chris Young, my buddy from officer training school, had a maintenance class here for the next month. He joined me Friday night and after the party, knowing we had another party Saturday night, made the comment, "Not a bad life... work hard all week while flying airplanes and party on the weekend."

Week 9: Grounded

Week 9 was a relatively disappointing week as an unexpected delay emerged.

We had the second instrument test and I flew Monday and Tuesday, all of which went well and I was on schedule to solo Thursday. However, after I flew with Capt. Baumann Tuesday, he had another flight with a kid in my class, Derek Olivares. Olivares, an Embry Riddle ROTC grad from Detroit had established himself as one of our class clowns. As they were coming out of a spin, Derek felt a pop in the control stick and he lost control. Capt. Baumann was able to take control of the plane and get it flying straight and level using trim. He could turn the plane, but the elevator—the control surface controlling the plane's vertical movement—wasn't working for him. Some serious mechanical malfunction had occurred and it appeared to have no solution.

After planning to eject and going through the checklists, they discovered Derek still had elevator control while Capt. Baumann had aileron control.

In simpler terms, Derek could only make the plane go up and down while Capt. Baumann could only turn. After lots of practice in the air, working as a team before shooting the approach, they successfully landed the plane, salvaging $4 million and potential problems with an ejection. Obviously this was great news from a safety standpoint and those two would go on to win numerous safety awards throughout the next year. Unfortunately, it also meant that all T-6s in the USAF were grounded due to the unusual and dangerous problem. I had confidence we would fly next week but obviously had no idea. They have said that if the Air Force came up with a fix, maintenance would work all weekend to get the planes ready.

A couple of quotes and a story from the week:

We always do a Lessons Learned talk at the end of each day. Sitting in a circle, each of us stood up and tried to tell and teach everyone what they learned that day. Our throttle had about 8 switches on it to control everything from the radio, to the rudder and speed brake. In the first week, I had tried to make a radio call with the rudder trim, throwing the plane and my instructor to the side. There are a significant number of buttons and switches on the throttle and stick and it can be easy to confuse them, especially under stress.

This week, Morrison's lesson learned was, "Remember, you can't make radio calls on the speed brake." This simply meant that he had tried to talk on the radio and instead, deployed the speed brake.

Another kid piped up, "Wait, so we have to fly and talk at the same time?"

On Monday there were very strong crosswinds so landing was significantly more difficult. I was on downwind and watching one of my classmates land when I saw him slam it onto the runway and bounce back up in the air. Next, the controller on the ground got on the radio: "Blade 34, that one looked pretty rough, are you sure you don't need to taxi back to the chocks and have maintenance look at that one?"

Pause. "No, that was only 3.5 Gs."

Capt. Baumann and I laughed, not aware there was a G-limit for landing. I hoped I never found out what a 3.5 G impact on landing felt like, mainly for my ego's sake.

Lesson Learned: Critical Self-Evaluation

My grandpa, from his time in the Air Force almost sixty years ago, taught me critical self-evaluation on my very first flight when I was eleven. The ability to objectively look at your performance to determine the strengths and weaknesses is crucial to professionally developing in any craft. In this profession, it will save your life. Just as I have adopted this structure for the book, not only was I learning lessons about aviation, the Air Force threw in many lessons applicable throughout life for free.

The lessons can be a realization of what works and makes things better or more efficient. Something as simple as, "it is easier to put our G-suit on right leg first, instead of left," to things more complicated at this stage like setting up our avionics to more effectively shoot an instrument approach. Any improvement to an operation was fair game and it could save money, improve safety or maybe even create a little more fun. At this juncture, most of our lessons learned were learned the hard way. We were making a lot of mistakes and it was expected—just tell your classmates so they won't make them too. This class had been outstanding at communicating and we were quickly outperforming our peer flights. The Air Force was stronger because our small group was helping each other, raising the lowest common denominator.

Week 10: Lucky

We showed up Monday morning not knowing how long the planes would be grounded but ended up flying in the afternoon. I almost soloed Tuesday but an Air Force paperwork issue arose and my solo was delayed all the way until Friday.

Jeff Witt, a Harvard graduate and Alabama Guard guy who had taken the job I'd first applied for, was the first up to solo and the flight sure lived up to the hype. On his third touch and go landing, immediately after airborne, he said he experienced a significant yawing motion to the right (propeller planes normally yaw left). He said it took everything he had to keep the plane under control. The IPs thought it was just a solo flight jitter but he swore something happened. A few of us were in our flight room listening on the radio when he made the following call which has been made fun of repeatedly, "Lucky 45, outside downwind with possible rudder fail, or TAD [Trim Aid Device]." We all perked up and began to listen but also chuckle at the vagueness of the radio call. In his defense, talking on the radio is not an easy task under stress and his adrenaline was undoubtedly high after a scary moment like the one he just experienced. The controllers told him to go to the chase pattern where another plane would rejoin him and look his plane over for any serious problems.

The downfall had occurred not with the possible trim problem, but as a result of the timing of his little scare. It occurred just after takeoff, a time normally reserved for raising the landing gear. Much of aviation is about habit patterns and when something disturbs those habits, the risk of forgetting or missing a step increase dramatically. Ultimately, this is what occurred and it meant he left the gear down and over sped them.

As this situation was developing over the radio, one of the IPs in our room jokingly said, "c'mon buddy, don't say the E [Emergency] word. Don't do it buddy. I really am not interested in a lot of paperwork today."

Five seconds later… "Lucky 45, emergency, possible gear problem."

IP: "Shit! Well, I'll be back in an hour or so."

Plenty of laughter ensued as the IP stood up and left. Witt was fine in the end as it was just an over-speed of the gear. Unfortunately, it meant he hooked his solo ride. Your first solo ride is generally regarded as a great flight in your career and without an instructor to grade you, should be a pretty easy ride to pass. For Witt, however, it just made for a good story.

The dunking tank is a tradition dating back to before my grandfather was flying. As a class, we spent an afternoon painting the tank and the area around it, personalizing it to our class. The idea behind the tradition is this: if you could get back to the flight room after getting out of the plane without being captured by your flight mates and thrown in the tank, everyone owed you a case of beer. Due to scheduling issues with our flight, there weren't people present to defend the room and generally it was not much of a fight to get back, so we threw everyone in anyway.

My solo flight was a great time. It was a good feeling, looking at USAF written across the wing and knowing that you were commanding this machine alone. The Air Force is pretty strict with shenanigans so it was a pretty tame flight. My one attempt at "a little extra" was the following: we generally fly 200 knots in the pattern and before each turn I would generally go max power, roll 85 degrees of bank and pull 4 Gs at about 230 knots. I probably wouldn't have done that with an IP in the backseat. After I landed I had to hold short of the T-38 runway for about ten minutes as sixteen T-38s did touch-and-go landings, which I was not disappointed about having to watch at all. As I was sitting there relaxing, watching the jets land with my mask down, I realized that I had 100% oxygen just sitting there at my disposal. "Hell, people pay money to breathe this stuff." So I put the mask back on, getting a little high off the O2, watching the jets land.

I actually hadn't seen an F-16 fly since I'd been here but in a strange twist of irony, as I taxied in, my T-6 followed a T-38, which followed an F-16 preparing for takeoff. A perfect symbol of the evolution I hoped to go through over the next year and a half.

MY FIRST SOLO TAKEOFF IN THE T-6

Lesson Learned: Building Habit Patterns

I have always been a strong proponent of habits and their effect on peoples' lives. Generally, we only hear about bad habits and their negative influence on our lives. Whether it is biting your fingernails, watching too much TV or a late night ice cream snack, most people have a few undesirable habits.

Conversely, good habits can be a tremendously powerful tool, making life significantly easier. I haven't had soda since 4th grade and generally drink water—my doctor told me if I wanted to be a great basketball player, I should quit. Eighteen years later, I am not a basketball player but my teeth are better for it, I undoubtedly struggle with my weight less than I would and I have saved a significant amount of money. After establishing this habit, soda never even crosses my mind. More applicable to this profession, we all have habits we develop under stress. Public speaking is a great example. The 'ums,' 'errs,' 'likes,' wild hand gestures, swaying and countless other bad habits emerging when one is under the spotlight can be detrimental to effectively communicating a message. These are overcome through training and practice, much like pilots must practice to create habits for operating an aircraft.

Having great habits in high-stress environments not only allows you to effectively complete these tasks, it also frees your mind to do and think of more possibilities. Some actions need to be so habitual, they require no thought. In an emergency in the airplane, numerous distractions are pervading every second and certain actions must be instinctual to avoid further disaster. Whether it is a quick glance at the fuel or to program the right radio frequency for an instrument approach at the right moment, when stress is high, things are forgotten unless they are thoughtfully developed habits. Even outside of emergencies, actions requiring no thought, just habit, allow your mind to think and plan ahead for what is coming next, not worry about the mundane details of the present.

Week 11: Heroic Disappointment

I had two stand-ups this week. A stand-up is pseudo quiz for one poor soul during the formal brief in the morning. An instructor calls a student up to the front of the room, in front of all their peers and instructors, and describes an emergency situation. You must then stand up there, with only the resources you have in the plane: the checklist, an in-flight guide, and instrument approach procedures. As the student, you ask questions about the scenario and then describe, in excruciating detail, what actions you would take to remedy this made-up situation. With the goal of trying to simulate the stressful environment of an emergency situation in the airplane, I will say it is relatively effective at getting the heart rate up. If at any point you 'fail' and make a poor decision, you are told to take a seat and a new student is called up to hopefully finish the emergency.

There was also an airshow on base over the weekend. It featured John Mohr and his legendary Stearman aerobatic performance, which I had heard so much about, and was as amazing as advertised. Having flown the Stearman as much as I had, I could really appreciate the skill required for the performance in such an underpowered airplane. Like a kid meeting one of his heroes, I was able to talk with him for ten or fifteen minutes. He is probably sixty years old and is currently an airline pilot and FAA examiner. He told me he had about 10,000 hours in the Stearman alone and to my pleasure, when one of my buddies asked him of all the planes he has flown, which was his favorite, he concluded with the Stearman.

I did ask one question garnering an interesting answer. Being in my flight suit and obviously in pilot training for the Air Force, I asked if he had ever flown in the military or would he have liked to. He casually replied, "Oh no, I have been flying since I was five and by twenty three I had 1,000 hours of flight time. There was no reason to go that route."

I am finally getting to the point of maturity where I don't just nod to people in agreement if my opinion differs—unless they are filling out my grade sheet of course—and this was one of those situations. I just smiled and looked back, trying to read him. It was an odd feeling as I couldn't relate in any way and strongly disagreed with his opinion. My mom has pictures of me flying well prior to age five and I too had about 1,000 hours at age twenty three, so I had the capability to understand, but simply couldn't. I considered flying a fighter jet to be in a whole different league. Not only is the flying on a completely different level with afterburners, formations, weapons and fighting, but you are serving your country. For him to say he had no reason to go that route bothered me.

Lesson Learned: Ignorance is bliss?

It is hard to fathom how someone as experienced as John Mohr could be so blind and arguably disrespectful to military aviation. He has no idea what it is like and won't ever know but has still convinced himself there is no reason to have done it. I am writing this lesson learned after becoming an F-16 pilot and can say, without hesitation, flying these jets is a whole different level of awesome than any other type of flying I have been associated with. I have flown corporate jets with passengers, performed in airshows and been in formations as a civilian but all of them pale in comparison to the amazing experiences a jet, and group of guys flying these jets together, can create. Almost everything in life is about perception and hopefully you have an optimistic view of most things but denial can't be healthy.

Week 12: Check Ride

The days were long but the weeks were flying by. Every day this week started at 0600 and ended at 1800, including a flight with the Ops Group Commander (OG), a check ride and the first couple instrument rides.

The first check ride finally arrived. We all had heard horror stories of people hooking their ride for not bringing the right form to the check ride or something ridiculous. Further, if something abnormal was going to happen, it would inevitably be on your check ride. My callsign was Venom 34, and yes, just as I feared, my abnormal situation occurred checking the maintenance forms of the airplane before flight. Not once had there ever been a problem with those forms on my flights leading up to this day, nor had I ever heard so, except in those random stories. As I looked through them, I noticed the date of the last preflight was 4 days ago. I checked, double-checked and finally brought it up to my Norwegian check pilot, trying to sound as knowledgeable as I could. "Sir, the last preflight on this plane was 4 days ago and they are only good for 48 hours if the plane hasn't flown, and until the end of the day if it has. We can't take this plane."

He peered in and said (in my best Norwegian accent attempt), "Ahhhh vesss, guude catch. Dis iz berry interezting."

The crew chief came over and we asked him. While not verbatim, this is close to what he said. "Hmmm, that is weird. Oh wait, ya, this plane was definitely preflighted this morning. Did you guys see that ambulance this morning? No? Oh, well, the guy who preflighted your plane has been having some heart trouble the last couple years and was acting really strange all morning, making mistakes and not making sense. Anyway, we ended up calling an ambulance as he was having a mild heart attack. But don't worry, you are good to go, I am sure he just made a mistake and put the wrong date."

Well this put me in quite a predicament. I guess I was supposed to assume the rest of the checks were perfect even though he had missed the date by four days? The Norwegian quickly replied, "Ah, grreat. So ve ah gooood to go. 'ow iz ze guy doooing?"

He and the crew chief continued to chat while I stood deciding what the hell to do. Looking back, I regret my decision but the Norwegian was adamant everything was fine so I just rolled with it and everything worked out. I think I made the wrong decision but I just tried to read his face like I would in poker and he appeared totally cool with it.

The rest of the flight was uneventful, less one instance leaving the airspace after doing some maneuvers. There was a lot of traffic and the controller was having trouble getting us down to the airport below to demonstrate landings. The Norwegian check pilot took control, assuring me I had done nothing wrong but was going to expedite the process a little. He made a couple radio calls while I began relaxing for a second as we got a 10,000+ foot descent. Without warning, he rolled it over and put us in a 5G descending turn for three full 360-degree turns. I had yet to experience any amount of Gs for more than about one turn and in all of those situations I knew what was coming. In this instance, not only did I not know they were coming, but once they began, I assumed he was just turning us around with a 180 so I didn't bother with much of a G-strain (flexing legs and proper breathing). Not to mention, I was borderline sick and stressed, both negative influences on G-tolerance.

So about 1 to 1.5 turns in, I started greying out. First, I started losing color, then tunnel vision occurred. If it had continued to worsen, I would have lost sight but remained conscious until you finally G-LOC, or lose consciousness altogether. I could have easily told him of my situation but that would have resulted in an "unsafe" situation and I would have either hooked or had to redo the ride, along with a visit to the dark side— as the flight doc is often regarded. So with all my might, I flexed every muscle from heart down and the color slowly came back. All the while I was still wondering why the hell he was still turning. He rolled out and immediately gave me the plane, in a 2000-foot-per-minute descent, 600 feet above my level-off altitude. Still in a daze from the Gs, I blew through the altitude by 300 feet, making one of my two obvious errors on the flight. I think he knew he had put me in a bad spot and said it was fine and to let him know when I was ready and then he would resume grading. Whew.

Overall, the check ride went very well. We are graded on approximately 40 things and I received one downgrade on my emergency landing pattern. I just didn't perform it well. I didn't know if the one downgrade was good or not at the time but ultimately learned the next closest kid had settled for five downgrades, with around six students failing the ride. Most students passed with around 10 downgrades.

At this point, everyone in my flight had hooked a ride, except one Italian and me.

The day after my check ride I had my first instrument flight. For these rides we wore this leather bonnet-looking device that velcroed to our helmet so we couldn't see outside the cockpit for the entire flight, simulating flight inside a cloud without external references. We'd sit in the back seat while the IP did the takeoff and landing so it gave us time to relax and enjoy a few minutes of stress-free flying for the first time.

As I was going through a few of the maneuvers, the IP, a Lt. Col. who was retiring that year, was quiet for a while before saying, "Dude, this is stupid. We are just wasting taxpayer money. I feel like I should just give my extra flight pay to your grandpa because I am obviously not teaching you anything. I can't do it this good." This was obviously a nice thing to hear and my stress level dropped dramatically. Another example of prior flight experience really paying off once I got to military pilot training.

We had to deal with formal release every day. It is a time where students share things they learned and the IPs and Flight Commander make announcements before we are allowed go home. Our tough German Flight Commander announced he was going on vacation for the next two weeks and had rented an RV to take his family to a national park in Utah. We also had a bar in the flight room with a "beer light" the Flight Commander could turn on when everyone was done flying. With most of the first check rides behind us and since he was going on vacation, it was a truly relaxed atmosphere for the first time and he flipped the light on around 1400 on Friday. Formal release on this Friday was the scene I pictured two years ago when I started the journey of applying to be a fighter pilot. A group of pilots in their flight suits telling stories with a beer in one hand, inhibiting their ability to use two hands to describe their tall tale.

One of the older IPs, joking with the German Flight Commander, said "just remember, if you put the RV on cruise control, you can't walk back and grab a beer."

The Flight Commander replied, "I call my autopilot Shannon and it works great (laughs all around)… funny though, I call my dishwasher Shannon as well."

Lessons Learned: Proficiency Advance

I get it; large bureaucratic organizations who are training many people must produce and ensure a baseline quality product. I also understand there would be far more politics, jealously and added anxiety as people lobby to get on the fast track and proficiency advanced through syllabus items but there has to be concern about waste. Out of my own pocket, I had trained and flown more instrument flights than many of my instructors in the Air Force. The Air Force's main focus is not flying instrument flights as this type of flying is just a footnote in the greater mission of combat, whereas instruments are the pinnacle of much of civilian aviation. Ultimately, I will get around twenty flights in the instrument phase, thousands of dollars spent on learning something I already know, when I could be getting challenged with something new and becoming a valuable, mission-ready asset to the Air Force sooner. There would obviously be hurdles, especially legally, but at some point a cost-to-benefit analysis should be done with any type of training to see if it is worth the proficiency advancement.

Week 13: Turbo

Tuesday was my first advanced contact ride, the first flight geared exclusively toward aerobatics. I was flying with Capt. Baumann for the first time since my initial solo. He is one of the more relaxed IPs, and as we got tail #007 for our flight, I immediately started making Bond jokes and start talking like Sean Connery on the radio. Almost poetically, the ATIS code indicating the current reported weather was Whisky. I did nothing more than make an idiot of myself but Baumann and I shared a laugh at my expense.

Friday at around 1500 things generally wind down and the beer light comes on. I got the raw end of a scheduling situation and had to do a simulator ride to Amarillo and had been helping the Italians study for it all day. Feeling over-prepared, I was enjoying the time leading up to the Sim, already acting like it was the weekend when Lt. Iwersen, our flight scheduler, came running in saying one of the students couldn't do his solo today. Lt. Iwersen is a hilarious German and instructing is his first assignment after pilot training.

Scrambling around the scheduling board he determined I could solo today. "Are you ready to solo, Fox?"

"Sure, what time?"

"Oh shit! You step to the desk in 9 minutes and I still have to brief you!"

Up until this point, I had known about every flight at least 12 hours in advance. He rushed through the brief, which in summary, said, "don't do anything daring, dumb or dangerous." He gave me one last, "are you sure you feel prepared? I am sorry for the rush" and 9 minutes after finding out about my flight, I was putting my G-suit on, simulator postponed until Monday.

The area solo was everything I had hoped it would be. Each time I was wings level for more than four seconds in the airspace I would ask myself why, and quickly do an aileron roll. I played in the area for about 50 minutes which, after constant Gs and maneuvers, was plenty of time. With air conditioning and being up around 13,000 feet doing these maneuvers, you could keep the plane pretty cold. However, even at max cold, I was in a full sweat and out of breath from constant maneuvering and pulling Gs.

I took a little break about thirty minutes into the aerobatics and feeling a little dizzy after 7 aileron rolls in a row when it dawned on me this was my job. It's like a friend saying, "Here, play with my $4 million dollar-toy for an hour and a half, I will pay for the gas and here is $150 for drinks to celebrate after."

I left the throttle at max almost the whole time and landed with 200 lbs less fuel than is normal in a shorter duration flight. As I was taxiing back I glanced at my watch to note the landing time, 5 o'clock, Friday evening. Perfect. As soon as I walked in the flight room, a beer was waiting along with a couple IPs and six students, all sitting around telling the latest exaggeration of their heroics. It was a nice Friday afternoon.

Lesson Learned: Do What You love

People always say to do what you love growing up but having the opportunity to do so makes it clear. I have to spend most of my day at work but getting to fly these awesome planes is amazing. It's fun, interesting and rewarding. It makes studying and trying to be better far easier if you like learning about your career. If I could have an unlimited amount of money, a significant part of it and my time would want to be spent doing this exact thing.

Week 14: New Orleans

For the past few weeks I have had two events per day. Either Flight/Flight, Flight/Sim or Sim/Sim. On top of that we get other briefs and classes almost every day making the schedule very busy. Out-and-backs started this week which means we fly to a destination of our choosing for lunch and then fly home. The Italians chose Amarillo so I followed, as it is generally more fun to go in groups. Not only are these type of trips fun, they are more comfortable for me than pretty much any other type of flying we do, because most of my civilian flying involved going from point A to point B. For the kids who hadn't done that, this turned into a huge ordeal. Furthermore, to hear the poor Italians try to communicate on the radio is a disaster and wildly entertaining at the same time.

I flew with the Lt. Col. whom I had numerous times before and this was the week of his retirement. He is a huge Rangers fan and I, a Cardinals fan, so along with my experience, our brief and debrief over lunch consisted of banter about the World Series. The poor Italians had all their charts open and were constantly talking with their IPs over details and we just relaxed and enjoyed the meal. Feeling I could probably handle another IFR (instrument) departure, and again, on one of his last couple flights, the Lt. Col. opted for the canyon tour departure. Apparently the second largest canyon in the US is just southwest of Amarillo and while we weren't below the canyon walls by any means, it was low enough to make it fun.

Then came the much-anticipated cross country. Four students and four IPs headed down to New Orleans on Friday around noon and got back Sunday afternoon. It was a perfect group of IPs who were willing to go out and have a wild time and four of the single guys in our flight who had a similar attitude. I will keep the majority of the stories quiet but it was fun hanging out with the IPs in a non-professional setting. One even made the rule that if his student ever called him "sir" on the flight down there, it would cost him a beer. Ten 'sirs' later he had a $70 drink tab and we all got a free drink out of the deal. The airport where we landed, Lakefront, has a runway sticking out into Lake Pontchartrain, which made it fun to shoot approaches into.

Saturday morning after going out, with everyone feeling below average, Capt. Baumann walked up to the table at lunch with a hat pulled down, shook his head and quietly said, "I spent hundreds of dollars." Not five minutes later, Lt. Iwersen, the German scheduler, who had called this trip his "Welcome to America Cultural Experience," tried to use the ATM next to our table. After typing in his pin the screen read, "Your withdrawal limit has been reached." The entire group rolled with laughter.

Besides Friday night, the other highlight of the trip was the visual flight rules (VFR) leg out of New Orleans which I was responsible for planning. On a leg that was supposed to take us home, northwest, I ensured my first turn was southeast, straight for the swamp and the coast. For the next hour we flew the minimum altitude we legally could, at 250 knots, over some of the most remote country I have ever seen. We would come across houses with a 30+ minute boat ride to their nearest neighbor, not to mention a grocery store. I had planned a route with visual waypoints for navigation that were islands off the coast and grass strips that had a crossing runway for seaplanes. It was a type of flying I had never experienced before, and one that had we lost the engine for whatever reason, would have not turned out so well. Knowing what we would've had to deal with waiting in the swamp below, I would have considered just going down with the plane, rather than ejecting.

The one other kid in the flight, an Italian, who had not hooked a ride yet, did so this week and took it really hard to the point of tears. It was another reminder of how important this is to everyone here.

Lesson Learned: Setbacks

No matter how well things are going or how great your job is, setbacks happen. Often out of your control, it is imperative to not dwell on them as you may compound the problem. Further, how one reacts to setbacks can be critically important, especially in a leadership role. People are always watching. If you react poorly as a leader, the entire organization may be affected negatively as morale declines. If you react poorly in a lower position, leadership and peers will take note and remember the reaction when considering promotions. In our business, knowing someone will break down in tears if they fail is a considerable red flag. Nothing goes perfectly in war and we need to know our wingman will continue to perform.

Week 15: Borealis

Monday started with a night out and back to Tulsa. This was our first night flight in the military. By coincidence, Tulsa had been the destination of my first night cross country when I was getting my private license, eight years prior.

Having flown a significant amount at night as a civilian I wasn't expecting too much of difference in the experience but I was very wrong. I completely underestimated the view with a full glass canopy compared to normal airplanes. It was like flying a planetarium. There was no moon and it was a perfectly clear evening which made it all the better. As we were leveling off at 18,000 feet I began to notice an odd blue color to the north, off our right wing. The next ten minutes involved nothing but constant staring and guessing as to what it could possibly be. It slowly transformed into almost half the sky and more of a red color. At this point Lt. Iwersen, my IP, made the comment, "this is almost hard to believe—we better make sure the oxygen system is still working properly and we are not hypoxic." But then, as quickly as it appeared, it disappeared. We had no idea what it could be, considering the Aurora Borealis is generally in Canada or farther north.

After getting home, I googled our odd visual phenomenon. Lo and behold, it was indeed an extraordinary occurrence of the Aurora Borealis. Besides the area solo flight, I would call this my favorite flight thus far in pilot training.

Week 16: Copter

Thursday we flew to Fort Worth for lunch and since I was in the backseat, Capt. Baumann landed. As soon as we touched down, I looked inside the cockpit and start playing with the GPS, setting it up for the next instrument approach I would have to fly. Not five seconds after we are airborne, Capt. Baumann violently pulled the plane up and banked right toward the tower. As my head was already down, this action further threw me forward toward my lap.

Having no clue what was going on, I said a few choice words.

Capt. Baumann simply replied, "helicopter!" I looked up and saw a helicopter, now at our 10-11 o'clock, same altitude.

The tower quickly got on the radio: "don't worry, he is taxiing to Alpha," a response hardly good enough for us as the helicopter was "taxiing" 200 feet above the ground, the same altitude we would have been at our moment of convergence and the runway and taxiway are about 100 feet apart and he took it upon himself to head toward the runway and our flight path.

Regardless, all was well. I got my first pseudo "buzz the tower" *Top Gun* moment in pilot training as we banked toward the tower. My IP filled out a safety report for the incident.

This was the first week of relatively cold weather with a few mornings of below-freezing temperatures. In an example of the Air Force bureaucracy, if the temperature is in a caution zone, hot or cold, there are rules. Caution for cold: all of the pilots must wear a jacket out to the plane. But one degree more and they don't need to. Yes, we are responsible enough to fly it, but not smart enough to get out to the plane in these treacherous conditions.

Week 17: Instruments

Week 17 was another exciting week. It started with my last instrument flight before the check ride on Tuesday. The forecast for these two days was the worst since we began flying—tornadoes on Monday and our first real instrument conditions with low clouds since I had started flying in Texas. I was one of the fortunate ones on Monday with an 8 AM takeoff so I avoided the severe weather and got puffy cumulus clouds in the practice areas. Why was this good news? Well, after practicing the maneuvers for the check ride the next day, Lt. Iwersen and I decided to "investigate the clouds." 20+ minutes of diving, rolling around and pulling 4-5 Gs throughout the clouds will turn any good day into a great one. We treated the clouds like cliffs or crevasses, trying to get as close as possible and move with their undulations. I really wish I could have had a camera for this one.

The check ride was supposed to be at 8 AM Tuesday. The brief started at 6:30 AM and I was ready—the problem being the lightning storm passing through. I didn't think I was going to get the flight in, even after the storm passed, leaving low cloud ceilings. Finally, with a new check pilot, 11:30 AM was set as my takeoff time. We briefed and got out to the plane with intermittent rain. It is hard to describe the anticipation you feel for check rides—you just want to get them over with. While the weather made for difficult conditions, I was more than relieved to get going. Having said that, I was preparing for the instrument takeoff when I noticed my oxygen system wasn't working properly. We always verbally check it between both pilots right after engine start and whether I said it without actually checking or the fault happened during taxi, I was not sure. So what do you do?

A) Admit the situation and try and fix it? Well if I did this, it would show I might have not been attentive enough to do the checks previously. Further, if the fix doesn't work, the check ride would probably be postponed to the next day.

B) Try and fix it without telling him? This would involve me disconnecting hoses which could make the situation worse and he would probably wonder what the hell I was doing.

C) Keep your mouth shut and deal with it to get the check ride over.

Of course, I went with C and got away with it. I rationalized that since this was a specific instrument flight, the highest altitude we would ever reach would be around 10,000 feet. We technically didn't need oxygen below 10,000 and I kept my mask on for appearance and ejection seat safety's sake.

This would turn into a story we all laughed about over beers, telling stories of our buffoonery. The scariest confession over these evening beers was of Cheech forgetting to connect his harness after getting in the plane. The harness connects to the parachute. A kid in the class ahead of ours did the same thing and the IP realized it while they were flying, so the kid was forced to wear his harness around the squadron for a week.

Anyway, check ride passed. Supposedly the hardest phase of the T-6 is now behind us. This instrument check ride was the first time I legitimately had to use instruments of out necessity in the Air Force as the clouds went down to about 700 feet above the ground. Next, onto low level and more advanced aerobatic rides.

Week 18: Cowtimeter

Monday, the taxpayers gave me the gift of a solo flight on my 25th birthday. However, as my flight went along, the weather continued to deteriorate. While it was never bad, I got rained on for some of the flight and the ceiling dropped. While this would normally be a limiting factor for the aerobatics I could perform, I decided to bend the rules a little and make it a little more interesting by starting the loops, Cuban 8s, cloverleaves, barrel rolls, and Immelmans below the clouds and then as I climbed, I would rise through the thin layers of clouds. It was awesome. Since I was flying near the clouds, the temperature/dewpoint spread was small so clouds would form from my wingtips when pulling enough Gs, creating trails of vapor off the plane.

The rest of the week was a bit slower-paced as the rest of the flight was finishing their instrument check rides. Just like the first check ride, our flight had ten passes and three hooks.

Low level flights began on Tuesday and they were a nice reminder this is military flying. We briefed the flight like we were going to bomb a target at X time and used satellite images to pinpoint the exact position on the bridge we wanted to hit. The routes were generally 40 minutes long with 6-8 turn points and then a target. We planned to fly at 210 knots groundspeed, using a technique referred to as 'clock to map to ground.' We labeled our map with times and assuming we were flying the correct speed, we would check the time against where we should be on the map and then look outside to verify we knew where we were.

While it shouldn't have been too difficult, I had never tried to navigate by visual references at 500 feet above the ground before with a map. It really is pretty damn low and difficult to see things more than a couple miles away which makes it tough. The Texas countryside has hundreds of cell phone towers and it's a constant struggle to find them all. We had to point them out to our IP, "Contact tower, right, 2 o'clock, 3 miles, black on grey." We tried to gauge 500 feet by a couple of different metrics. My favorite was the

Cowtimeter. Can you just make out all four legs of a cow? Yes? Well you are about 500 feet, obviously. Every IP has his own trick with houses or cars but the cowtimeter is my method of choice.

Week 19: Billhillies

Monday I was scheduled to fly low level, out and back, to Fort Worth with four other guys. Out-and-backs involve a lot of planning and low level flights require a lot of planning. The weekend had obviously been busy preparing, only for the weather to be bad and for me not to fly at all. Frustrating. Tuesday, repeat same process and result as Monday. Wednesday, weather was looking better except for a layer of fog, conveniently placed over the beginning of the low level routes. Since these flights were flown 500 feet above the ground and were completely reliant on looking at and avoiding the ground and our beloved cell phone towers, this is a problem. However, my IP was determined to fly so we pressed on and the first two legs were entirely fogged in. We were flying at 500 feet above the ground in clear skies, which is pretty low, and the clouds were below us. I was forced to navigate purely off the cell phone towers sticking up through the clouds, which was an eerie sight.

As soon as we landed and debriefed, Cheech and I ran home, packed and hopped in the car for Missouri as it was late November and this was Thanksgiving break. For the first time, the Italian experienced hot tubs, biplanes, Bass Pro, more of my friends than he could believe would like me, Thanksgiving, and as his language barrier put it, "Billhillies" (Hillbillies) on his trip to the greatest state in the Union. He even got a ride in my grandfather's Stearman.

Week 20: Everyday Friday

A week full of stories but most not associated with flying.

We had our mid phase reviews. Everything about our life was graded and they gave us an update on where we stood. First, a flying review. They told us where we stood based on thirds of the class. We all generally had an idea where we stood but it was tough seeing the guys get told they were in the bottom third of the class, especially since they were competing for airplanes. It left an awkward buzz in the flight room for a day or two. We also received feedback on our officership qualities: professionalism, leadership, teamwork and motivation. All of the IPs ranked us on each category on a 1-7 scale and provided comments. I had no idea how this would go since I hardly know anything about the military compared to the rest. It went well and I was rated most highly for motivation. I was pleasantly surprised as this is almost 25% of your grade. Most guys were downgraded due to professionalism issues at the wrong time and while not great, it does make our flight entertaining.

I had only two or three flights this week as we were weather-cancelled a couple days. One was an advanced contact ride, which, as most of the maneuvers were relatively easy, was just a fun excuse to go fly. The other was a low level flight. I have three low level flights before the low level check ride. Overall we would have five check rides in the T-6, one for each of the different areas of training: Contact, Instrument, Low Level, Formation and Advanced Contact.

This left us with Friday afternoon and the weekend where we had our first roll call. I was still learning what a "roll call" was but I think the tradition started among fighter pilots in WWI or WWII. After coming back from battle, they would have roll calls for accountability because many would not return. They would drink in their honor, tell stories, sing songs and participate in many other traditions. I could write pages about what goes on in them. There is an appointed Mayor who runs the show by setting and enforcing rules. Break a rule, take a shot. There was a round for storytelling which was hilarious as everything was fair game. Witt told the story of my instrument oxygen problem on the check ride. People confessed to all kinds of things and the whole place was generally rolling with laughter.

There was also a "What if" round. Witt, the guy who had oversped his gear on his solo, stood up and said, "what if I had raised my gear every time I took off?"

I stood up and said, "what if the Cheech hadn't asked my father to join in him the bath tub?"—last week, when I took him back to my parents' home, he kept calling the hot tub a bath tub.

If someone says something about you, you have a chance for rebuttal. Cheech tried to defend himself and ended up earning a call sign out of his attempt at a defense. In his broken English he said, "This is not true, I asked Steve [my father] if he wanted to join me in the bath t…"

You couldn't even hear the rest of what he said as the whole place erupted in laughter at his misspoken response. Someone yelled out that at our party the next night, at Capt. Baumann's house, there would be a hot tub.

Cheech replied, "Yes, I will be in Baumann." After saying what he had about my dad and then that comment, the room exploded. No one said a word for at least five minutes as everyone was crying from laughing so hard. So Cheech was named BASS. It stood for not only his Bass Pro visit and the billhillies comment, but predominately, Baumann's ass. I came away from roll call with no voice.

The next evening was all about the call sign naming ceremony. A huge board was placed behind a chair and the person in the chair couldn't say a word. If he did, he took a shot. If the Mayor told him to take a shot, he took a shot. If someone told a lame story about the person in the chair, they took a shot. There were probably more rules but as you can imagine, my memory faded throughout the evening. Hawk, my buddy going with me back to South Dakota, was the first poor bastard up and had missed the roll call so he didn't understand the rules. He kept talking and not following the procedures, so he kept taking shots. We told stories about him doing various things like going into a women's restroom, dumb things he'd said, and when I told the story of having to constantly hear him call his wife "Punkin" 80 times per day over the phone at our last training, that sealed it. He is now "Punkin."

To select a call sign, each person received about six names up on the board and then the volume of cheering determined the winner.

We got to my name and the following names were thrown out there. Megan, Bond, Jose, Hose, Hick, Fang, Snoopy. It was down to Bond and Hose and Hose won. Capt. Baumann told a story of my first ride, struggling to get in the plane. Trying to strap in, I got all of the belts, oxygen hoses and radio cords in a big knot and he had to uncomfortably help untangle them in my lap.

The rest of the call signs were awarded as follows:

Hulk – Smallest guy and tried to open the canopy without rotating the handle. (Culbertson)

Smoka – His last name is Grassi. You do the math.

PBJ – Parking Brake Jackass—he pulled the parking brake while moving.

BJr – pronounced BeeJayer. Blue Jr. Looks and acts just like a Lt. Col. in our flight. (Morrison)

Cane – Our captain who is old. A play on his real callsign, CAIN.

Salsa – Stupid ass with Low SA "Situational Awareness." (Olivares)

Fish Lips – Made out with a girl on cross country who someone thought had fish lips.

Dip – His last name is Schiess… or shit in German.

TAD – Witt's callsign, derived from his solo emergency and claiming it was the trim aid device's fault.

All in all, it was two hours of straight laughter, more shots than we all care to remember and thirteen names.

Lesson Learned: Camaraderie

When you work so closely with a group of people, in such a high stress environment, it is great to let off steam and laugh at ourselves. I had never seen an entire room of happiness and real laughter like I did those two evenings. It taught me the importance of organized group entertainment amongst friends and for an organization. We got a lot closer after this weekend and it did nothing but help in the future. We built stronger friendships and trust that can be utilized in and out of work.

Week 21: Cancelled

One interesting aspect of pilot training was how little the students influenced decisions regarding the weather. There was generally one instructor up in the tower who decided if, where, and when we could fly. The students essentially had no say in the matter. Considering weather is the cause of most aviation-related accidents, this surprised me. I understood the need to cover everyone's ass, but I felt we were missing out on a big part of being a pilot. I said this during a week of multiple weather cancellations. It was a very slow and disappointing week as I saw my low level check ride continue to get pushed back for unnecessary reasons. The check ride was now scheduled for next week, another week with rain blanketing the forecast.

I ended up flying twice last week. Thursday was my first flight with a Lt. Colonel who had ridden a mechanical bull in New Orleans on our trip and was a great guy to be around. We even had a couple beer bets based on my performance. I forget a certain radio call, I owe a beer. It ended up being my best low level flight with no beers owed. It was one of those unfortunate one-way bets.

Week 22: Trust

It was another interesting, weather-filled week. It started Monday with my pre-check ride flight for the low level phase. The flight went fine and I was ready to check, even though the forecast for the next two days was rain and low ceilings.

This left the check ride for Tuesday. It was scheduled for a 1400 takeoff, so I slept in. I was sitting in my boxers, drinking a smoothie, using Google Earth to look at various angles of my target to ensure I wasn't going to miss it and thinking there was a 1% chance I would get to fly because of the weather when the call came in. It was our scheduler saying the weather was just good enough at the moment and if I could be ready to brief in 30 minutes, I would have a check ride. Ten minutes later, I was in the flight room with Schiess handing me the stuff I needed. I had prepared two low level routes, Alpha and Charlie, but unfortunately, the weather was too low on those routes. I had taken satellite pictures of each turn point and had them all prepared but now had to switch to another route, 15 minutes before the brief, where I had to explain, in detail, the entire route. I actually hadn't even seen the target, via satellite or in person, as I walked in to brief the check ride. If I didn't see the target on the flight, I'd hook. To make matters worse, it was the first low level flight we'd had with poor weather. Ceilings were forecasted to drop each hour and they were 300 feet above the minimum when we took off.

Schiess and I had the same takeoff time and were flying the same route, meaning there had to be a five-minute takeoff separation between us. While this seemed insignificant, it proved to make a huge difference. I requested taxi 15 seconds before he did and as we were parked next to each other before taking the runway, we gave a few last-second head nods as it began to rain. We made radio updates along the route for traffic deconfliction and while I'd expected to hear from him throughout the flight, those head nods were the last communication we had with one another during the check ride.

I took off and made it onto the route, but not three minutes later another guy in our flight ahead of me had to abort for low ceilings and visibility. Three minutes later, another guy did. Further, they just announced Sheppard had gone to instrument conditions, meaning I would have to get approach plates out and shoot an instrument approach upon return, in the clouds. Ironic, since the only time I'd shot an instrument approach in real weather was on my last check ride. Regardless, we were pressing on and the lower cloud ceilings actually made the towers easier to see with their strobe lights on top against the grey background. We made a couple of turn points and then as I climbed a couple hundred feet for a few towers, a cloud deck went underneath us.

Me: "Sir, we obviously don't have the weather to continue."

Lt Col: "Ah, ya, hmmm, just descend through this layer and continue."

Me: "Ok, but I wouldn't descend because of the towers."

Lt Col: "It will be fine, I will help."

So we descended through the clouds, in the rain, on a VFR flight 800 feet above the ground, with towers all around for another five minutes or so before we called it off. I got ahold of a controlling agency on the radio and picked up an IFR flight plan and climbed into the clouds, essentially beginning another instrument check ride. Even though low level is completely visual, I could still hook for an error here. We flew in the clouds for a good 30 minutes and they even made us hold for traffic and do a circling approach. All things that seemed to only happen on a check ride.

All went well but it might have been for nothing as we didn't finish enough of the low level to be graded. But my IP, after looking at my grade sheet and along with what he had seen from previous flights, felt I could handle the "low level military environment" and passed me. I picked up two downgrades, with one for mission planning which is ironic because I did none. The 15-second difference in ground ops between Schiess and me created a five-minute wait he had to endure before takeoff. This five-minute difference allowed the first weather abort call from another airplane on his route, meaning they couldn't start the low level. They turned around and landed after a three-minute flight. He had to check on Thursday, so essentially a 15-second difference in ground ops resulted in Schiess having to wait 48 hours to check. Check rides require skill and luck.

I wrote the following email to my flight the next day.

"I called my grandpa on the drive home to tell him about my check ride. While applying the 10% rule [when telling stories, only 10% of it needs to be true. This rule obviously makes stories far more interesting] everywhere I could, I finished the story about 10 minutes later, awaiting feedback.

Paraphrased- "The one thing I really love to hear is how much your buddies helped you prepare for that. It is great to see that bond and camaraderie among the flight."

I didn't realize it at the time of stress, but it is pretty amazing that on the check ride requiring the most planning and preparation, I essentially did none of it and had the confidence to say I was ready when our Flight Commander asked prior to step. Further, our Flight Commander not only saw, but essentially approved, knowing everyone involved, at least 5 that I know of, could be trusted to send someone to a check ride.

I know we do it for each other all the time but I thought it was cool that even after all the 10% rule I applied to my story, the main thing Pop noticed was the one thing I didn't apply the 10% rule to, our camaraderie. Pretty cool guys."

Morrison had his check ride on Thursday and it was forecasted to have heavy crosswinds. I taught him how to handle crosswinds in the simulator in September but he wanted a refresher since the winds have been calm and we haven't flown much recently. We talked through the controls and then I added, "If you want to be real shit hot, when the right main wheel touches down, add even more right aileron input and dance on one wheel as long as you can down the runway."

A few hours later and not knowing how his check ride went, he called and said, "I was feeling pretty good about myself coming into the landing, direct crosswind. Big crab but for once in my life I get the x-wind corrections right and touchdown on one wheel and all I could think of were the words from Mr. T. Fox. So I put in more aileron and no shit, that bitch rolled in on one wheel, totally sealing the deal."

After some laughter and hanging up, I realized this call had undoubtedly made me feel better than passing my check ride. All thirteen of us passed our low level check ride.

Finally, I had my first formation flight on Friday with the Flight Commander and Morrison in the other plane with an IP. Fortunately, it was the first beautiful day we'd had in a while. In total, I probably had 3-5 hours flying formation in the Stearman and it helped. We practiced turns, pitchouts, echelon turns, turning and straight ahead rejoins, and all of the communication and choreography necessary to fly formation. All in all, it was a great and incredibly fun flight and far easier than I was expecting. I even got the famous words from my Flight Commander of the performance being "shit hot."

At the end of practicing in the airspace, lead told us to go to fighting wing position. The position is about five hundred feet behind lead and you try to stay 30 to 45 degrees off his tail, so not directly behind him. It is akin to a car's blind spot. My instructor took the plane from me and proceeded to do two barrel rolls around the lead plane. As we were inverted on top of their plane I could see Morrison with his head tilted back, looking at us and just shaking his head. While I couldn't see through his visor, I could definitely see him laughing. It was awesome.

Lesson Learned: Trust

It is a liberating feeling to have complete trust in someone. In this business it almost comes naturally as there are so many instances in which you are forced to trust your wingman. Whether it is not bumping into you during basic formations, to later on, not accidentally shooting you instead of the bad guy when there are many jets tied up in a furball, trust is essential. It makes our flight and the Air Force so much stronger. Imagine having to constantly watch the other airplane in your flight for fear of him hitting you, when the flight lead is responsible for the more important tasks of navigation and tactical decision-making. The same is true in business. If the leadership can simply hand a task off to someone and trust it will be done properly, it allows them so much more flexibility and time to strategize and move the company forward. If they must micromanage everything, it creates significant inefficiencies. Part of our class's ease in trust is derived from knowing we have all been through the same training and have spent a lot of time together, getting to know one another. I don't want to let the other guys down because it would look poorly upon me and hurt the Air Force's overall mission, but more than anything, I don't want to let my friends down. Team building and social settings at work, while sometimes seeming irrelevant and a waste of time, can help make actual work more efficient and effective.

Week 23: Posit

With two formation flights and two night flights, it was a fun week. In formation, I led my first wing landing which was a rewarding feeling. You bring your wingman down from 30 miles away all the way to land with him ten feet off your wing the whole time. He must trust you completely as he is forced to focus exclusively on staying in the proper formation and not hitting your jet all the way through touchdown on the runway. We practiced these in case of emergency so one plane can lead another back to base if it is having problems.

Both night flights went well with one embarrassing exception. It was a cloudy night and the strobes on our airplane were blinding when we entered the clouds, especially at night. This bright light was designed to be seen from miles away so when it reflected off water particles just a few feet away, it was very distracting. So as we were climbing through the clouds, I flipped the lights off and once we emerged above the clouds, I flipped them back on. This is not a big deal unless, on the descent back to base, you do the same—less remembering to turn them back on. So we were entering the traffic pattern, making the standard radio calls, my IP and I were chatting it up since I have seen a lot of night flying and it wasn't too foreign to me, when the runway tower made this call to us: "inside initial, say posit."

I knew he was referring to us but was confused. He just said our position and I didn't know what "posit" meant. So I did what I am told and replied, "posit." It turned out that posit stands for "position" and since they couldn't see us, they were looking for an update. In all honesty, it was one of the bigger mistakes I made in pilot training as the traffic pattern was based on seeing other airplanes to avoid them. To say the guys had a great time making fun of me on this one would be a dramatic understatement.

The next night flight went far better. Most guys stayed in the local area but I chose to do a little extra planning and fly to Oklahoma City as bigger cities are more interesting and beautiful to fly over at night. It was a great tour of the neighborhoods and their Christmas light decorations. My IP also let me shoot an instrument landing approach (ILS) at 170 knots as opposed to the normal 110 knots so I could see what it would feel like in a T-38 and F-16. The older IPs generally have the bigger picture in mind and therefore let us do different, but still beneficial things.

In a note on Air Force bureaucracy, we must fill out approval forms if we are going to do anything hazardous. In our final briefing before the holiday break, they reminded us that building snowmen was on that list. As my mom would say, "he can fly a jet, but he can't build a snowman without permission."

Lesson Learned: Spice

While something may be more difficult and require extra work, it is often worth it. I chose to put thirty more minutes of planning into this night ride and got a far better memory than the rest of the guys who stayed local for their night flights. Don't be lazy because it's easier; make life more interesting.

Week 24: Old School Fight

We started back from the Christmas holiday break with only the instructors flying to get current again before flying with students on a warm up, ungraded ride, Wednesday.

I had two formation flights this week, both with Cheech as my wingman. I also flew the second flight with a Dutch IP, a nice, happy guy with whom everyone wanted to fly. He flew the F-16 for nine years so once he found out I was in line to do the same, he requested we fly together again.

My flight with him on Thursday included the formation maneuver called Extended Trail. Essentially, the #2 airplane flies 30-45 degrees off lead's tail about 500-1000ft back. They are allowed to maneuver however they choose to stay within this area while the lead plane can basically do whatever they desire. Essentially my first taste in the realm of dogfighting, lead maneuvered into barrel rolls, cloverleaves, and loops while #2 had to stay within that cone or he would bust on a check ride. The best part is our joystick having a trigger switch that could be pulled without negative consequence. We had fun imagining the lead plane as a P-51 or Spitfire, chasing them down as they did in WW2. I wish I could eloquently describe the feeling and conversations we had doing this stuff but I couldn't... yet. A lot of Gs were pulled during this maneuvering.

We all heard a Guard guy was eliminated from Introduction to Fighter Fundamentals (IFF). IFF would be the 10-week course after this one introducing us to dropping bombs and dogfighting in the T-38. It would be one more hurdle towards the dream of piloting a fighter jet and while I was confident it shouldn't be a problem, my prior experience would no longer be helping me and wild things can happen. I shouldn't have let it get me down, but I will admit it did some. Anything standing between me and the goal of an F-16 was the enemy.

Week 25: Ring of Fire

Formation training continued to get more entertaining. As students, we were getting better in the wingman and lead positions, which in turn, made it easier for the other guy with whom you were flying. The same IP who bet me a beer on a low level flight had a new deal for our flight on Wednesday. Every second I was out of position, he would start singing. As he warned and I later discovered, this was indeed a punishment. So at one point in my wingwork, flying closely off the wing of the other airplane while they did large climbing and descending turns, I got out of position and *"The Devil Went Down to Georgia"* crackled over the intercom. I was directly above another airplane, less than 20 feet away from it, in 90 degrees of bank, and this terrible noise came through my headset. I got the plane back to a position I thought was suitable and the singing continued. Frustrated, I continued looking at all the references for the proper position. For example, we align the other plane's wingtip light with the exhaust cowling on the engine. But he was still singing.

Frustrated, I eventually asked, "Sir, what is wrong with this picture right now?"

"Oh shit, I forgot. Nothing, but I think I'll just keep singing anyway."

I ended up getting to solo in formation on a Friday with the same singing IP. Just he and I walking out to a couple planes sitting by each other, taking them up for an hour and having a great time. I led the formation out and for the first thirty minutes of the flight before passing him the lead responsibility. It was one of the quicker hours of my life, which is unfortunate, but speaks to how much fun we had. He led the descent back to Sheppard and Air Traffic Control gave us a steep descent, so in reference to his singing to me on Wednesday, I keyed the mic on our private frequency and started in on, *"and down, down, down, the ring of fire, the ring of fire."*

I could see him nodding his head and throwing a thumbs up.

We pitched out to land, meaning we flew directly over the runway at 1000 feet in close formation and then he turned away from me aggressively. I waited five seconds and then followed him with an aggressive circle to land. As lead, he gave me the signal indicating he was going to pitch away, which is just twirling your pointer finger vertically in the air. Not only did he do that, he followed it with a stationary middle finger as his plane snapped away. The atmosphere in our flight was pretty relaxed and enjoyable these days.

I had 93 hours of flight time in the T-6 now, with 21 flights to go.

Weeks 26 and 27: Karma

We had 0600 show times and I flew in the morning each day, meaning I was done by 1130. With most classes complete at this point in training, the schedule was pretty nice as most days as I would go home, work out and just relax.

The last simulator ride is notorious for being a fun emergency ride. The IP throws all kinds of issues at you and you do your best to figure out the solutions, often ending in ejection. My grade sheet simply said, "Afterburners are better, happy landings."

I also heard a terrible story this week from H flight, our sister flight, on Friday night over a beer. I hadn't really known before, but H flight didn't share the same camaraderie as G flight. I'll tell the story via abbreviated dialogue:

H flight student: (Talking to the group. A good guy who has just said he absolutely hates student X, another kid in H flight) "Have you guys ever, even once, taken a picture or video in the plane?"

Me: (Smiling) "Of course not, none of us have."

H flight student: "Well I had one of those Go-Pro Cameras and took it with me on a solo. Not a big deal, everyone does it. Student X finds out about it and in some fucked up way, decides he needs to tell the IPs, because it is a safety issue. Yes, a bro in my flight went straight to the IPs; not me, not anyone else in our flight, to tell them this. So the Flight Commander comes to me and says, 'Look, Student X came to me and told me you are filming in the plane. I thought you would want to know that. I don't condone it if you are and you probably shouldn't. However, we have all done it and I thought you would want to know he is going behind your back like that.'"

Lesson Learned: Being a Bro

The amazing part of the camera story and the lesson I am learning comes from the Flight Commander's response. He couldn't have cared less about following every little bureaucratic rule the Air Force sent down because someone needed to cover their ass or have something done for their resume; he cared about going to war with the right kind of guys. He didn't want his wingman to be a guy who stabbed his last wingman in the back to get there. It is why the snitch never won in elementary school and even more so within the uniformed services. Should the camera rule have been broken? Probably not, but Student X needed to be a man. In his attempt to help vault himself above his peer, he lost the respect of all the students and instructors in our class and his reputation would follow him.

When I wrote this weekly update, a retired Marine colonel was one of my recipients and responded to this post in the following way:

"Interesting story about the kibitzer Student X. There are always some 'safety tattletales' around and I hated all of them. The missing key issue with these guys is 'unit integrity,' that willingness the infantry troops display against a common enemy; it is what gets you through tough combat situations. In the fighter community (any service), it is an absolute essential. Guys like Student X destroy that sort of cohesiveness—they ought to be shot at sunrise or sent off to count beans. His was an attempt to curry favor with the instructors on what he hoped they would react to in the name of safety. The instructor reaction was correct and appropriate; your instructors are a competent lot of officers, what I would have expected. Maybe H flight has a chance at some unit cohesion now.

One important rule of military leadership is never to make a rule you can't enforce. Rules on the honor system just don't work, everybody knows you can't get caught. The military is particularly fond of making trivial rules, and it just makes 'the rule maker' look foolish and petty."

Week 28: Knock-it-off

My first of three flights this week was Wednesday and we got a taste of fluid maneuvering. This is an exercise where, for about four minutes, we would chase the other aircraft as he essentially tried to block us moving in on him for "the kill." We had been chasing the other airplane every flight in extended trail up to now, but previously he had always tried to make it easy for our wingman. More of this would come in the T-38. I left the flight exhausted and had a weird soreness in my teeth from pulling Gs for an extended period of time.

The next day we flew formation in the evening. It was one of those pre-storm evenings where a colorful sunset was in full display with a backdrop of exploding clouds. It just so happened the puffy clouds were at the bottom of our airspace, 8,500 feet, creating a floor of faint red and purple cotton balls. Practicing fingertip formation in a 90-degree bank turn and looking down on the lead airplane with the clouds just below him was an amazing sight. I mentioned to my IP, Lt. Iwersen, that I would kill for a picture of this but he had left his phone in the room. I almost asked him to take the controls so I could get mine out but decided against it.

Hawk discovered he and his wife would be having a boy in June, six months from now. He had to delay his check ride until the afternoon to go to the doctor to find out the good news. However, after he moved the check ride back, the weather rolled in, making the flight more difficult. He was given a non-standard clearance on departure and botched it, hooking the formation check ride. I would imagine most days didn't have as much emotion as this one did for him.

Hawk's examiner was an Italian instructor who questionably downgraded him for many other mistakes as well, infuriating our Flight Commander. After hearing the news, he returned to the flight room and threw a binder on his desk. After pacing the room he finally exclaimed no one would fly with that Italian check pilot again, even if it meant delaying check rides.

By some miracle we were able to fit in a flight on Friday despite forecasted thunderstorms. It marked my first experience of flying through clouds in formation and it was incredible. During extended trail, Morrison, my flight lead, did his split S relatively low and when he realized he wasn't going to be able to stay above the clouds, found a hole and hoped I would be in the proper position to follow. Well it didn't work out quite as planned and I descended through the clouds having to call a "knock-it-off" (a safety call-out to stop maneuvering as an unsafe condition was developing). Not a big deal, and it happens occasionally, but it was wild to watch him 500 feet in front, pull Gs near the clouds, causing the wingtip vapor trails to form and extend past me. It was as if he was drawing a road in the sky for me to follow.

Half of our flight had their two ship low-level cross-country flight to Oklahoma City this weekend. A few of us drove up to meet them for shenanigans on Friday night. We met them at a bar and a couple executives from Waste Connections were in town for business and, upon discovering our group was from the Air Force, demanded we not buy another thing. There were around fifteen of us along with many others and they kept inviting more over for a good time. We estimated they spent at least a few thousand dollars.

Lesson Learned: Stand up for your People

There is a clear delineation between students and IPs, and IPs generally never talk poorly about each other in front of students. However, when our Flight Commander had his rant in our flight room over the questionable check ride, it was inspiring. Our Flight Commander saw an injustice and was willing to fight for his student. I will never forget how good it made me feel to know he was willing to stand up for us. It motivated me to work even harder to not let him down. I would think any time a superior supports a subordinate on a public stage, it is a great opportunity to create a loyal follower and friend.

Week 29: The Downgrade

As last week was relatively quiet, this week was quite the opposite. Morrison and I had our final two flights leading into our formation check ride on Wednesday, followed by one contact ride on Thursday and our formation low-level cross-country trip over the weekend.

The final two flights before the formation check ride fine-tuned all of the procedures and techniques we had learned. Thus far, formation check rides had been ugly for the other students, with five downgrades being the best score and eleven or so being the average. This check ride was really important to me as formation is a huge part of the fighter world and most of the T-38 flying would be in formation. Morrison and I had heard all the horror stories of our flight mates' check rides; both planes not being able to see each other, not leveling off at the right time and busting airspace boundaries. Our two ship had flown cleanly but Morrison started getting his left and right radio calls backward. Combine this issue with deteriorating weather which changes some formation rules and the nerves had started showing up for both of us.

We briefed the check ride and headed out to the planes, first checking the damn maintenance forms. Yes, the same forms with errors only on the check rides. I was looking at one page as the IP said, "Hmmm, how long is the tire pressure check good for?"

I had honestly never heard this rule and tried to come up with a number before giving up and confessing. The tire pressure check had expired by 20 minutes. Yes, this was the first time this had happened for anyone in our flight. I looked over and saw my buddy already starting his engine when my IP said, "you know, I actually need to go use the restroom, I will be back in a bit." Awkward. I ended up sitting in the plane for five minutes, cold, thinking I had already hooked my check ride for the damn forms. I found out later that Morrison was freaking out because he couldn't see me from where he was parked and didn't know the dilemma. I was supposed to be checking him in on the radio but was silent for ten minutes as my IP was taking a leak. It was a lovely start. We ended up taking off and the rest of the flight was uneventful. Granted, there were numerous things I wish could have gone better, but besides my maintenance forms debacle, I knew things had gone well.

Considering the bloodshed on the rest of the check rides, and we were the last, we had set a goal for 10 downgrades combined. I ultimately got one downgrade for ground operations due to the forms and Morrison got four downgrades for a couple discrepancies in the air. So not only had we beaten our goal by half, but as a pair, we got the same amount of downgrades as the next best individual. It was a good day.

Over the weekend we flew out and back to Fort Worth. While I still had four more flights and a check ride in the T-6, this weekend was supposed to be the culmination of everything we had learned and a good time. We took off in fingertip formation, sent the wingman to tactical formation (2-3000 feet away), flew a low level for 40 minutes at 500 feet, dodging towers for not only yourself but your wingman as well, found a target and simulated bombing it. Then we had to fly to a foreign field, dealing with approaches, weather and traffic, all with a wingman you had to be responsible for. It was pretty impressive some of these guys came here with 15 hours at the controls of an airplane and could handle all of that with 120 hours in the T-6. We had four flights over the weekend doing this, two of them as the lead aircraft and two as wing.

As I mentioned earlier, while this trip was a learning opportunity, it was also meant to be fun. I had previously secured one of my favorite IPs for both of those reasons long ago, so when he fell out two days prior and some random guy from the reserves jumped in, I was disappointed. Further, every time an IP from my flight asked who I was flying with and I replied with Ernie, I got the same, "that sucks" look. The poor guy meant well but when I think of the word "Goober," nothing could have fit his description any better. I could go into countless examples but the one I will give involved us landing after our first flight in Lawton, OK. We were in a room of eight guys all debriefing the flights when he looked at me and said:

Ernie: (Nerdy but always nice sounding) Do you want to get punched in the face?

Me: Uhhhhh, no?

Ernie: Well if you did and I let you put on your helmet, would you want your visor down?

Me: I don't know, will it shatter? (My eyes glancing around the room, looking for sympathy.)

Ernie: Well I saw you have a clear visor and a dark visor. Wouldn't you put both of them down to shield you?

Me: Well, if they don't shatter then yes, probably.

Ernie: Then why, when I looked into the front cockpit today, did I see your dark visor down and your clear one on top of your helmet, not protecting your face?

Me: Because if both of them are down, I get double the glare, dust and scratches.

Ernie: Just clean them better and you will be fine. If a bird comes through that windshield you will thank me.

I told this story at dinner that night because Ernie went home instead of hanging out with us. Further, I confirmed every IP only used one visor for the same reasons as me. The canopy was tested up to 270 knots with a four-pound bird. The entire weekend with Ernie was that kind of "well, you should have worn your static discharge suit because you never know when you might get hit by lightning" bullshit. I finally learned to just nod and not say anything further.

Morrison was leading one flight and called out a tower, "Contact, tower, my 12 o'clock, 3 miles, uhhh lots of little white balls on it." I burst out laughing at the thought of Morrison describing a cell phone tower with balls on it and replied on the radio, "I am visual," while laughing.

Ole Major Ernie didn't skip a beat, finding no humor in what occurred. Meanwhile, I could see Morrison's instructor, Capt. Baumann, laughing all the way from my plane.

We stayed at the Gaylord Texan and went to a club on the grounds. Our group of ten younger guys, all on the dance floor, made for quite the hit in the predominantly 40s crowd that was there. We may or may not have gotten on stage with the band and been thrown off.

Lesson Learned: Always Be Personable

You can be the smartest, most competent person in your field but if you can't effectively communicate to peers or subordinates, your value diminishes quickly. I have no doubt Ernie knew procedures and great techniques to make me a better pilot but the way he addressed me and delivered his messages made him repulsive. My natural reaction was to tune him out. When pointing out every single rule infraction or possible improvement, while good in intent, it must be delivered in the proper tone and time to be effective. No one likes the guy walking around correcting everyone in an odd tone.

Week 30: Complete

As of Thursday morning I had one solo, one ride with an instructor and my check ride left in the T-6. However, there weren't any IPs available to fly with me so they paged the entire building trying to get someone for me. One IP was available. My last image of the T-6 instructing core was going to be none other than Major Ernie. When Lt. Iwersen got off the phone and told me the news, the entire flight room burst into laughter.

The flight with him went fine and my solo during the afternoon was awesome. Weather was moving in so there were clouds in the airspace, making it a pilot's paradise. Six of us soloed at the same time, creating a fun atmosphere on the ground and in the air as we chatted up the radios.

Now Friday morning, and as expected, the weather was terrible. My check ride, and hopefully final flight in the T-6, was scheduled for 1430 but they moved it up to 1300 in hopes of getting airborne before the really nasty weather arrived. Twenty minutes before my brief, there were reports of ice, snow, and three miles visibility in the airspace. Not good for a flight based off visual references.

By miraculous luck, good or bad, the weather was deemed good enough to fly. I got the same check pilot as I had on my very first check ride, the Norwegian former F-16 pilot. We took off and ended up finding a few holes in the weather, fitting in half of the maneuvers. Fortunately, he said he had seen enough but had one more challenge. "Fox, let's see how good of a pilot you really are. Lock your harness and really make sure everything is secured."

He proceeded to roll upside down and hold the negative G for 10-15 seconds, with the challenge being to hold altitude inverted. When you perform this maneuver, the blood is rushing to your head and it seems no matter how tight your seatbelt is, you are still loosely hanging from it in the cockpit. I repeated but lost about 500 feet doing so.

"Oh God Fox, you suck. That was terrible. How did you make it through this program? Try it again."

I tried again, this time adding a lot of nose down trim. Naturally, the plane climbed 500 feet.

"Fox, horrible. Now give me a second, all of my papers are everywhere back here."

I replied, laughing, "Sir, in my defense, if you put the two attempts together, I am at my original altitude."

He said, "Sure, if that makes you feel better about yourself, now get us out of here."

We flew to the auxiliary field and I did one approach before he took the airplane and did one for himself and flew us back to Sheppard. We talked about the Guard, F-16, T-38 and everything in between as I enjoyed relaxing on my last T-6 flight. Or, as he kept saying, "*hopefully* your last T-6 flight."

After we landed, the crew chief came over and shook my hand, saying it had been a privilege working with me and I would really enjoy the T-38. In the debrief, the check pilot's general knowledge questions were from a sheet with questions from the first day of training. It was brutal but intended to be comical as the first day questions were tiny details meant to haze us. After the check pilot finished asking questions, he asked how I felt. I said I felt like I got punched in the face. He replied, "Good. Since I can't do that to my wife, I like to take it out on you guys at work as often as I can." In the end, he gave me a zero downgrade check ride so it all ended on a high note in the T-6.

After walking back to the flight room with an extra kick in my step, I was talking about the flight and weather with my buddies when the check pilot walked in. My Flight Commander asked him how my check ride went and in front of everyone he replied, "Well, let's see. How did it go? I asked Fox to fly straight and level for ten seconds and he lost 500 feet. I asked him to try again and he gained 500 feet. You tell me, how do you think it went?"

In the upcoming weeks I'd begin to crack open the books for the T-38 but with the weather being nice, the motorcycle would also get warmed up.

AN EVENING MOTORCYCLE RIDE WITH A T-38 LANDING IN THE BACKGROUND

Week 31: Roof Stomp

A relatively normal week as flying wrapped up for the rest of the students in our flight. In total, I'd logged 122.2 hours in the T-6. 6.4 hours were solo, and I'd spent an additional 50.6 hours in the simulator.

I began studying the T-38 and the procedures surrounding it. I discovered that in afterburner, we were burning 1,628 gallons per hour, which was 27 gallons per minute or almost a half-gallon per second. The afterburner is the flame you see come out of the engine on military fighters, producing a significant amount of extra thrust, and we are required to use them for takeoff. With a full tank being around 558 gallons, in afterburner we would be out of gas in 20 minutes.

Friday we had our final roll call and followed this up with a roof stomp. I am not sure how this tradition started but for a Flight Commander a class or group likes, it was tradition for everyone to go to their house and jump on their roof until they come out with free food and beer. Ours wasn't a complete surprise as we had warned his wife so she could have plenty of food ready for us, obviously. It was still nice to see our Flight Commander a little more relaxed with his family around. With everyone in our class finished with the T-6 program, he didn't have to be his "commander" self and I overheard him tell another IP, "I hope this next class is half as good as these guys."

We also had "international night" this weekend. All of the participating countries here at ENJJPT set up a booth serving their traditional food and alcohol. Countries represented: Spain, Canada, Germany, Italy, Norway, Turkey, Netherlands and Greece.

Lesson Learned: Popularity

There were times I disliked our Flight Commander. There were more times I was scared and nervous around him and he had no intention of being popular with the class. In the end, we all loved and respected him. He was tough and stern but taught us great habits and I give him a lot of credit for molding us into a strong class He wanted to create the best officers and pilots he could and we all knew he had and are forever grateful.

Week 32: The Fuge

This week started with our final T-6 feedback on officership and flying skills from our commander, both of which went well for me and the guys with whom I was closest in the flight, putting everyone in a fine mood. Tuesday, we had our first briefing in our new T-38 flight, nicknamed the MOB flight. We would have an Italian Flight Commander and what appears, on the surface, to be a good group of IPs.

I began to get sick on Tuesday with a fever and bad cold. Very poor timing, considering the proximity of the centrifuge run this same week. The T-38, due to the significant power increase, could sustain more Gs and for a longer period of time so additional training with the centrifuge was necessary.

Everyone, less the Italians, (they didn't participate) car pooled down to San Antonio on Wednesday, twenty guys in total. Witt, Schiess, Olivares and I took advantage of the time and studied T-38 info for a majority of the drive.

We took Wednesday night pretty easy and I had to quit taking my cold medications. I was getting nervous about the fuge, not only because of my body structure and height, but now the sickness continuing to get worse. They told us in week one of pilot training that tall, skinny, marathon runners had the most trouble with Gs and the centrifuge. Check, Check and Check. Further, the only times I had a problem with Gs in the T-6 were when I wasn't feeling well. I was nervous.

The next morning we sat through two hours of class learning about techniques to deal with, and the physiological reactions of G-Forces. They thought it was hilarious to show us video after video of students G-locking (passing out). While I generally find these things humorous, I was not laughing. I was fourth to spin in the fuge. All of the other students sat in a waiting room looking through a window to see the fuge spinning and a TV, with audio, allowing us to see and hear the person currently in the fuge. Hawk was the first to finish and after five minutes, threw up. Perfect. My squadron commander told me the kid before him actually shit his pants while on his fuge run. After a twenty minute delay, he got in the terrible machine with the seat still wet, smelling of Lysol.

The fuge affects everyone differently. The feeling is far worse than pulling Gs in the airplane. When the little bucket you are riding in rotates, so all the Gs hit you "from above," you begin to feel this tumbling sensation. It is a terrible feeling. You've just finished 30 seconds at 6 Gs and all of the sudden you feel like you are tumbling forward because the centrifuge is slowing down so quickly. It is the same terrible feeling you get when the room starts spinning after a long night of drinking. Now you have to ramp back up and do 7.5 Gs. I asked guys to try and describe what it feels like:

"It is like all your muscles are being ripped off your body."

"It is like you are 20' underwater, no air, trying to swim up but chained to the bottom."

"It is like you are under a pile of linemen for a long time and the hit that got you there was in the head, hard."

The flight doctor had a variety of ways to observe us; video, audio, and some pressure sensors in the G-suit to see if we were straining properly. Why didn't they connect us to more medical sensors to observe each of our reactions more closely? The Air Force has found that if they did this, we would all fail acceptable standards to allow us to continue. Apparently our bodies are truly freaking out, for lack of a better term.

After each run, the docs always asked how much light we lost in our vision. It was a juggling match in your mind deciding how much, if any, you wanted to admit. If you admitted you lost some they could teach you how to get better. However, you didn't know where the threshold for, "This guy needs to spin again" was. They asked Olivares the light loss question and he gave this conflicted response, "uhhh, well, I probably lost 0% if anything." Obviously this made little sense and the whole watch room roared with laughter.

Once it was my turn on the 7.5 G profile, I could only see a soda straw of light directly in front of me. As I saw my vision shrinking I remember thinking, "there is no f%$&ing way I am doing this again," and flexing my legs and butt harder than I thought possible. I may have downplayed my struggles slightly to the doc. I wanted to get better at the anti-G straining maneuver but not at the expense of having to go through it again while sick.

When the last guy was up to spin, we convinced the machine operator to play a prank on him. They had told us many people don't even realize they'd passed out until they watched their own video. So when his ride ended, the controller began to ask if he knew where he was and if he realized what had happened. His confident face turned to panic and the entire class was rolling with laughter.

We also got to experience Geasles for the first time. Looking a lot like Measles, they form where the blood pooled during the high G portions of the fuge.

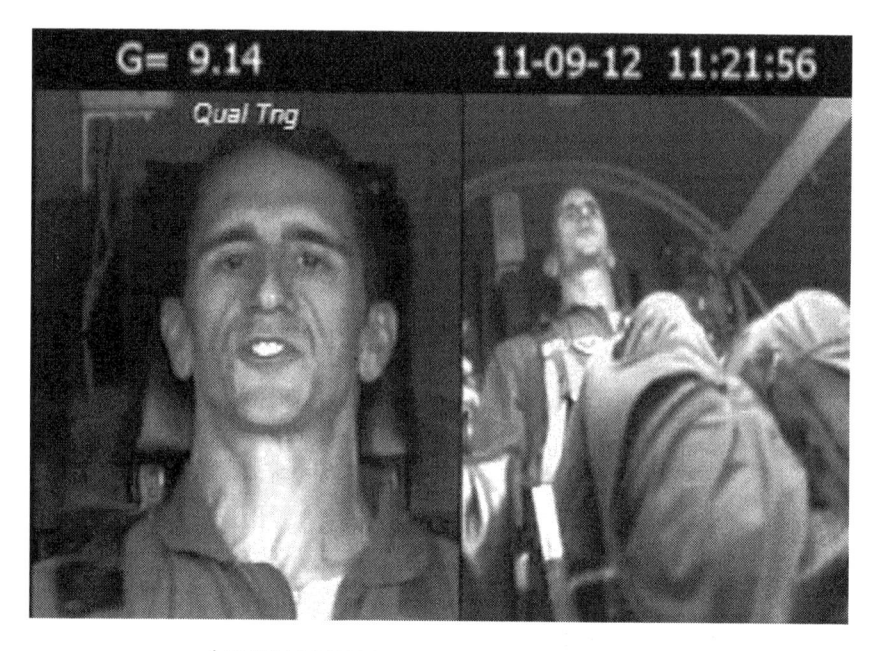

AN IMAGE FROM MY CENTRIFUGE RUN

Week 33: The Tickle

A throwback to July and August, this week was all classes and computer lessons, but now on the T-38. The days were long and full again with class from 0730 to 1700 but the studying continued at home until bed. The T-38 is the transition plane for aspiring fighter pilots. It is a sleek, supersonic jet trainer that rolls faster than any jet in the Air Force. Besides the avionics, the systems were actually easier to understand than the T-6. They let us into the simulators and I played in them until they kicked me out at seven on Friday night. I could already tell it was going to be a sweet plane. As one of the IPs said, referring to the speed, "if you are ever flying and not doing something with the airplane, you are getting behind." The missions are only about an hour long and there is a lot to cram in during that hour.

For all the pilots reading, we all know a plane generally buffets before it stalls, a mild vibration that turns into shaking, especially when adding G during a turn. Since the T-38 wing produced no lift by itself, the pilot had to create the lift with angle of attack and airspeed. So in the final turn to landing with full flaps, we would be anywhere from 180 to 200 knots, 45 to 60 degrees of bank, and in the buffet (the tickle) the entire way around. Final approach speed ranged from 160-185. No flaps, add 15 more knots to those speeds.

Not much else going on but I will explain one interesting thing about the pilot training selection process I have learned this week. At Sheppard, we all took the T-38 for granted. It was the plane we'd all go to regardless of where we are ranked in the class. I was reminded by the active duty guys this was the most coveted training base in the world for that reason. The ROTC kids competed for pilot spots and around 40 per year got a spot at Sheppard. They all said the day they were selected was one of the best of their life because it meant they had the best shot at a fighter jet. Currently, about a quarter to a third of them would get a fighter from our base, even after flying the T-38. The rest would get bombers, tankers, refuelers or special ops planes.

Let's compare this to another training base. You have a class of 24, they compete in the T-6 to "track" fighters. Four of them will get the T-38. Four out of twenty four. Twenty of the twenty four will never fly another plane with a G-suit and will never feel an afterburner. Then of those four, two or three will get fighters.

I am sure glad I went the Guard route.

Week 34: Changeover

A week full of simulator missions, the aircraft systems test and aerodynamics classes. The sims were going well but I did, however, end up respectfully arguing with the instructors about standardization after each sim. In my opinion, this had been the weakest part of the Air Force flight training experience. The sim instructors were all retired Air Force pilots with thousands of hours flying F-16s, F-15s and everything else. It was an impressive collection of resumes and they were very good at what they did. However, they were all set in their individual ways and you were wrong if you didn't do exactly as they said.

Further, I was repeatedly told, "I don't care what they are doing on the actual flight line, this is the way you should do it."

So I'd respond, "Sir, I understand your technique and it sounds great but we are here to prepare for the airplane and the flying IPs said to do it the opposite way. Further, the guy I simmed with yesterday said to do it a different way."

Every sim was an appeasement to each IP and the way they thought things should be done. The T-6 sim instructors had been the same way and it was the most infuriating part of pilot training.

Our class threw a changeover party at one of the maintenance guys' barns for the newest class at ENJJPT last night, as they were replacing us. The class graduating the T-6 and starting the T-38 would throw the "baby class" a party as they became the new G and H flights. A few kegs and a lot of food allowed everyone to mingle and reminisce with their old IPs, followed by an awards part of the evening. As a class, we gave out serious awards like "Most valuable IP," but also gave out gag awards like, "IP with most stick time during student sorties"—translated, they'd be most likely to take the airplane away from you when you screw something up.

After the students were done, each Flight Commander came up and gave serious awards, in ultimately, the last formal thing we did as "G" flight. The awards were: Top Academic, Top Officer and Top Stick awards. CAIN came away with Top Officer, Witt was Top Academic and I was Top Stick. It was a relieving affirmation of performance thus far.

Lesson Learned: Consistency

The larger an organization becomes, the more difficult it is to ensure consistency and reliability of service but it is critical, especially in a training environment. Even the most motivated and talented personnel can be weakened and ultimately driven away if they aren't allowed to excel. Having numerous "experts" and diverse opinions can be invaluable but there are limitations. In this specific situation, we had a different instructor for each mission, only aggravating the problem. Assigning just a few instructors to each student would have prevented this problem and reduced time wasted, as each new instructor had to determine the level of skill of their new student. Instead, I was working really hard to please the instructors and improve but left every simulator ride frustrated.

Week 35: Afterburner

Week 35 marked the return to flying with my first afterburner experience. We had sims all week with our Aerodynamics test on Tuesday which I was relatively nervous about, as you would hear of guys failing it every once and a while. With that finally behind us, we had the flights to look forward to.

The T-38 went operational in the Air Force in 1961 and my Dollar Ride aircraft had 19,000+ hours on it. The plane was interesting and exciting to say the least. The switches were worn down, the air conditioning didn't really work, it rattled and vibrated and made popping noises all of the time. Compare that to the T-6 we had just flown, which had state of the art everything and was just a few years old. The T-38, however, had some dramatic improvements, mostly regarding power and speed. The takeoff was an amazing experience. By the time you made sure both afterburners lit, you were calling out 100 knots and once airborne at 165, if the gear and flaps weren't raised immediately, you would probably over-speed them at the 240-knot limit. Climb out was at 300 knots and then 350 after passing 10,000 feet. The power, however, came with its price tag, as we burned 475 gallons or so per 1 hour and 5 minute flight—probably around $3,000 in jet fuel.

The wildest sensation about the plane was the buffet I previously mentioned—the shaking that occurred right before stall. The buffet is a result of air no longer flowing smoothly over the wings and when it detaches from the wing surface, it doesn't do so evenly. Most planes have a slight tremble right before the stall as a final warning. This plane, in its old age, felt like it was coming apart. I had never experienced anything like it. The buffet would start very lightly, like mice were running around on the wings, a slight vibration. The vibration would escalate to the feeling of cats, then dogs, and then it felt like children were jumping on the wings. The instrument panel would sound like it was breaking and we weren't even to the stall yet. The moment when the now massive shaking, became irregular, was the moment you would do something about it (add power or lower the nose).

If you remember from T-6s, I got my call sign "Hose" for failing to strap in properly on my Dollar Ride. Well they cleared us, Kent 23, for takeoff and as the IP was taxiing onto the runway I leaned forward to hit a switch when I looked down to see all of my harnesses and seatbelts were just lying in my lap, not hooked up at all. Yes, here came my first afterburner takeoff, in an ejection seat aircraft, and the only thing I was connected to was my oxygen and communications cord.

Thinking to myself, "Shit, shit, shit... should I tell him? How does this even go together? God, not again. Alright, if he gives me the airplane and I am not done hooking up, I will tell him."

On the last snap of the buckle he asked if I am ready. I gave all of the harnesses one last pull to check my work and proudly exclaim, "yes, sir!"

The schedule ramped up and free time was almost non-existent at this point. Thursday night I got home from my flight around 7:45 or 8 PM and started preparing for the next day when I felt the first real stress in pilot training since back in September. I had not had dinner or showered and wanted to tell people about my flight when the next days' schedule was emailed out. Flight planning class at 0745, I had to give the morning brief after that at 0930, my first instrument simulator ride from 1030-1300 and my second flight at 1500. I nervously laughed because I thought it was joke. Needing to go to sleep in about an hour and a half with nothing prepared put me on edge. The Air Force had a policy of getting 12 hours of continuous rest so I couldn't even go in early the next morning to prepare. Busting crew rest is one of the most sacred violations.

A couple stories to close:

Olivares, the kid who grounded the entire fleet of T-6s and almost had to eject with the mishap after a spin, had his Dollar Ride on Thursday as well. They took off and the heater was stuck on full hot. He was guessing it was 150+ degrees in the plane and the IP was furious, thinking Olivares didn't know how to turn the heat off. It got so bad they thought about jettisoning the canopy and flying back convertible style. When they got back one of the publications with a plastic case had melted to the paper.

Culbertson, a witty, outdoorsy, Arizona ROTC grad whose dad flew fighters, had to abort a start because the fuel never ignited. They let the engine "rest" for two minutes and then tried again. This time, the crew chief grabbed the nose of the plane and was using all of his body weight to shake the plane. Sure enough, the $8 million plane, with state of the art avionics, needed an overweight crew chief to hump the nose to get started.

Finally, the final turn to landing was probably the most hazardous aspect of flying the T-38. It was a 180 degree turn, losing 1800 feet at 45 degrees of bank and was in the mouse-to-cat running on the wings amount of buffet. Most fatal accidents occurred here, as major errors could not be salvaged, even with ejection. Therefore, a huge emphasis was placed on not only flying the final turn properly, but in the event you were about to stall, knowing what to do. One evening I was coming up on my last landing and the IP wanted to do the last one and show me a few things. Well, one distraction led to another and we got slow. Based on our weight, we should have flown the final turn at 180 knots and final approach at 160. Still in the final turn, I looked down and saw 157 knots—23 knots slower than where we should have been. Significant considering students were castrated if we got one knot slow, ever. I decided I should interrupt and emphatically said,

"Watch your airspeed." Not one second later, the stall horn went off. It was nice to get a lesson learned at the IP's expense. He apologized and used it as an example of what not to do.

Week 36: Retired Mafia

Four flights, five sims and two tests this week. I would have flown each day but had a weather cancel when it was clear blue skies less one cloud in our pattern, exactly as I was next for takeoff. Can't make your takeoff time exactly? Taxi back and try again some other time, usually the next day. It was really frustrating but I got to blow ~$350-worth of jet fuel just taxiing the jet around.

The simulator missions were now predominately instrument sims with an emergency sim thrown in every once in a while. I had built a decent rapport with most of the sim instructors despite my constant, but respectful, arguing about various things, namely checklists. All of that bantering had started a few weeks ago and, unbeknownst to me, led one of them to start quite an email thread that ultimately landed at AETC (Air Education and Training Command). One thing led to another and AETC came out with the first abbreviated checklist for the T-38C yesterday. The normal checklist was in a thick book and probably ten pages long, unusable at 400 knots. As my sim buddy said to me, "Never underestimate the power of the retired mafia."

I had another sim yesterday with a former fighter pilot who characterized all of the stereotypes. He essentially dropped the F bomb every sentence and had crude analogies to make all of his points but it was hilarious. He was making a point to save all the gas you could on instrument approaches so if the weather was bad you would have more chances to try and land. He illustrated with the following story: "If you save your gas, you will make it home that night while your buddy, who didn't save gas, will have to divert to another airport. He will have to stay at some rat-infested motel while you will be staying at his wife's house" (drastically paraphrased and cleaned up).

Further, I landed a little long and when he asked why, I told him that it was the instruction I had previously received for that scenario from a different instructor. "It is F%&$ing bullsh%&, we can't wash out pilots any more so we have to make all of these Fu%&ing rules so anyone can pass. Before you know it, we are going to have paraplegics, blowing straws, flying air force jets because it's politically correct."

Being relatively new to all of this I couldn't fully appreciate his comments but they were hilarious and anything besides talking about my mistakes was always welcome.

Lesson Learned: Respectfully Object

I knew there was a problem with the checklist training from the day I started T-38 training. One would think an airplane over 50 years old would have something so simple figured out but alas, this one didn't. Inefficiencies can be built into habit, especially with older guys stuck in their ways. Unless someone fresh is willing to stand up and consistently protest the issue, nothing will change. I think because I knew I was doing well in pilot training, I had just enough confidence to fight back. The strong military culture of respecting authority, along with being students in a training environment willing to do whatever it takes to get good grades, limits some of this creative potential. Often, those raising questions or protesting the status quo don't have all the information to make the best decision but simply accepting things is not great either. It is a fine balance between questioning the current system and respecting authority, which is very important as well. I have heard you get one "yes, but" response to a leader or manager shooting down your request. After that you shut up.

Week 37: Jimmy and Snort

Six years ago I decided to make a bucket list. It had various goals like get a Master's degree or run a marathon, but one was to fly a jet airplane by myself.

Flash forward six years and after some unexpected life decisions, Jimmy 01 was cleared for takeoff, afterburners and all. My dad and grandpa traveled down to watch as three of us, Schiess, CAIN and I, all soloed for the first time, blasting off in succession. We had to hold short of the runway for about five minutes, allowing us to just sit there and take it all in. Sitting in a supersonic jet with the guys who've been your best buds for the last few months in theirs, all about to blast off together, was a pretty cool feeling. I enjoyed every second of that afterburner takeoff and gave a little wing rock after takeoff so my family knew which one was me.

Afterward, we joked that it was a standard evening, just three friends blowing $20,000 for an hour of fun. To top it off, the schedulers gave me another solo the next day. This time the boys of the South Dakota Guard, Snort 12 and Snort 13—Fox and Hawk—had another moment of foreshadowing by taking a pair of military jets to play around with for an hour. My mom asked me the next day what was different about the T-38. My response: "the speed, the power, and feeling like a badass taking off and climbing out of that machine."

LEFT TO RIGHT: MATT "CAIN" OLDE, ME, AND SEAN SCHIESS AFTER OUR INITIAL SOLO IN THE T-38

Week 38: Broken Planes

The unpredictable weather continued this week and I was only able to get in three graded flights. The 4:30 and 5:00 AM wakeup calls were rough and would continue but the weeks were flying by.

Monday we were weathered out but Tuesday was a beautiful day for an aerobatic flight—assuming one had a good plane to fly. First, we had to abort the start due to a lack of ignition. Then, a generator fell offline a couple times while we were setting up the avionics. Now we were holding short of the runway and noticed the right nozzle, the circular aft component where the exhaust flows out of the airplane that changes in size, was not in the proper position for being at idle power. We elected to abort the mission and taxi back. As we did, the nozzle corrected itself and after calling the operations supervisor, he gave us the green light as long as it stayed in a good position for takeoff. So we blasted off, all things running normally—for about 20 seconds.

If you remember Olivares's flight when the heat control got stuck on full hot, well the opposite happened to us. I set the temperature to full hot and absolutely nothing happened. As we were flying a simulated single engine emergency pattern for practice, the master caution light illuminated with "Engine" flashing in my HUD and instrument screens. We had been through enough emergency practice that it doesn't get you too excited but it was definitely a moment that made you say, "oh shit!" I scanned the engine instruments and realized our nozzle issue had returned. The indicator was telling us it was 100% full open, and then rapidly changed to 25%, then back to 85% and so on. I got the checklist out for the single engine approach we were going to simulate for my practice but now was for real. We still had both engines operating but weren't going to use the right one unless necessary. We landed uneventfully, just 5 minutes after takeoff, but as we were pulling off the runway, our nose wheel steering broke. We ended up stopping on the taxiway and got a ride back in a pickup truck.

Friday morning we had a 0700 takeoff. There was a broken layer of clouds so it was still pretty dark. When the jets ahead of us blasted off in the twilight, we saw full afterburner glow raging down the runway, flames sticking out a few feet behind the plane.

Morrison hooked a ride on Friday which was hotly debated. We had been introduced to advanced handling characteristics, higher level maneuvers max-performing the jet. We were not graded on them and the IPs were supposed to talk us through them. Morrison was doing a maneuver called a slice back, which, without going into too much detail, had them turning around by aggressively pointing down and pulling through in full afterburner. Morrison didn't pull enough G so he began accelerating and losing too much altitude. Not a big deal as he had never experienced it before and we had always been briefed to not over-G the plane to keep it in the airspace. So Morrison, recognizing his problem, ended the maneuver and started recovering, but the IP took control of the plane and immediately yanked the stick back into an over G. The lowest they got was 10,200 feet, 700 feet above the airspace floor. So he hooked Morrison for area awareness on an ungraded maneuver he had never seen and was supposed to be talked through, for something the IP ultimately screwed up. Even our flight IPs were not impressed with the decision.

Lesson Learned: Never blame others for your mistakes

No one is proud of their mistakes and we often try to deflect some of the blame onto other people or with excuses. I have never, so instantly, lost respect for an instructor or leader as I did in this scenario. My perception of him for the remainder of training was of weakness and pity. He seemed physically smaller and while I was always respectful, I had a negative opinion in the back of my mind. It can show more strength and definitely builds more trust to publicly admit your mistakes and how you plan to learn and improve from them.

Week 39: Toro 14

Week 39 was one of the busier weeks of pilot training, having flown nine times in the last six days, including lunch in Fort Worth and a cross-country to St. Louis.

The 3rd solo was another great time but mine paled in comparison to the excitement of Culbertson's two solos this week. In his first, he was inverted during a loop when he realized he was going to bust out the top of the airspace, so he yanked the stick back, trying to save it. When you are slow at the top of a loop, not much air is going into the engines anyway, so when you yank back on the stick, going slow, and relatively high at 23,000 feet, you really reduce the amount of air going into the engines. Ultimately both engines flamed out and he was gliding back to earth with no power. I am not sure of all the details, but he got them both fired back up and flew it home with a chase plane. Based on the look on the IPs faces, you could tell that an emergency like that was pretty rare. After they watched the tapes and data recorder, they hooked him for all of the things he did wrong to get into that situation.

The very next day, Culbertson got another solo. The base was going through a huge inspection and besides the student pilots, the results could determine a lot for people's careers. The students just had to deal with an influx of bullshit rules as a result. Apparently while Culbertson was out flying, our Squadron Commander, this grumpy German, was having his own check ride with one of these inspectors. This is hard to explain but our pattern was essentially a 360-degree oval and it was more "badass" and "fighter pilotesque" to make this oval as small as possible. Everyone had been complaining that our new class messed the pattern up because we were conservative and made this oval too big. Well Culbertson, a day after a dual engine flameout and still wanting to be a fighter pilot, tightened his oval up and didn't notice the Squadron Commander out far wider than he was and essentially cut him off. Obviously, this infuriated him and he hooked Culbertson on the ground for it. It was a tough week for him.

This led us to the cross-country flight to St. Louis. I flew with my German assigned IP, Lt. Christian Pal. We blasted off to Fayetteville, Arkansas to shoot approaches and refuel. On the descent into St. Louis just prior to sunset, they leveled us off 50 feet above an infinite cloud deck. The setting sun created a cool orange glow on the clouds and we could really feel the speed of 400 knots, being so close to something relatively stationary.

We hit the town with some dancing and gambling during the weekend. Olivares, a self-proclaimed, borderline professional gambler, walked away up $1300 and Schiess was up $1100. I had never seen anything like it and it made my proud $90 in winnings from craps look pitiful.

Lt. Pal and I requested the 'Arch departure,' a special vector that air traffic control could give us to fly directly over the St. Louis Arch. But with rain, low clouds and restrictions about flying over cities, I wasn't expecting much. We tried anyway after everyone else in our flight opted out and were rewarded. In and out of the clouds, just 800 or so feet above the arch and downtown St. Louis skyline, we popped out as we were coming off the river directly over the arch and city, banked up to 90 degrees and got a fantastic view of Busch stadium and the entire downtown area. It was awesome. Lt. Pal was going crazy as he hadn't seen much of the country yet and I couldn't believe they would let us fly that low over downtown.

The nine flights with no days off in seven days caught up with me a little on this ride. I was forgetting to switch altimeter settings and missed leveling off at my assigned altitude for the first time in a T-38. Embarrassingly, this was all after Lt. Pal had given me some of the nicest compliments last week during a contact ride, saying, "It is amazing what you do with the aircraft," and, "that was the best no-flap approach and landing I have ever seen."

Today's debrief was more like, "you know you weren't as sharp as normal and you know what you did wrong so I am not going to remind you but do you have any questions?"

I was slightly down about the flights but had no time for that as my next check ride was coming up.

Week 40: Check Riding

My first check ride in the T-38 was Tuesday. Mother Nature decided to introduce a crosswind for the first time in the new plane but it was a beautiful day otherwise. Overall, the flight went well and I passed with three downgrades. After we finished doing the aerobatics in the MOA (Military Operating Airspace), it was time to do unusual attitude recoveries. The IP took the plane and put it in an unusual attitude, around 70 degrees nose high and in a 60-degree bank turn. However, this IP, wanting to have a little fun, did 8-10 aileron rolls in a row and then stopped in something similar to the aforementioned attitude. When the spinning finally stopped, he gave me the plane and it was borderline impossible to determine which way was up with my head still spinning. He also showed me the reason many people have died in the T-38. With the gear down, at final turn speed, he stepped on a rudder and within two seconds, we were upside down and sinking. Obviously a bad situation to be in had we been just a few hundred feet above the ground.

I walked out of the debrief from the check ride and was already late for the brief of my next flight in the next phase of training, called transition. Transition is a fusion between contact and instrument flying, mainly geared around out-and-backs to other airfields. For example, I flew to Oklahoma City with our Flight Commander yesterday. We took off, practiced an emergency single engine landing, then flew to Oklahoma City and practiced instrument approaches before landing and having breakfast. When we left OKC, we flew to the MOA, performed some aerobatics, and then returned to Sheppard to practice patterns. They had been flying me quite a bit and I was scheduled to have the transition check ride Friday. I was sure lunch with the check pilot before flying back home would be a touch awkward. Our Flight Commander called me his scheduling "Joker"—with a touch of language barrier he really meant "wild card."

"Fox, you will fly immediately after your check ride. You are my Joker. I try to make scheduling fair for everyone but you are Guard so it doesn't matter." He said this because I already had a fighter spot reserved so if I happened to falter a little due to his aggressive scheduling of me, it wouldn't be a big deal compared to the guys competing for spots.

The Italian Flight Commander was quite a personality contrast to our German Flight Commander in T-6 training. I couldn't really say which I preferred but their personalities were strikingly different considering they were both former fighter pilots in the same role. The Italian was a relatively nice guy, always smiling and joking, and a machine with scheduling with nothing bothering him. We spent most of the flight cracking subtle jokes and having a good time. The German Flight Commander would teach at every opportunity he could and would only relax and unwind on Friday afternoon.

Overall, Cheech the Italian had been the only hook of this check ride with the average number of downgrades being around eight. Poor guy tried to start the engines without the boost pumps on.

Week 41: Ze Germans

This week was full of out-and-back flights. We woke up at 0430 each morning to be ready to brief by 0530 for two flights with breakfast in between. I went to Oklahoma City, Dyess AFB twice, Fort Worth and Longview, Texas just this week. It was exhausting with the early wakeup calls and significantly higher level of planning required for these flights compared to local flights. I was supposed to have my check ride Friday but after we landed in Fort Worth on Thursday, we found the piece connecting the landing gear door to the landing gear had sheared off. That left my German IP and me with a rental car and a two-hour conversation back to Wichita Falls. Fortunately, we both like airplanes, marathons and triathlons so we had plenty to talk about. He also told me about how poorly the German Air Force and military are regarded in their country. He said if seen in public wearing his uniform that it would be plausible to be spit on or called Nazis. That treatment is a far cry from us wearing our uniform publicly in the U.S. While it is rare that we do and we are generally discouraged from doing so, we always get plenty of smiles and are often thanked by numerous people.

I've had quite the run with German FAIPs (First assignment instructor pilot) through pilot training. I can't remember the last time I flew with an American IP but loved flying with all of the Germans except one. While the exception was a nice guy, he treated me like a child and as if it was my first flight in a T-38. I have definitely figured out my preferred method of instruction, which I will try to apply when on the other side of the table. Some IPs mention every little mistake, immediately when it occurs, throughout the entire flight. While I see the advantages of instant feedback, there are negative consequences possibly not considered. It is almost embarrassing for me to say but as this guy was coaching me through every minute detail of flying, I had a feeling of resignation. I knew whatever I did, he would have a comment so why not just let him tell me what to do? The more he talked, the less I was thinking for myself and therefore unable to think about what was coming next. The more he talked, the more I'd have to critically listen and if you know me, I often question and disagree when I deem appropriate. The problem is at 500+ mph, you don't have time for this type of exchange.

The one saving grace to this flight was watching two B-1 bombers take off right in front of us. I had never seen one fly and with four, yes four, afterburning engines just a couple hundred feet away, the amount of noise and vibration through our airplane was indescribable. It felt like my chest and our plane were being torn and shaken apart.

Compare him to my assigned IP, Lt. Pal, one of the German FAIPs. He was the youngest and newest instructor in the squadron but I would argue one of the best. Did he have all the answers? No. But he had a demeanor in the airplane allowing the student to perform their best and then once on the ground, provided useful feedback geared toward helping you learn instead of making you feel like an idiot or wasting our time. In the plane, his communication was almost always praise for things done well and he had an upbeat attitude. He only taught airborne if he felt I needed to learn a lesson in the specific moment. Otherwise we talked about it at 1G (on the ground) when I had time to think about it.

Another example of why I respected him was exhibited on our flight yesterday evening. It was an evening of thunderstorms and clouds building from cumulus into cumulonimbus. Our clearance had us flying through some of these and we were bumped around pretty well flying through the first one. I could hear a little hesitation in his voice as we approached the next one and he said, "Ooo this one is going to be really bumpy huh?"

I replied, "No sir, I think this one will be pretty calm after the last one." Sure enough, it was quite a bit smoother and he couldn't believe I knew. I explained how my civilian experience flying passengers in a corporate jet taught me a lot about what to look for in the clouds and whether or not to fly through them with passengers or a military fighter. Once on the ground, the debrief was split 50/50 on my mistakes and teaching him about reading clouds, something I have mentioned before as a major weakness in this training program. I don't think many IPs would have had a conversation like that with a student but now I knew Lt. Pal wasn't full of bullshit and genuinely wanted to make himself and those around him better.

Our no-flap final approach speed into Dyess AFB with wind gusts was 193 knots. I believe the T-38 is the fastest-landing airplane in the Air Force inventory. At those speeds, even a two-mile-long runway looks pretty short. I just looked up the space shuttle and its touchdown speed was 195 knots.

Lesson Learned: Instructing

Having the title of "instructor" doesn't always mean you need to be talking. Knowing when, how, and how much to speak is often more important than the message itself. You must earn and maintain the respect of the student to be an effective instructor or teacher.

Week 42: Swagger

This week was probably the best of pilot training thus far. The torrid pace had slowed considerably and I had three very different but enjoyable flights. Twice this week I didn't even set an alarm in the morning.

Monday kicked off with my transition check ride. Often regarded as the most difficult ride in the program, it the holds the most weight in final rankings. Naturally, it was my first time flying in clouds in the T-38. It was a flight to Oklahoma City to shoot three approaches followed by a return to Sheppard to do aerobatics and patterns. The cloud ceiling forecast was 1,500 feet broken in OKC but when we made it up there, 15 minutes later, it was 700 feet overcast. In fact, the weather required to shoot two of the three approaches was 700 feet, so we were emerging beneath the clouds at the minimums for the approach. I had the same check pilot as I did on the previous check ride so our lunch was a little more fun after a successful first flight.

I passed the check ride with two downgrades; the loop wasn't great and altitude level off wasn't smooth as I was trying to deal with a clearance change. However, he was generous and gave a special distinction to the grade by calling it an "outstanding" check ride. This is earned by displaying above average "airmanship" throughout the flight. Airmanship is difficult to describe but it is about making decisions and taking actions in unusual circumstances, improving the quality, safety and efficiency of flight in ways not necessarily required. While I've made that definition up, you get the idea.

After work I was mostly hanging out with Schiess and was really hoping he would drop a fighter come July. He always did well on normal flights but mediocre on check rides and had some problems in the T-38, so I was getting concerned. He was a nice guy and had a tendency to not act as confidently as he should, letting IPs walk on him a little. We had a little pep talk over steaks Sunday night and I saw a different swagger all week. Not that I had any idea what it was like to be a fighter pilot, I did remind him we are aspiring to be fighters on the front lines of the Air Force. Don't stop being the nice guy who does what he is told, but have some confidence and the attitude of someone going to war with these check rides and flights. He came away with a three-downgrade check ride on Thursday and you could see the glow radiating from his face. Thus far, most guys are getting eight-ten downgrades and many have hooked so he distinguished himself with this important check ride. His thank you for the pep talk made for a nice week.

I ended up getting another solo on Wednesday but I would never again be graded on what we call "loops to music" (aerobatics). Instead, I practiced turns in afterburner pulling Gs. That morning I actually went to the Aerospace Physiology building on my own to get additional, individual training on my G-Strain in fear of the upcoming 9G centrifuge experience in September. They taught the breathing and muscle straining technique designed to keep the blood in your head and air in your lungs, something easier said than done. So after getting a few tips, I practiced them in the jet, spending ten minutes straight in some form of 4-6 G-turn, turning my head back, pretending the Russians were maneuvering behind me and I was evading.

Friday, the weather was pretty bad with low clouds and thunderstorms so my first formation flight appeared to be cancelled until the last second. My mom was driving in and literally made it to the squadron as I was hopping on the bus to fly. We had 3-foot wingtip clearance in fingertip formation and it sure felt close. A significant portion of the flight was bouncing through some of the thickest clouds I have seen. You would think at 3 feet the other airplane wouldn't be hard to see, but I could tell it even made my IP a little nervous.

We also got our mid-phase officership feedback and they said I had the highest "motivation" ranking which I appreciated. Being in the Guard, many might have assumed I didn't have to work as hard because I knew my future airframe. One of the Italians ranked 10 or 11 and said he was happy about it because the officership grades don't matter for their overall score when determining airplanes. He claimed he would rather the Americans have better rankings. The Italians were known for being independent and not working with the group, which annoyed most of us. It appeared selfish and while there is some language barrier, we were a flight all helping each other get through the program. I let him know my thoughts and got into an argument about it but when I saw there was no changing him, I let it go. It just pissed me off as he was justifying not helping anyone the last nine months by claiming he was helping with the rankings, which is complete bullshit. He will go back to his Italian squadron having no clue how to work with others in the flying environment, something critical in war. Sure the F-16 and most fighters have one pilot but we always go out in formation.

LEFT TO RIGHT: DEREK OLIVARES, ME, MOTHER, ANDREW MORTON, JEFF WITT AND SEAN SCHIESS BEFORE A NIGHT AT THE OFFICER'S CLUB

Weeks 43 and 44: Banger

My next couple formation rides were with the wing commander and we were scheduled to fly a third day but our wingman's plane broke after starting.

I double-turned (two flights) Friday and with lots of large, puffy, cumulus clouds in the MOA, it made for a fun day. All of our formation maneuvers involved dodging and playing around clouds, which was a nice bonus.

This short week included five formation flights in four days, with one being the coveted formation solo. The amount of preparation going into flights was now minimal and I had noticed some complacency in my work ethic. Hopefully this four-day weekend would help rejuvenate the motivation.

The formation solo flight in the T-38 is regarded by many as the best in pilot training. I wouldn't go that far as there had been many other great flights, but it was awesome. Further, my IP made the flight all about me and helped make it a memorable experience. The formation position of fighting wing, 500-1,500 feet behind lead, was essentially a cone to maneuver within. I could be to the left, right, above or below and could move around as much as I liked. My IP would send me to the position any time we were just flying level, so I could "play" around his jet.

He initially radioed, "Fox, want to go fighting wing?"

Me: "Yuuuuuup."

IP: "Banger 2, go fighting wing." And with that I pulled away and up, then turned back into to him, doing three barrel rolls in a row around him, throwing the engines into afterburner during the last. During the portion he led, each time I would rejoin on him, a different beautiful woman was plastered against the side of the canopy. It was great.

To end the week I had my first advanced formation flight. We are now practicing tactical formations and learning how you move them. These are the formations fighters generally fly in combat, more spread out, versus the formations you see during airshows.

Week 45: Zoom and Boom

This short week was full of the unexpected. I flew three times in two days and each morning I would show up expecting a certain flight and would fly something completely different. It started on Wednesday when I was scheduled to fly advanced formation with the Squadron Commander, the grumpy German. Just five minutes before brief, the schedule fell apart and I was going solo.

The solo was as fun as the rest. I hardly did any aerobatics but spent most of my time pulling Gs and practicing various maneuvers as I begin transitioning toward dogfighting. However, after I returned to Sheppard, I had gas for two landings. The closed pull-up is a maneuver performed after you have made a touch-n-go landing and want to immediately circle back around to land. Generally done around 240-280 knots, the maneuver can be performed passively or aggressively. If done aggressively, you pull up using 3-4 Gs, then immediately roll 90 degrees to begin the circle. As you can imagine, on a solo, I might be a little more aggressive, especially being as comfortable with the plane as I was at this point. The more aggressively done, the more impressive it is to watch from the ground as well. Since I was getting one closed pull-up on this flight, I was determined to make it a good one. I pulled hard enough to get a strong buffet and a little wing rock, pulling the nose 30 degrees up in about one second, then rolled to 90 degrees of bank, with everything working out just as I wanted. However, the same Squadron Commander I had been scheduled to fly with was flying with another student, holding short of the runway right where I began my closed pull-up and got a front row seat to my performance. He was less than impressed with the alleged showboating and wrote my call sign down on his hand in bright red ink so he could investigate when he got back.

The moment he got inside he called our flight room and asked one of our IPs, "is Snort 21 one of yours? I want you to review his HUD tape in the pattern immediately and get back to me." Apparently, he just hung up without even waiting for a response.

Ten minutes later, thinking nothing was wrong, I was greeted by Lt Pal in front of the whole class asking if anything happened on my solo I needed to tell someone about. Honestly a bit surprised, I denied any wrongdoing but he asked if we could go to the back room and watch the HUD tape.

Nerves firing a little, I was pissed my first hook in UPT could come on a solo but I was still relatively confident in my innocence. Pal and I reviewed the tape and agreed that while my maneuver had been aggressive, I had done absolutely nothing wrong and since we were in fighter pilot training, what exactly did they expect. Still, it was not his call and he kept my tape as I double-turned into a formation flight which sucked as I had the incident on my mind.

Ultimately Lt Pal said he spoke to the Squadron Commander in person, defended my flight and put all concerns to rest.

The next morning I was opted for the Zoom and Boom flight with Lt Pal as my instructor. This flight calls for us to leave in afterburner for the first ten minutes as we climb out and blast through the sound barrier for the first time in our lives. My grandpa was among the first generation to do this in an F-86 and still has his certificate on his wall.

The most impressive part of the flight was the climb out. While we use afterburner for every takeoff, we usually take it out relatively soon after getting airborne and have a gentle climb out. In this case, we left the afterburners lit until 38,000 feet. I spent half of the climb looking behind me, soaking in how quickly the earth was falling away from us. By the time we leveled the plane off at 38,000 feet, I looked down and we had already broken the sound barrier. It was that easy and anti-climactic.

What happens? The instruments started acting a little crazy, showing fluctuations of altitude around 400 feet without them actually occurring and various other irregularities.

When an aircraft passes through the air it creates pressure waves behind it, similar to the bow and stern waves created by a boat. These waves travel at the speed of sound and as the speed of the object increases, the waves are forced together, or compressed, because they cannot get out of the way of each other. Eventually they merge into a single shock wave, which travels at the speed of sound, a critical speed known as Mach 1.

The controls for the airplane were also pretty sluggish compared to subsonic flight. I ended up seeing Mach 1.1 and as my grandpa later pointed out, about .08 more than he saw in a vertical dive in the F-86 around 55 years ago. As we slowed back through the sound barrier to a subsonic speed, there was a noticeable bump in the airplane as we traversed the shockwave. I would compare it to a little bump in the road. Overall, a very fun and enjoyable flight with Lt Pal made for a great time.

Week 46: Banger 53 Solo

Tuesday there was a significant amount of rain and we had a blast flying in close formation through the clouds. It was wild to be that close to another airplane out of necessity. Normally, if we got out of position, we'd take a deep breath, relax, and move back in closer. If you got out of position in the weather by just a few feet, you could no longer see him and would have to de-conflict by turning away blindly. Not only difficult, it would mean you just ruined a lot of training because it can be difficult to find each other and join back up with all of the clouds. With the pressure of staying in position, you couldn't afford to look inside to see where you were going or even know if you were turning, climbing or what your speed was. You just trusted the flight lead. It didn't take long to get spatially disoriented and think you were turning to the left and descending when you were actually doing the opposite. It is a tough feeling to describe but know it was uncomfortable.

I had my second formation solo on Friday with a cool IP and Morrison, the kid with whom I had flown most of my T-6 formation with. I was starting to feel sick but adrenaline always counteracts those effects and it was a pretty good flight. Since we were doing tactical formation, a majority of the flight was spent about a mile apart. There were times we had the 3 feet wingtip clearance formation, but not for long. What does flying a mile in formation feel like? A potential analogy is being on a five-lane highway with a few lanes separation. You aren't overly concerned another car is going to hit you but within seconds things could get ugly and you always keep an eye on them. We did a maneuver called a cross turn that had us turn directly at each other. We passed at 700 knots closure when #2 flew directly over the top of #1, just a couple hundred feet away. Flying fingertip (3 feet wingtip clearance) was like riding a bike on half of a sidewalk, not too hard but any loss of focus and you would have a problem.

The only story I really have from the week was on Schiess's solo formation ride when he earned his IP an FAA violation for busting an altitude. Schiess was leading but the IP was ultimately responsible for everything the flight did. They were in fingertip formation so his focus was not as close on altitude and they climbed through the assigned altitude. Fort Worth Center asked them to write down their phone number and give them a call when they landed. Our call sign naming party was next Friday and Schiess had a good candidate of a name with "VAJ," standing for Violates Airspace with Judy—Judy being the call sign of the IP.

Week 47: Bag

Another full week of pilot training complete and as of Friday night, we were the next class to have their drop night coming up, which was surreal. Monday I had my last solo in UPT. There was a chance I would have a solo in Introduction to Fighter Fundamentals (IFF) but if not, the next time I would fly a plane by myself for the military would be in the F-16.

We had our T-38 naming party last night. It was a similar scene from the T-6 naming party but we were outside and there were a few more stories told. I was in the hot seat for about 15 minutes and heard the full spectrum of stories. From girls past and present, to not strapping into the plane, I ended up with "Bag." To say most of the names were not as G-rated as they were in the T-6 would be an understatement. Mine is an acronym with G standing for Guardsman. I joke it stands for Bad Ass Guardsman—I'll leave you to guess the real version.

A quick rundown of some of the funny (and cleaner) names:

"Colt" – stands for "Cheech Only Likes Teens." Enough said.

"Fish" – stands for "Fox is hot." On our cross country there was this girl Morton kept saying was hot and that she looked like me. Rules of logic say he was calling me hot as well.

"SHOTZ" – stands for "Student Has his Own Time Zone." Witt is late for everything and never in a hurry.

A REJOINING T-38

Week 48: Broken Planes

A long, fun and frustrating week as there was a little bit of everything. It was the first week of two where we night flew, not showing up for work until 1430 each day. Monday I had my first night flight in the T-38 and sure enough, I was scheduled with the Squadron Commander. Yes, the same Squadron Commander who was on my case for the closed pull up a few weeks ago. We flew to Oklahoma City, shot an approach, and few home for patterns. It wasn't exactly a fun flight as I was focused on impressing him but it went very well and he thanked our schedulers after the flight for giving him his first "low maintenance" flight in a long time.

As we were walking back in from the jet around 11:00PM, he asked in his German accent if I drank beer. After replying I did, he told me to meet at his desk in 15 minutes with a couple beers for debrief. When I went to grab the beers out of our flight room, I noticed I was scheduled to fly with him again the next day so when he offered to pay for the beer, I quickly declined.

This ultimately led to the rash of broken jets for the week. Just the next day, I had two broken jets with the Squadron Commander and we didn't get to fly. Between my formation partner and me, fourteen of our jets broke this week. Sometimes we found a problem with the plane on the preflight or sometimes there was gas pouring out of the engine during start. On Wednesday, my afterburner didn't light on takeoff and we aborted takeoff at 70 knots. While this was a rare occurrence, the same thing happened to me the very next day. When doing a formation takeoff, the other plane almost never "sympathetic" aborts with you as it can create a more dangerous situation with two planes trying to stop on the same runway at high speed. I broke on two of the night flights as well when the HUD didn't work properly and some of the lights in the cockpit weren't working correctly. It was a terribly frustrating week.

This brought me to the next two night flights, each I flew with my favorite instructor, Lt. Pal. The first night we flew to Lubbock, TX for an approach and then back to Sheppard. It was a beautiful, clear night less a huge thunderstorm off in the distance which created an amazing lightning show. Further, there was no moon so you could see far more stars than normal. Each time I flew at night in these military planes, I couldn't get over how amazing it was to be in a canopy where you could see all around you. On the return leg, I turned off all of my lights in the cockpit less the altimeter (altitude) and HSI (course guidance), leaving them just bright enough to make out what they said, and soaked in the view. We could see full arms of the Milky Way galaxy, shooting stars and the lightning storm off in the distance. We were quiet except for the occasional exclamation of, "did you see that?!" It was awesome.

The second night flight, my last of UPT, was with Lt. Pal and I had already finished all of my syllabus requirements so it was essentially a free flight. The military does some amazing things with airplanes but they have their weird fears as well. Class B airspace and doing "different" things scares military pilots. Class B is the airspace around busy airports like DFW and Love Field in Dallas. There are endless rumors of guys receiving violations in class B airspace because they are more stringent with rules due to the higher traffic volumes. But flying over cities at night is beautiful and the challenge and mystique of going, due to opposing Air Force opinion, had sold me. I really wanted to go now. I mentioned it to Lt. Pal and we talked to a few of the other IPs and heard the following responses:

"There is no way they will let you into Love."

"You might as well throw your wings on the ground trying to fly into class B airspace."

"Good luck with that."

All of those comments just pissed me off and in my opinion, were ignorant. I wanted to go but I didn't want to pressure Lt. Pal into it. He is a relatively new instructor and ultimately, it is his responsibility. Further, he is a lieutenant and had captains and majors telling him the things I've written above. I finally asked Lt. Pal what he thought about trying the adventure and while I could tell he was nervous, he decided it would be fun to try anyway.

Once airborne, I told air traffic control I was willing to do anything they needed to get to Love Field for training, motivated to prove the other IPs wrong. We got great vectors all over the city and shot an instrument approach into Love. I didn't realize how close downtown was to the departure end of runway 13R and it left us in astonishment how close we were to the buildings. We stayed low after the touch and go, co-altitude with the tops of the buildings and just a few thousand feet away horizontally.

On the HUD tape, after the touch and go, you hear me say, "Ok, gear and flaps are up at 210, annnnd holy shit, this is awesome." Pal exclaims, "F$%&ing sweet!"

We then requested the downtown tour and while I had expected Dallas again, they thought we meant Forth Worth so we were able to fly directly by both downtowns. It was pure luck but worked out beautifully.

Afterward, Lt. Pal told me there is no way he would have tried it with any other student and it was one of those flights we got out of the plane high fiving and hand shaking each other as it was so fun. Further, I overheard him saying it would be a flight he will remember for a long time. Same.

Lesson Learned: Push the Envelope

Pushing the envelope can take many forms, especially in the aviation world, but the intent is always the same. There is a comfort most people develop in doing things the way they have always been done. While there is benefit from the reassurance, it is difficult to grow, improve and have a great time doing things you or other people have always done. Not only is it often good for you, this effort can also help an organization. Had Lt. Pal and I simply listened to the leadership's suggestion, we would have missed a great learning opportunity and a significant amount of fun.

Week 49: Sundog Check. Two, Three, Four

The two ship check ride was definitely my ugliest check ride of UPT as I came away with five downgrades, four of which were due to one poor decision. I was leading and our two ship was approaching an airspace border off our nose. #2 was a mile off my right wing so I made a 90 degree turn to my right, I placed him a mile to my left and a mile closer to the border than I. Either way, he was possibly out of the area and I took a big hit for it. Everyone had passed the check ride so far except an Italian. Lt. Pal had been out of town the last few days in Washington D.C. doing something with Congress and our Wing Commander. When I got home and checked my phone after the check ride, he was the first person to text and see how I had done. Good guy.

Friday I had my first four ship ride. I was #2 and students were only allowed to fly the #2 and #4 positions. It was amazing. We did some of the airshow "fingertip" formation where we all had the 3-feet wingtip clearance from each other but it was mostly a variety of tactical formations in shapes such as a wall (all four jets separated by a mile, line abreast), fluid four (#1 and #3 are a mile apart and #2 and #4 are like annoy flies on each one of those jets, much closer at 500-1500 feet). Box and offset box (from the ground looking up, this formation looks like a rectangle with 1 and 1.5-mile sides). The crazy part was maneuvering four jets in these different formations as sometimes it looked like there were airplanes going in all kinds of directions.

I was now down to low level and four ship flights. Most of low level is in a two ship formation.

Lesson Learned: The Little Things

When you are leading or supervising people, taking a few extra minutes to make a phone call or send a quick text message can make a considerable difference in morale and how people feel about you. Even better, send a hand-written note. We may do this with friends but when a superior makes an effort to care about you and your performance, it can have significant meaning.

Week 50: Birds

I had a few low level and instrument simulator rides leaving me with only two sims left in UPT. I had three flights including a four ship, an instrument and my first low level flight.

I was #4 in the four ship for the first time, which made for nice views looking down three other jets in fingertip formation. Being #4 in fingertip is often described as being on the end of a whip. #2 is always correcting to be in position off of #1. #3 is correcting off #2, so each time #2 bobbles, #3 has to correct as well, but generally a little more. #4 corrects off #3 which is an even further, exaggerated correction. Each little error by anyone flows down the formation and is magnified.

The low level flight on Friday was simply incredible. I had a laid back Major for an IP and it was an easy route, making the reacclimatization to the low level environment stress-free. I knew it was going to feel fast but it was still hard to put into words how fast it felt when you were just 500 feet above the ground. Most of the route was flown at 360 knots but the final run towards the target was at 390. At one point, as I was correcting for winds, I was showing 420 knots across the ground, or 483 miles per hour. The towers appeared a lot quicker and it was cool to approach the target and have an "air-to-ground weapons mode" in the HUD and simulate dropping a bomb on target.

I flew well and as we were riding the bus back from the jet to the squadron, my IP asked if I had any questions.

"No sir, not that I can think of."

"Sounds good. Well I hope you have a fantastic weekend. Good flight."

And that was the end of the debrief on a Friday at five.

Witt was also flying low level and nearly hit a bird. After the flight while watching his HUD tape, we could see the bird try to dodge the jet but instead dove right toward it in a suicide attempt. Witt quickly pulled up, avoiding the bird. He pulled 6.5 Gs and was 0.1 G away from an over-G. It would have been interesting to see if the instructor would have passed him had he over-G'ed.

On Monday, another student hooked a four ship ride when his lead told him to turn left and he turned right. Since lead thought he was going the other way, he turned left, creating a dangerous situation of over 700 knots closure between the jets and less than 100 feet of vertical separation. The student's IP took the jet, rolled and pulled to avoid the other jet, over-G-ing it in the process.

This Air Force training program was incredibly well designed and safe but those stories quickly humble everyone. It was a turn we did all of the time and a simple left from right mix-up almost ran two jets together and cost four lives. While training was safe, it could be terribly unforgiving.

Week 51: Fox 2

I was on the schedule four times this week for 1800 takeoffs, the last flight of the day on base. Monday and Tuesday's thunderstorms cancelled the flights but Wednesday and Thursday left beautiful evenings with the airspace all to our four ship formation for Heat to Guns—arguably the highlight of UPT.

Heat to Guns was an exercise where we tried to get a missile kill and then move in closer to get a guns kill. During this block of four flights before the check ride, which would be Wednesday of next week, we took off as a four ship, went to the airspace to maneuver for twenty minutes and then separated into 2 two ship elements to practice Heat to Guns.

In Heat to Guns we started one mile apart, heading the same direction as the bandit when an instructor, by himself in the other plane, called "Fight's on" and turned aggressively away from me. I chased by aggressively executing a 6G turn in afterburner, pulled him into the missile reticle in my HUD as quickly as I could, uncaged the reticle and fired a simulated heat-seeking missile.

After my Fox 2 call, he broke the other direction and I climbed slightly to avoid his jet wash, attempting to start my turn after him in the same exact spot in the sky he reversed his turn. This was called entering his turn circle. From there, I drove on his turn circle, getting closer to the range of the gun, 2,500 feet. Once I approached that distance, I ensured I was not closing too quickly and then pulled my nose in front of him and gunned him. I needed bullets hitting him for half a second to count as a kill. It was the first time I was able to call "Fox 2" and hit the pickle button, simulating the launch of a missile and gun someone, for my job. While the process was very canned, Heat to Guns was a baby step into the next year of fighter pilot training. There is a different level of adrenaline running through the system when you are trying to kill a bandit and we often said "the fangs come out" as the fight is on. It was a nice reaffirmation I picked a great career.

The active duty guys in our class would find out which planes they would be assigned to fly in two weeks and were given a few days to consider the options and had to list, in order, their preferences. The following list did not mean all of these planes would be assigned but they could be. The choices were as follows: F-22, F-15C, F-15E, F-16, A-10, T-38, T-6, B-1, B-52, C-17, KC-135, U-28 and MC-12.

It was interesting to watch the guys debate and argue for the different airframes. Fighter jets are amazing machines and we do incredible things in them. You get to be the tip of the spear in combat. It is fast paced and high adrenaline flying but also more stress, work and some guys just don't like pulling Gs. We have heard cargo and refueling planes have an easier pace to life. They get to travel around the world and see amazing things but the flying is not so exciting. Bomber pilots probably have it somewhere in between. My buddies could also choose to become instructors in the T-6 or

T-38 again. Most wanted to move on to the combat Air Force but instructing can be rewarding as well.

Week 52: Puffy Clouds

I flew seven times in five days this week and my four ship check ride was Wednesday. I made it through with two downgrades but Witt, the other student in the four ship was not so fortunate. He'd originally thought he hooked after the four ship separated and we were doing the Heat to Guns exercise. He flew through the bandit's jet wash and thought he had over-G'ed. They returned home early but after landing and reviewing the HUD tape, he was within limits. However, the check IP hooked him for the first rejoin after takeoff after he over shot the three of us by about 2,500 feet.

After the check ride I started formation low level again. It is pretty hard to describe how fast and low it felt, especially when you had another airplane near you in a formation. It was like the world was in fast forward reaching speeds as high as 500 mph, just 500 feet off the ground. It was hard to believe but I had just two more flights left before the check ride and would be done with UPT Wednesday, two weeks before graduation.

We received our final officership reviews and I was happy to hear I remained second behind our class leader, CAIN. The Flight Commander said I received the highest motivation score he has ever seen. Often considering myself pretty lazy, I felt like the fact I had already "dropped" an F-16, was in the Guard, and had prior flying experience gave me numerous reasons to be lazier if I wanted since I could simply pass rides and get through the program. Since I didn't, I think I appeared extra-motivated in their eyes.

In more somber news, a guy in the other flight washed out of pilot training this week. He had struggled from day one, his grandfather passed away and he had a kid which didn't help with distractions. It was tough news as he was a guy everyone liked. He was also in the reserves with an F-16 waiting for him. Our flight has had one guy on flying CAP (Commander's Awareness Program), a program designed to give continuity in training with a struggling student, in all of T-38s. We knew that having only one guy on

CAP was strong but we didn't know how strong. We found out the two newest flights in T-38 had 4-6 guys on CAP already in each flight.

Witt was leading a two ship back from a low level on Friday afternoon when Air Traffic Control asked for a PIREP. (Pilot Report: essentially they are asking about the weather where the plane is.)

Having never been asked the question before, Witt replied, "Banger 55 is... uh... just skirting along the tops, it's uh very puffy up here, scattered clouds." The other plane's IP, a former F-15C pilot, replied over the inter flight radio frequency, "Ya, I have definitely never heard the word puffy on the radio before." Witt hasn't heard the end of it from the guys and we have saved the video clip.

THE MOB FLIGHT

Week 53: The Drop

I started the week with four flights left in UPT and concluded the program Wednesday afternoon. The two ship low level check ride was Wednesday morning, and besides a few small errors, went very well. After 10 UPT check rides beginning last September, I was done and had one last, relatively free flight with Lt. Pal to conclude UPT.

Besides the slight self-induced stress of not hooking the ride, the flight was purely meant to be a good time. Lt. Pal and I spent 10-15 minutes cloud-chasing, shot a couple instrument approaches and then Lt. Pal showed me some basic fighter maneuvers I would learn in my next class starting in October. They were max rate of turn maneuvers, in afterburner, with my head back looking for the enemy, pulling 6 Gs. It puts a decent amount of strain on the neck.

In other sad news, another kid was removed from the program the day before drop night. Overall, our class had lost three guys to medical problems and two to performance during the past thirteen months. All of the attrition was in our sister flight so I didn't know the guys nearly as well and didn't know the details. Guys are typically removed for repeated safety of flight issues. Nonetheless, it was somber news so close graduation.

The thousands of grades we have each received during the past year led us to drop night, one of the most important nights of many of our lives. The Guard guys found out if they were "fighter qualified" and the active duty guys discovered the airframe they would fly. Fighter jets were the dream for everyone here and they competed for a year to get a shot at dropping the plane of their choice on drop night. The party was a "Christmas in July" theme in a multi-purpose room with a few hundred people in attendance and our drops were hidden in presents. We played Christmas music, had eggnog, a snowball fight, an ugly sweater contest and the works. It was a fun, lively atmosphere as rumors of a good drop were causing quite a buzz. I opened a present and found my F-16. Since I was hired by the Guard I knew I was getting one as long as I passed the course. I could write for pages about each individual drop and the stories behind them but I will pick three.

1st: Schiess, my buddy whom I had given the pep talk to a couple of months ago, experienced the night's most disappointing moment. Of all the guys in the drop, I wanted him to get a fighter the most. His brother was an F-15C pilot and he wanted it bad. He was an all-around good dude who did everything he could, all year, to help others and himself get what they wanted. He dropped a T-38 instructor job, staying here in Wichita Falls for the next 3-4 years. The worst part is the Air Force has a rule that to be an instructor you must be in the top 50% of the class so there were guys who performed worse than him, many of them in fact, who dropped fighter jets. He and his fiancé weren't taking it well but I had no doubt it would work out.

2nd: CAIN, our Captain and class leader who was a Navigator in the F-15E Strike Eagle prior to pilot training, had his heart set on the same plane. Midway through the drop, he got an F-16. Obviously a huge achievement to get a fighter but at the end of the night, "Santa" pointed out one last present under the tree. They had played a joke on him. It was the Strike Eagle for the old man.

3rd: Cheech, the red-headed Italian and a closer friend to me than most, was part of the Italian early exit program because he didn't perform as well as some of the other Italians. As a result, he didn't get to fly in a four ship or two ship low level during the training. He had the best "Christmas morning face" upon finding out he was the first early exit student in the history of ENNJPT to drop a fighter, the Tornado. He had his mom in Italy on the phone, 3 AM her time, when he got the drop and after all of the pandemonium of us all tackling him in joy, he picked up his phone and softly said in his Italian accent, "Mama, Toooornaaaadddo." Easily the coolest moment of the night.

Otherwise, our Flight Commander said it was the best drop he has seen here in the four years he has been at Sheppard. Off the top of my head, this is what I remember:

- Five F-16 (3 Guard)
- One F-22
- Four F-15E
- One F-15C
- Two A-10
- Two Eurofighters
- One Tornado
- One T-38 Instructor
- One T-6 Instructor
- Two MC-12
- One AC-130 Gunship
- One Unmanned Aerial Vehicle (Italian)

Everyone was now finished except one. Hawk has been out the last few weeks taking care of his newborn in Fort Worth. Now flying again, if he double turned every day this week, he would finish the day before graduation. Throughout pilot training we had been taking weekly tests called EPQs (Emergency Procedures Quizzes). At approximately 45 questions, we had to get an 85% or face remediation and a reputation of not putting forth enough effort. In a cruel twist, we were given one Monday morning, when we were not expecting it. We were 30 minutes into the test when our Flight Commander looked at the instructor who gave us the test like he was evil and told us to shred the test. It was a nice head-fake to the last real grade of UPT.

I found my digital logbook and this is what I finished UPT with:

Hours in the T-6: 122.2 with 299 landings. An additional 56.2 hours in the simulator.

T-38: 98.1 hours with 211 landings, 47.8 simulator hours.

I had spent most of my free time the last few weeks working out due to fear of the centrifuge. For the first time in my life, being skinny wasn't the first thing people noticed as I had thrown on an additional 10 lbs.

Graduation was this week and a group of ten family and friends from Missouri were coming down for it. Unfortunately, this was a good time for the IPs in our flight to take leave and Lt. Pal would not be in attendance. We both sent each other a letter and small gift before he left for Germany.

Lesson Learned: Life is Not Fair

We were told the harder you work and better you perform at pilot training, the better chance you have to fly the jet of your dreams. The one exception in our class was hard to swallow for our buddy who dropped the T-38 instructor job. The same is true about college or anything you work hard to achieve. Sometimes the result is a matter of luck and timing. Life is a journey and Schiess will undoubtedly get his shot in a fighter on this path but it will be delayed. It was terrible to watch how down he and his fiancé got over the issue but at the end of the day, he was still being paid to fly a supersonic jet airplane and would have the satisfaction of teaching people something pretty cool. Life isn't fair but everything is a matter of perspective. I encourage you to look at things from the optimistic perspective as often as you can.

CHEECH, THE ITALIAN, THE MOMENT HE FINDS OUT HE WILL FLY THE TORNADO

ANOTHER ITALIAN CLASSMATE LEARNING HE WILL FLY THE EUROFIGHTER

Week 55: Wings

The final week finally arrived. Hawk finished his last flight late Thursday night, the day before graduation. Of the 27 in our class, 22 finished the entire program and received wings. Approximately 140 family members traveled to Wichita Falls and Sheppard Air Force base in support of the twenty-two graduates.

Friday, red carpet day, was a look into our lives over the past year. We spent a little time in the T-38 simulator which my cousin Arlen, entering second grade, was a master at flying low, supersonic, and buzzing the tower. When he got out of the simulator he said, "thanks! That was awesome!" It was another reminder this was a good choice of profession—many kids would not call work awesome unless it was pretty fun. The families also saw a mock morning brief, met the leadership, saw a mock emergency procedure stand up, walked out to the planes, tried on my helmet and parachute, toured Air Traffic Control and got to go up in the tower. I'd had some tiring days in pilot training but this last one might have taken the prize.

The ceremony in the evening included a few speeches by colonels and a general, our class video, hours of thanking people, awards and finally the wings. The awards went pretty well from my perspective. They handed out six total. CAIN and I were the Distinguished Graduates given to the top 10% of the class. CAIN also won the Military Officership award. He earned this for the tremendous job he did as our class leader and always acting in the appropriate manner of an Air Force officer. One of the Italians, from "Roma, like the empire," won the Academic award, which was a cumulative grade on all academic tests throughout the year. In addition to D.G., I came away with the Flying Excellence award given to the person with top flying grades, top formation award and the overall award, called the Commander's Trophy, combining officership and flying scores.

I will admit it felt pretty good to win those four awards in the company I did. In undoubtedly the most competitive pilot training base to attend, flying the airplanes and doing the things we did in them, in one of the best classes ENJJPT had seen in the last few years, it felt pretty damn good to be recognized in such a manner. I know the group of guys in my flight helped me and themselves perform at a higher level than any of us had expected.

MY GRANDFATHER PINNING MY WINGS ON MY CHEST. YOU MUST HAVE BEEN AN AIR FORCE PILOT TO GIVE SOMEONE ELSE WINGS.

After graduation we all went to the Officer's Club to celebrate well into the evening. One tradition, the wing-breaking ceremony, was held soon after we arrived and only people having earned Air Force wings could attend. All of us just receiving our wings took our first pair and broke them in half, the idea being it would be better to ruin your first set of wings there rather than doing something dumb in the air. Someone made the following toast as we took a shot, all 125 pilots in the room: *"Fight on and fly on to the last drop of blood and the last drop of fuel, to the last beat of the heart"* – The Red Baron.

The rest of the evening was spent with classmates and IPs finally treating us as peers. It was a nice feeling. The humbling news is that I started at square one in the next class and would still have a long way to go in order to sit in the F-16 and ultimately be combat ready—hopefully around 14 months from now.

Lesson Learned: Celebrate

We achieved quite an accomplishment this evening and a formal ceremony helps put it in perspective. I hadn't yet reached my goal of flying the F-16 but celebrations could still be had. Becoming an F-16 pilot is a journey. Starting a business or getting through college is a journey. While milestones may seem insignificant or not the end goal, I felt the pride within myself and saw it in my bros that evening. We had a great time celebrating a great year. We had worked hard and the evening was a great reward in front of family and friends.

Don't overlook the value of these occasions and their potential to motivate people.

PART 4: INTRODUCTION TO FIGHTER FUNDAMENTALS (IFF)

Pre IFF

After graduation, I drove to Missouri and my grandpa and I flew our Bonanza out to Yosemite National Park. It was my first experience with actual mountain flying in a small aircraft. We flew through canyons and around peaks we couldn't climb above, a fun challenge as we navigated through various passes. I also planned our route to fly over ten national parks. It was an interesting way to see the country as we were usually flying at the lowest legal altitude over these areas. It's nice when the vacation from your job is doing more of your job, just in a different way.

My grandpa and I spent the majority of time talking about the flying of the past year and what an incredible experience it had been for me, and for him, to be able to follow. He and I, having shared elements of this experience in our lives, have a special relationship as we can understand each other. Military flying is difficult to understand for even commercial pilots so I was very fortunate to have him to tell my stories to.

1,663 lbs

Another few weeks passed as I continued to wait for the next IFF class, still at Sheppard AFB. I would fly with IFF instructors in the back seat, called sandbagging, typically once per day. I had developed a decent relationship with a number of IPs which I hoped would pay dividends once I actually entered the class as they took note of my motivation.

Some of the rides have been pretty amazing. On one, a surface attack ride, we went to a bombing range and dropped simulated bombs. For the last target, the ranger (the simulated troop on the ground calling in air support), came over the radio with a slight panic in his voice, just how it sounds in the movies. "Satan 1, we have an urgent target!" He proceeded to talk our eyes onto a truck, a real truck, driving around on the range. "We need a strafe on this truck immediately. Wait. The truck has stopped! Three men are getting out, it looks like one has a shovel and they are planting an IED."

No kidding, we were orbiting at 10,000 feet and as he was saying this, I could see the men getting out of the truck. "We need the strafe now, come in from the north, you are cleared hot!" I had chills it was so exciting. We roll into a 30-degree nose-low dive shooting the gun, pulling out of the dive at about 4,000 feet, with our wingman, the student, following to make sure we took out the target. The ranger told us it was successful and we headed home. It was incredible how dramatic a fake scene could be.

I continued to learn more each ride but I was also riding along to pull Gs. The 9 G centrifuge, round two, was last week and I felt it was the biggest threat between me flying an F-16 and not. My body structure was not built for it and the 7.5 G centrifuge six months ago had not gone well. However, I'd spent these last two months working out regularly, a workout geared toward the muscles supporting an anti-G-Strain. I had even flown the morning I left for San Antonio so I could get one last shot at pulling Gs and further maintain my G-tolerance.

Hawk and I showed up for the centrifuge and I was just as nervous as expected. By some miracle, I did well. The workouts had paid off and my breathing technique was considerably better than the first time. I hardly had any light loss during the whole experience. I would have described the first centrifuge, at only 7.5 Gs, as the worst thing I had ever experienced. This one still sucked and three days later my arms still hurt and my butt was still bruised, but it was tolerable. I should never have to go back to the dreaded centrifuge again. We celebrated appropriately with Coronas on the rooftop pool at the Riverwalk.

Free Flying

Another few interim weeks down and only 1.5 weeks away from the beginning of IFF. I continued to fly once or twice per day, generally in the backseat, but occasionally a front seat ride. There were 18 graded rides in IFF and I had seen them all, some a few times.

In more somber news, a kid in my Guard unit a year ahead of me and whom I have referenced numerous times, had washed out of F-16 school in Phoenix two weeks ago. I'd spoken to him a few times since and he was understandably distraught and was looking at various options. We were not completely sure what his options were but he would probably join a Guard unit flying a C-130 or refueling aircraft. Somewhere along the training pipeline, he developed a reputation of having a bad attitude and attitude is one of the more critical elements of being a fighter pilot. CAIN had looked through all of his grade sheets when he flew the F-15E and noticed the first comment on each was not about his flying skills, but his attitude.

With this news and a couple of kids washing out of IFF, I was concerned about the future. However, we had come find out those students struggling at the next level had struggled in UPT as well, something I didn't have to worry about. Further, I was sandbagging and studying more than anyone I knew during my time off, something many said was unnecessary. Because my fear of failing was so high, I generally ignored those who questioned why I sandbagged so much. It was this paranoia which ultimately made UPT relatively easy for me. I had even been teaching some of the students in IFF certain things they have already had class for that I haven't. I didn't understand how they could be so ill-prepared.

Week 1: Witt's Boyfriend

Now late October 2012, after two and a half months of waiting, I started IFF with eight new students. I had begun my Air Force Training 21 months ago and finally got to start the nineteen-ride introduction to dogfighting and bombing. IFF would be the last hurdle before the F-16. I had two simulator rides to start, an instrument and emergency simulation. The instructors gave a variety of problems: fire on takeoff, complete electrical failures, tire failures, a variety of engine malfunctions and more.

The rest of the next week and a half included a variety of classes introducing the concepts of dogfighting. We started on a Wednesday and on Friday the squadron had a roll call. If you don't remember, a roll call is a closed-door event, with a Mayor running the festivities. It is used to tell stories, sing songs, and take shots for almost everything and a variety of other shenanigans.

We had a couple of these roll calls in T-6s and one in the T-38 training but this was the first in a "fighter squadron." Basically, it was a mild hazing with the IPs ridiculing us for everything regarding the event's setup and then telling stories about themselves or students. The students typically hovered as far away from the front to avoid the spotlight and ridicule associated with it. Students almost never willingly told stories unless they had to because they had an over-G. So there I was, six hours prior to the roll call and I realized I had a story about something stupid an instructor had done while I was sandbagging. I rehearsed the story no less than five times throughout the day and agonized over whether I should tell it.

Pros:

1. I was a student who hadn't even flown yet, willing to stand up and tell a story.

2. If I told it well, it had the potential to be funny.

Cons:

1. If stories were even moderately not funny, you would get booed and heckled the rest of the night.

2. It might have actually pissed the subject IP off—not a great way to start IFF.

3. I didn't even know whether they wanted students to tell stories.

While the cons won in my mind, I decided I was going to make the call in the moment, based on the vibe of the crowd.

The roll call began and it was going just as terribly as I imagined. Students from all three classes were hiding in the corners of the room and the IPs were doing all the talking. The Mayor hit the gavel, announcing the beginning of story-telling. My adrenaline started firing and no one was talking. They started yelling at us for not having a story so put my beer over my head, signaling I wanted to speak. The Mayor pointed at me and I stepped in front of 40 students and 30 IPs.

I apologize mother, but this is even the tempered version of the story. Hopefully there won't be too many inside jokes among the pilot community as I retell. Also, realize the storyteller is expected to use the 10% rule. This means you can make the story better by making some stuff up as only 10% needs to be the truth. All stories start the same way...

"So there I was (crowd says, "in the shit!") no, no. I wasn't in the shit, I was actually in the backseat of Major Smith's jet on my 69th sandbag ride. It was Katarina "Quick Pickle" Witt's Offensive BFM solo flight and we were in the middle of an engagement. Bullets were flying and we were jinking [quick, unpredictable movements to avoid bullets] when all of the sudden, Witt calls a Knock-it-off.

The fighting stops and he begins to describe all of the things going wrong in his airplane. Witt says, 'Nisan 2 has a left generator and left fuel pressure caution light on. Left oil pressure and fuel flow indications are off. Engine and caution is flashing on my Heads up Display.' So knowing I have Major Smith with me, I drop my mask and turn off the microphone because I know he will save the day.

Before I know it, we have declared an emergency and are heading toward Altus. I hear this and realize a serious problem is developing for me. I think to myself, oh god, they teach heavy pilots at Altus. [Heavy airplanes, cargo etc. Something fighter pilots don't want to do.] Even worse, I don't know any girls at Altus, this is terrible. I immediately put my mask back on and get on the intercom.

Having no idea what the real problem is because I am an idiot student, I say, 'Sir, I think this is just a left generator failure with no crossover, tell him to simply reset the generator.'

He replies, 'Shut the F$%^ up, back-seater.' [This got one of the biggest laughs from the crowd as I had to pause my story for a good 15 seconds.]

There is a silent few seconds before Major Smith quietly tells Witt to reset the generator. Witt reports everything is now working normally again. I chuckle to myself and in the end, I got to go home to my girlfriend, Witt got to go home to his boyfriend [the room exploded and no one could hear my final line of...] and Major Smith was the hero and got a bullet item for his officer performance review."

I took a bow and the IPs applauded while explaining to the room that was how a lieutenant should tell a story. It was a good night—a good night right up until I was hustled out of $80 in some card game called four, fix, six.

With my first flight tomorrow, the dogfighting should start Wednesday.

Week 2: Kill Mig

My first flight was Monday evening and it went well. One carry over from civilian flying had been my fuel awareness and consideration. On numerous flights in UPT and this one in IFF, IPs had been complimentary of my fuel-saving habits. In the civilian world, saving fuel is saving money, something I was always conscious of as I may have been paying the bill. For example, when air traffic control gives you a descent, you could either descend rapidly making things easier because that is one less thing to worry about later, or you could descend as slow as possible until the last minute to save gas. The latter could rush you as you approach to land but it saves gas, something the IP on this flight loved.

We had academics each day and I flew my first offensive BFM (Basic Fighter Maneuver) on Wednesday with an infamous IP.

It was the most fun I'd ever had in an airplane. It was challenging both physically and mentally but an incredible game to be playing as well. Not only are you focusing on the parameters of your airplane, but every move you make is in relation to the bandit's airplane as well. I got six fights in and killed the bandit five times. I had residual adrenaline from the fight lasting well into the evening as I was trying to go to sleep.

I had my second ride the next day and we started the fights from a farther distance away, one mile as opposed to 3,000'. It was another fun flight but a lot more painful with the G forces. People often ask if it is like what we see in movies or video games and to some degree it can be, but I'd never expected the physical demands this type of flying requires. I ended most fights almost out of breath, drenched in sweat and could even be sore the next day.

I also was able go to home for the weekend for my grandfather's airport renaming ceremony. The city of Monett, Missouri had decided to call their airport "Fox Field" after his efforts throughout the past 20-30 years. Not only had he flown the F-86 for the Air Force in the 1950s, he had been instrumental in securing funding and improving the Monett airport for over forty years. Whether it was lengthening the runway, adding an instrument approach or flying his iconic yellow biplane around town, Jack Fox was aviation in Monett, MO.

Week 3: Taxpayer Presents

This four-day week included two flights, a sim, and academics. Wednesday was my third offensive BFM flight and happened to be my birthday. Two years in a row I had received quite the birthday present from the taxpayers. I flew with a new IP and he was pleasantly quiet in the plane. Further, in four full fights, I killed the bandit each time which made things more enjoyable. I shot nine Aim-9s, which is a type of heat seeking missile, and killed him with the gun three times. Expending that much ordinance means I killed him twice each fight but was too much of a pansy to call the kill earlier. If you call a kill but determine after reviewing the tapes on the ground you didn't kill him, you lose a bunch of points and owe the bar $5.

Ultimately, my main debriefing points were regarding wasteful use of ordinance. The obvious counter to this point was that if I had killed him the first time, he would have blown up. The other comical debriefing point was regarding the last fight that ended quickly because of fuel. The radios were busy and I couldn't make the "fights on" call because so many people were talking. Basically, fights are supposed to set up a certain way and this one was screwed up. My IP was yelling at me to go kill him but I didn't know if I was within the rules and the best way to hook a ride is to do something unsafe. Flash forward to the debrief where he said, "look, if the bandit didn't know we were fighting, then it is his fault. It's an easy kill if he doesn't know you are there. I go to the local elementary every other week and kick the shit out of a 5th grader because I can and it makes me feel good"—obviously kidding but trying to make a point. There is a famous fighter pilot quote I am paraphrasing: *"If I ever get in a fair fight, I didn't plan it properly."*

The IP cleared me solo against him the next day for my last offensive BFM ride. The solo was essentially a duplication of the previous flight, getting 4/4 kills. It was quite the awesome feeling, to be cruising around in a jet by yourself and to successfully kill every chance you get. Having not done any type of flying similar to this, I had some concern about how fighting would go for me. It was comforting to know I had out-prepared each of my peers through study and simulators.

Weeks 4 and 5: Jinking

It's now Thanksgiving 2012. As in UPT, they broke up the IFF flights into blocks. Along with even simulator missions, we had:

- Intro instrument flight
- Four flights for offensive BFM
- Four for defensive BFM
- Four for surface attack
- Two for CAS (Close Air Support is helping troops on the ground calling in airstrikes)
- Two for high aspect BFM (where the fight starts with us pointing at each other and passing at 950 knots of closure)
- Two air combat maneuvering flights (more than 2 aircraft in a fight)

If you hooked five events, you would be sent to a board and probably removed from the program, not to set foot in an actual fighter. Further, if you hooked a ride, you had to repeat it. At the end of my last weekly summary, I had just finished offensive BFM and was moving on to defensive BFM, generally regarded as the most difficult and least fun phase of the program. Instead of starting fights chasing the bandit, you are being chased and he is already in a position to employ weapons on you. Goal? Survive for a certain amount of time and in some rare cases, turn the fight around on him so you are offensive and can kill him.

Defensive BFM is tough for a variety of reasons. First, the G-strain. 5-7 Gs is a lot easier to handle sitting in a normal body position looking forward. When defensive, you spend most of your time looking behind you at the bandit, maneuvering in relation to what he is doing. Your diaphragm is twisted and it is much harder to perform the breathing and straining techniques we are taught. It was not uncommon to see students hook a ride for not doing the G-strain properly. Sometimes you could get by without doing the strain in this plane but in a 9G F-16, it could be very dangerous if you passed out, for obvious reasons. Besides tolerating Gs while flying, flying while looking backward was significantly more challenging. Imagine trying to drive by looking at the car behind you on a curvy road, your head weighs 100 lbs, it's hard to breathe, and the car is violently shaking the entire time. Further, the car behind you is shooting at you. Most guys ended up losing the fights by flying through the simulated "floor" because it is hard to keep your altitude under control and know when is the floor is approaching since you are looking backward.

After finishing the phase with a solo on Friday afternoon, I can proudly say I passed all four rides, didn't kill myself by hitting the floor and didn't over-G. The last ride I escaped all five fights unharmed and even got offensive on him on the last fight and killed him. Man, it was a lot of fun. The previous three flights were fun but not nearly as much as the offensive phase.

Physically, the week wasn't as fun either. I had been nursing a sore throat for a week but still couldn't get myself to pass up a scheduled flight and get behind on the timeline. My neck and back have also felt the effects of flying while facing backward under 6 Gs. On Friday, I could see the bandit a lot better on fights turning to the right rather than the left due to neck pain from Wednesday's flight. Compare that to another kid who was only on his 3rd flight because he continuously had an excuse for not flying. He had already hooked a ride or two and started the IFF program on CAP (Commander's Awareness Program).

Lesson Learned: Man Up

In many jobs, this one especially, it is critically important to be fully prepared to execute what you are required to do. Not only prepared with regard to study and planning, but physically and emotionally healthy as well. It is necessary in any line of work to get optimal performance but in a short course like this, when an emphasis is made to determine if we will be capable fighter pilots at the next level, it is essential or you risk the chance. Having said that, as I watched the kid in my class continually have excuses for not flying and falling further and further behind, I realized it was creating other detrimental effects. Not only was he flying with greater irregularity, which causes problems, he was damaging the instructor opinion of him and his own opinion of himself as well. Life is never perfect and while there are reasons you legitimately shouldn't fly, we are in the business of war and there can't always be an excuse. When it is time to fight, be ready. We can't determine the timeline and in a program looking for fighters, a persona of excuses is not what they are looking for.

Week 6: Hall of Fame

One of the best flying weeks I have had this entire journey in the Air Force. I had my first two surface attack rides with one of my favorite instructors and both rides went well from my extra practicing in the simulator. On these two rides, we did 10, 20 and 30-degree dive bombs along with the 30-degree strafe (gun) attack. The 30-degree dive is quite a feeling when you are accelerating through 420 knots as you release the bomb and the world is moving rapidly closer in the windscreen. On the 10-degree bomb, we were releasing about 1000 feet above the ground. I had another surface attack simulator ride on Friday for my flight the next day, which was a tactical pattern called "pops." We drove into the target at 440 knots, 500 feet above the ground, made a quick 30-degree turn and then "popped" up a couple thousand feet to acquire the target visually, roll in and bomb it.

Later, I had my two high aspect BFM rides. This means we started the fights neutral by pointing at each other doing 400-450 knots, flying by each other at what is called the merge. The idea being no one had an advantage as the "fight's on" call was made as we passed. Both rides went well and I avoided any over-Gs, the highest threat for failing the ride. Further, the second IP I had was another former Viper guy who I liked a lot. He set me at ease during the brief by saying, "alright Fox, how are you going to hook this ride?"

Me: "Over-G."

IP: "Yep, that's pretty much it. So don't do that and I want you to enjoy this ride. In 5 years I want you to look back and say, I actually did have a good time on that high aspect ride in the T-38. Sure, it sucks compared to the Viper I am flying now but those were fun airplanes."

With that comforting knowledge, and a tip from a buddy who had told me an atypical fight strategy, I was armed for a good time. The first two fights I didn't kill him but the third was one of the coolest things I have done in an airplane.

After turning to point at him to start the fight, I was 2-3,000 feet below. The atypical game plan was to start a loop directly beneath him and then after he chose which way to turn, I'd turn the same direction, doing a large barrel roll, which lengthened my flight path, allowing me to roll out directly behind him and shoot him with 3 missiles and a guns kill. It might sound more simple than it actually is—keeping sight of him is the worst part and it can be difficult to even know which way is up with all of that climbing and rolling around. Losing sight is one of the primary sins of a dogfight. If you can't see him, you can't maneuver your jet to a position to kill or to keep yourself from getting killed.

I was hopped up on adrenaline for hours after the fight. The IP even wrote on my grade sheet, "This one is for your memory's Hall of Fame."

Lesson Learned: Lose Sight, Lose Fight

You can't fight what you can't see. Whether it's in a visual engagement or on a radar scope, the actions of your jet are essentially a guess and random if you can't see the enemy. You need to assess, in detail, his speed, the rate at which he is turning, whether he is shooting at you and many other variables by the second. Not only keeping track of his jet, we need to keep sight of the mission objectives at all times as well. Primitively enough in this business, they are usually led by "Kill and Survive." The same is true with objectives and competition in business. To outperform the competition, you need to know everything you can about what they are doing. How much are they paying their employees? What is their pricing strategy? What kind of margins are they making? You also need to keep sight of your objectives on any project. If the whole team is aware of the objective, it makes decentralized decision making far easier as everyone clearly understands the goal.

Week 7: Fingertip

I ended up finishing three flights and a simulator this week, leaving me with three flights and a simulator left in the IFF program.

Tuesday I had the ACM simulator. Standing for Air Combat Maneuvering, it is essentially a 2 v. 1 fight. It simulated my flight lead and I cruising along and an enemy Mig sneaking up behind us. We actually connected three of the sims together—two IPs and I were all in different sims, all fighting each other. It was a video gamer's dream.

The next day I had my first of two ACM flights. My instructor was actually in another jet. There was an instructor in my jet as well, but he was referred to as a "breather," meaning he just sat there and didn't say a word unless safety was an issue or I felt like talking to him. His only purpose was to save me from crashing into other jets because I had never seen this type of fighting. It added quite another element to fighting when there was another airplane to keep track of, all in close proximity to each other. At one point, flight lead and the Mig were fighting each other, rolling around each other, trying to gain an advantage but it was a neutral fight. My job was to get a small distance away from the fight, reenter, figure out who was who, and then shoot the Mig without him even knowing I was there. All was going well until their fight oriented itself directly between me and the sun. I would see two jets enter the sun and disappear, one reappear, disappear again and so on. Very stressful, as I was responsible for the jets not hitting each other and would hook the ride if there was a close call. It ended up working out but not to my amusement at the time.

Thursday and Friday I had two more surface attack rides. Thursday was four ship which was another one of my big fears as you often hear of guys hooking four ship range rides if they lose sight of someone and don't apply the appropriate procedures. All went fine. Friday I awoke to a relatively low overcast layer of clouds, especially for a bombing mission. Frustratingly, this would mean I probably couldn't finish by Christmas break, so I twisted and bent the weather forecast as much as I could to convince the flight lead we should give it a try and ultimately he agreed. We had to do a close formation takeoff due to the weather and immediately after airborne we were flying formation through the clouds.

My job as #2 in the formation, at a minimum, was just to be in position and on the correct radio frequency. This was especially true in poor weather as I was flying within a few feet of his jet. If I deviated, flight lead could quickly disappear, causing quite a headache for everyone, including air traffic control. If you were "on the wing" in clouds like I was for a while, you often can't tell if you are in a turn, climbing or descending because all you can see is white and you are purposefully keeping the other jet stationary from your point of view.

At one point, unbeknownst to me, we were in between cloud layers but it was still all white around with no horizon line in the clouds. The only reason I knew we weren't in a cloud was the T-6 behind flight lead from my view doing loops and cloverleaves between the cloud layers, just a few thousand feet above us. It was a surreal feeling, an image you might have in a dream. The only things I could see were the jet I was a few feet away from, reacting to every flinch it made, and another airplane putting on an aerobatic show in the distance, everything else, every reference, whitewashed away.

We finally got vectored below the weather and had to make a pass to see if the clouds were high enough to execute the maneuvers we needed. If we omitted the steepest bombing pass, the highest we would be is 3,500 feet above sea level and we needed 500' above that per the regulations. As we drove over the target, one mile apart from each other in a tactical formation, at 3,500 feet I looked over and flight lead disappeared in the clouds. Dejected, I realized this mission was probably not going to work and I would have to try again on Monday.

Just as I keyed the radio to say I was blind, he reappeared and I kept my mouth shut. "Uhh Baron 1, the clouds are low but I am happy with it. Two, what do you think?"

I was already keying the mic in excitement saying, "Two's happy!" Damnit Fox, why do you have to sound like such an idiot? There were times I was at 3,300 feet, skimming in and out of the clouds but it made it more fun. In the current Air Force, with rules and regulations galore, it was always fun to interpret them liberally when everything was still done safely. The weather continued to deteriorate so we stopped bombing a little early but completed enough to call it a complete mission. Now we had to get home. We hardly ever flew in the close formation except for short intervals flying through the weather. However, today, the entire flight home plus an instrument approach, fifteen straight minutes, was in the close fingertip formation. My forearm was pretty tired from constantly making little corrections due to being so close to another airplane in the turbulent clouds. For the pilots, it was a no-gyro ASR approach, no less.

Week 8: Last Hurdle

32 months ago I had been hired to fly F-16s for the South Dakota Air National Guard. Even then, I had no idea how many more hurdles it would take before I was ready to start flying F-16s:

- Four medical exams
- Officer training school
- Air and Space Basic Course
- Flying Diamond Katanas in Pueblo for the initial pilot screening
- Thirteen months of UPT (Undergraduate Pilot Training) which included a couple hundred flights, ten check rides and probably 70 academic tests
- Had to finish UPT with a "Fighter Qualified" designation
- Two FACT Tests (Fighter Aircrew Conditioning Test)
- Two centrifuge experiences
- IFF (Introduction to Fighter Fundamentals)

I am sure I am leaving some things out, but as of yesterday, I successfully finished the eight week IFF program and there are no further requirements to fly the F-16.

I had three flights and a sim to finish up. My last 2 v. 1 flight occurred Monday morning and it couldn't have gone better. Every flight I got back from, I was annoyed about a couple of dumb things I knew shouldn't have happened but this flight was an exception. I liked my IPs, I was killing quickly and there were no real problems. It was the end of my air-to-air combat in IFF and a great way to go out. I drove home thinking about my future and how I would have to get a job in a few years complimenting my part time Guard job. I couldn't figure out how anything was going to compare to this.

This left me with two CAS (Close Air Support) rides. While neither were stellar based on performance, both were fun and interesting. I essentially just followed flight lead around in a circle at 19,000 feet above the target as we peered down, analyzing the "ground fight" going on below. We would then get talk-ons from either flight lead, the ranger on the ground, or my backseater, as to where and what the target was, where friendly troops were, and whether they wanted bombs or strafe. Once all of the details were sorted out, we rolled into a 30-degree dive and dropped a bomb or strafed at approximately 4,000 feet, before climbing away to re-enter the "wheel," or circular pattern above the battlefield.

The second ride, which I hoped would be my last, was the day a huge dust storm rolled across Texas. They forecasted winds gusting over 50 mph early in the day but they showed up late. My 4:00 PM takeoff happened to be at just the right time, for as we were approaching the bombing range, the dust storm was rapidly approaching from the northwest. It was like a scene from the movie *Independence Day*. This enormous dark shelf was barreling down on us and I only needed one bombing pass to call it a complete mission and be done with IFF. Long story short, I almost strafed the wrong target because visibility was so bad but was able to salvage the pass and we quickly returned to base. It wasn't the prettiest ride but I was able to get through all IFF rides with a pass.

On the first surface attack ride I actually bombed the wrong target. When we got back to debrief, the IP laid a map of the area on the table and asked which targets I had attacked. When he saw me point to the "wrong" one he gave an eyebrow-raising look and said that we'd check out the HUD tape. Fortunately for me, the HUD tape also included the radio communication of him telling me to bomb the wrong target. I sat there quietly holding back my smile as my innocence was confirmed.

IFF Graduation

It is January 2013 and almost a month since the last update. We had about two weeks off for the Christmas holiday break and it's interesting to get out of the secluded training life and reenter normal society. My life was so focused on one thing that world news, what other people are doing and unfortunately some personal relationships, had become a blur. At one party I attended at home this girl asked what I did and after telling her I was a pilot in the Air Force, her response was, "oh, wow. I am sorry to hear that." Dumbfounded, I pressed the issue momentarily but quickly realized there would be no decent resolution to the conversation. I always look to understand disagreements from the other perspective but I am still utterly disgusted by the comment for its intent and ignorance. I still can't imagine a job I would rather be doing.

After returning to Sheppard, I jumped in a few backseats to sandbag, got another T-6 ride with Capt Baumann and another ride with Lt Pal one evening. We had probably flown together 30-35 times in the T-38.

Graduation for IFF was on a Wednesday afternoon. We started as a class of nine, graduated eight. The follow-on airframes were: two A-10s, two F-16s, two F-22s and two Canadian F-18s. This graduation was far different from the formality and duration of the UPT graduation I'd had in August. This one lasted about 45 minutes in the squadron bar with IPs, students and usually just a handful of family and friends watching from the back. Our Flight Commander spoke about our flight as a whole and then to each of us individually as we received our certificates.

It marked the end of a great eight weeks for me. For most of it, I had difficulty sleeping due to the pure excitement of what I was getting up to do the next morning. In the end, my preparation for the class paid off and I came away as the distinguished graduate and won the Top Gun Air-to-Air award, for which they claimed I had the highest Air-to-Air combat score from IFF in the last couple years. I was second in the Air-to-Ground portion with a Canadian beating me out.

I felt like I had worked far harder than anyone else in the program and it was a great feeling to be rewarded accordingly. The Wing Commander and various other leaders gave speeches to send us on our way. In one story encouraging us to appreciate what we have, the Wing Commander told us that Bo Jackson was asked in a retirement interview if he had any regrets. He said he had one and it was not being a fighter pilot.

Next, I had land survival training for three weeks. After that, a month in Wichita Falls to hang out before moving to Phoenix and Luke AFB on April 1st. My F-16 class started May 2nd with a scheduled first flight in the F-16 on 5 June 2013. I was supposed to graduate as an F-16 pilot on 13 January 2014.

I heard about one of my friends from Sheppard who had blacked out (experiencing G-LOC) in the F-16 during training this week—providing a little more motivation for workouts as of late.

Lesson Learned: Different Perspective

I was at a concert and remember thinking I wouldn't trade places with a single person in that room due to my profession. It is an incredible feeling. Undoubtedly, there are people making far more money and making quite a difference in the world but at this stage in my life, being a fighter pilot is the ultimate. So, you could understand my bewilderment when the girl said she felt sorry for me.

This exchange taught me a couple things. First, people can have drastically different opinions about the same subject. What one person sees as beauty or a great deal could be the ugliest or worst deal for another. It is difficult to relate to someone with such a seemingly skewed view of the world but they exist and we must all still coexist. The exchange with this person also taught me the importance of this tolerance and an ability to respect the views of others. She instantly forced me to have a negative opinion of her after insulting me and many others I respect. It is not only an incredibly insensitive thing to say to a person, but even worse, to someone who has volunteered to risk their life for her, her family and her liberties.

Survive, Evade, Resist and Escape (SERE)

The last annoying hurdle the military threw at me occurred during the last three weeks of February in Spokane, Washington. SERE, or "survive, evade, resist, escape", was created after the Korean War in an effort to better prepare us for the situations listed in the acronym. Not known as a difficult class with respect to passing, it is a very below average way to spend a few weeks. Except for getting hoisted up into a helicopter, the first week was classroom time learning about building fires, how to eat and drink in various climates and most other matters relating to survival.

Week two created a little stress for me. It was an all-expenses paid camping trip to the mountains of Washington to learn how to survive and evade capture. While on the surface it sounded relatively fun, when you are limited on food, throw in four feet of snow on the ground and below freezing temperatures, it was less than appealing for me. I got lucky and they put me in a great group. Out of a class of 86, our group of eight included all the fighter pilots and one enlisted kid. Fortunately, our personalities got along well having the same career field and the enlisted kid was training to be an instructor of this school, meaning he already knew how to do all of the tasks which was helpful. We vectored in a helicopter during the day and night, built fires, navigated through the woods on snowshoes, used night vision goggles and other practical outdoorsy things. For a kid who honestly can't properly tie his own shoes, the course was a pretty big step.

The last two days in the woods were all about evasion. One day, two other guys and I had to move about 3 km through the mountainous terrain and snow with our 60 lb packs, to an extraction point. Simulating having ejected and trying to get to the point for pickup, not only was it an eight-hour ordeal, but we had people searching for us on the ground and via helicopter as the enemy would. One of my favorite moments was at the end of this exercise while we were waiting for pickup at the specific time and no one showed up. We stood there for a bit before getting cold and decided we should take advantage of our new fire making skills.

One kid started prepping an area while I went throughout the woods finding as much fuel to burn as I could. With both arms holding as much wood as possible I started heading back. As soon as I got to the road, ten guys came running up with large, automatic rifles, yelling at us to get our hands up. I was standing in the middle of the road and could hardly see because I had so much wood piled up in my arms so I didn't immediately oblige them. It only took one more armed request to get my hands up, for me to—just like you see the idiots do in comedy movies—obnoxiously throw my hands into the air, tossing the wood everywhere. The scene paused as all of my firewood was making an obscene amount of noise rolling down the inclined road in an awkward stalemate between us and these people of whom I was not sure of their friendliness.

On the bus ride home from the woods the real fun began as we were captured. Eight hours of torture fun followed by a few more days of classes before the thirty-six hour marathon of torture and captivity as a POW (prisoner of war). Most of it is secret information but I can tell you it was easily the ugliest thirty-six hours of my life. The Spokane weather this time of year and the prison camps they set up were exactly as I have pictured the concentration camps of WWII to look like. No color, grey days with little bits of snow everywhere. Not the pretty snow in the mountains but patchy, muddy, nasty snow. Everything was wet and it was either misting, windy or both. A majority of the time was spent with a bag over my head and it may have been a blessing as I probably didn't want to see my surroundings.

At one point, we were standing in some prisoner formation in front of the camp guards and this kid, male and my age, was simply crying. The head guard walked over to him and just stared at his face, inches away. He pulled his right hand up, took his pointer finger and wiped a tear off the kid's face. He proceeded to lick the tear-covered finger, never breaking eye contact with the kid before finally saying, "I live off my prisoner's tears." After the training, one instructor admitted to having nightmares for months after he began working there, for the things he does to us in this simulation.

While it was a terrible time, it ended beautifully. They had brought our entire group outside, in the cold mist, bags on our heads and in handcuffs. The bags and handcuffs came off and we were told to "about face" (a military marching term meaning turn around). We did, followed by the command "present arms," meaning salute. Our national anthem started playing and there was the American flag with the POW MIA flag beneath it. Having been through the last thirty-six hours it was, without question, the most beautiful version of the anthem I have ever heard. I had been joking with my friends by saying the only thing this prison camp taught me was that I wouldn't eject, I would rather go down with the plane than have to deal with this terrible scenario. After the anthem played they went on to point out those flags probably have a different meaning to us now. That almost all Americans don't know what freedom is because they have never had it taken away. We now know what it means and should be much better off for it. It is said this is the class worth millions of dollars that no one would pay a cent for.

I remember sitting in a cell thinking about how miserable this was when my thoughts drifted back to Vietnam. I had experienced thirty-six hours, a set amount of time with a light at the end of the tunnel, in a training run by the Air Force knowing they had already spent two million dollars on me and wouldn't risk really hurting me. There were POWs in Vietnam for seven years getting the shit beat out of them and not being fed. It was even more inconceivable to me now.

I finished up the class and spent the weekend in Seattle with Chris Young, the guy I had met two years ago at officer training school. Ironically, we spent March 3rd together, the day we were both promoted to 1st Lieutenant.

A FEW OF US IN THE WOODS DURING TRAINING

Water Survival

The next phase of training was water survival in Pensacola, FL. It was essentially a day of PowerPoint slides and two days of waiting, wet and cold. I got a phone call one evening from Emily, a friend from college, which pretty much summarized the week.

Emily: "Oh hey, I didn't think I would be able to reach you. Are you okay? How is it going? I thought you would be floating in some little raft, starving and trying to stay warm."

Me: "Just finished a little beach volleyball and now we are all going out to eat at some place on the beach. Drinks later. It's been ok."

Emily: "What?! Did you spend most of the day in the water? Did you have to eat raw fish? Did you parasail?"

Me: "Yeah, we parasailed and they left me in the water for a while. They actually had a delay so instead of waiting for 30 seconds to get picked up, it was closer to a minute or two. Super cold but then we got Subway on the boat.

I understand water survival sounds like a terrible and manly adventure but the above conversation should quell all fears you had about my safety and happiness. The last day we actually did have to jump in the water with our survival gear and wait to get picked up for an hour or two. One of my buddies had some problem blowing up his raft and he literally trod water for 45 minutes until he got it half blown up, sitting in the cold water the entire time. As for me? I had my raft blown up in a couple minutes, bailed all the water out and fell asleep.

To hear him tell this story now almost brings me to tears of laughter. "It wouldn't have been so bad except I could see all of you fu%&ers warmly floating away, enjoying yourselves."

Regardless, I was done with all survival training the Air Force had to offer and this was fantastic news.

The Move to Paradise

I write this on the eve of the move I have been waiting for throughout this entire process, to Phoenix and the F-16. After survival school and going home for a few days, I had about two weeks to try and get any flights I could and say goodbyes to all of the friends and instructors still remaining after my twenty months in Wichita Falls.

I was hoping to get just one or two more front seat rides in the T-38 but ended up getting one every day last week and two this final week. It was a miracle and the best week of flying I have had this entire journey. Having graduated from IFF, the instructors, especially those who flew the F-16, were willing to teach me higher-level maneuvers to kill the opponent and it made for a lot of fun. Hawk and I got into a dogfight against each other for the first time and at one point we were barrel rolling around each other and as I was directly above him, inverted in the roll, he disappeared as I flew into a cloud. The fighting resumed as the barrel roll continued and I popped back out, descending from the cloud as he began his climb to roll over me, both of us trying to get behind the other to create an opportunity to gun the opponent. I had many more stories from the week but most involved some obnoxious gestures with my "pilot hands," trying to describe what occurred.

The last couple days involved wandering around the squadron. I was mostly excited to be getting out of here but it was still bittersweet. I hunted down most of the IPs for one final "remember when we did this" and a handshake before leaving the squadron for the final time. There were a few I hoped to remain in decent contact with, especially some of the Europeans. I had lived there almost 21 months and would have been pretty upset to have to move on from this lifestyle if it wasn't for the F-16. The geography and town left much to be desired but the job and people within it made for an enjoyable time.

Best memories:

- Seeing the Aurora Borealis in the T-6 over Oklahoma
- Soloing the T-38
- The night flights with Lt. Pal
- Dogfighting in IFF
- Evening motorcycle rides after a day of flying

That list could go on for pages but those were the first five that came to mind.

Worst memories:

- Sub-5 AM wakeup calls
- Weekly tests about general knowledge
- Being restricted from travel
- Centrifuge the first time
- Air Force paperwork
- POW training

In total, I added another 89.2 hours in the T-38 after the 98.1 during pilot training—a number I am pretty proud of, and high enough most can't believe it. 187 hours isn't a lot in the civilian world but when you fly 50 minutes at a time, it makes for a lot of flights.

My Flight Commander in T-38s is now a student in IFF. I had told him about being so excited about dogfighting I couldn't sleep. A few weeks later, as he was having his first dogfighting rides, he said, "Damn it, Fox, I was lying there in bed last night, next to my beautiful wife in her underwear, and all I could think about was you because I was so excited about flying I couldn't sleep."

Lesson Learned: It is about who

People often ask, "If you could live anywhere, where would it be?" My experience in Wichita Falls taught me it is not about where, but with whom. Of all my traveling around the world, this town had easily been one of the worst. However, I had the best time of my life due to the nature of the work and the people with whom I shared it. Quit worrying about where you are and start worrying about those with whom you surround yourself.

PART 5: THE VIPER B-COURSE

Viper Mecca

It was April 2013. My first two weeks in Phoenix at Luke AFB included numerous days I had dreamed of for years. The first was the day I left Wichita Falls and made the pilgrimage to Luke Air Force Base, or Viper (F-16) Mecca. It marked a dramatic upgrade in living conditions but more importantly, a realization I had passed all of the hundreds of requirements to fly the F-16. Guys have said this upcoming year of training was the only part they would do over again as it was that great. I had been an officer in the Air Force for 27 months and personally, less survival and officer training, I would have done it all over again.

After arriving, I spent most of my time focusing on two things: finding a place to live and getting an F-16 ride. I had wanted a ride my whole life but had literally been working my ass off to get one for four straight years. I had one roommate and we were the two single guys in our class of nine. We rented a house on a golf course with a pool and waterfall.

The house hunting went great but after a week of doing everything I could to simply sit in the backseat of an F-16, I was more than frustrated. I had read numerous books and attended many classes saying you don't want "yes" people in your organization, people who simply agree with the boss so he likes them. No one ever challenges anything. I feel like a rant on this topic is in order after the two weeks I had but I will spare you slightly. The "yes people" lesson may be applicable and I am talking about a different dynamic but I heard from countless people that there was simply no way I would get to ride in a jet until the class started.

"No, we won't give you a medical screening until class starts."

"No, it would be an unfair advantage if you got rides." (For who? China, North Korea or Iran?)

"No, we have never had anyone here this early."

There was one enlisted airman at the medical clinic who simply reviewed our paperwork and was borderline belligerent in preventing me from flying. He had tens of reasons to keep me from flying, none made any sense and he knew it. I am not completely proud to say this but I wanted to pull him aside and say, "look, I think the reason I am flying fighter jets and you are in a windowless office reading about my blood type and lack of health problems is attitude. I am refusing to accept 'no' because it doesn't make sense and you are doing everything you can to do nothing." I obviously didn't say it but I think a pep talk would have served him well for the future. I even had Majors and Lieutenant Colonels say no, which was generally a good time for a Lieutenant to accept it and move on but I refused. It made no sense. I flew a jet in the Air Force last week and each day there were F-16s with empty back seats going flying. It took a letter from the Wing Commander and finding one Sergeant to be that "yes person" and I was on my way.

After decades of dreaming, years of training and a week of bullshit trying to keep me from the Viper, the day arrived. Two years and 355 days ago they had told me I would get to fly one and the day was here. I was so excited and nervous I could hardly put my G-suit on. It's difficult to describe the flight and how it felt but there were things more incredible than I had ever expected and others were not as overwhelming as I imagined. For example, the dogfighting was infinitely better than I had imagined. I had been dogfighting for almost six months in the T-38 but there was a reason this was a fighter jet—it could fight. Because it was so powerful, it had superior turning performance, keeping all of the jets in close proximity during a fight in comparison to the T-38. There were real flares shooting out of the jets trying to break a missile lock, there was a greater kick in the afterburner and the cockpit visibility was far better. However, it was still an airplane and just like Michael Jordan had to put one shoe on at a time, we still had to... well, I was going to say we still took off and landed like any airplane, or put on a G-suit and helmet like before, but no. All of it was different and better.

A PICTURE I TOOK ON MY FIRST FLIGHT IN THE BACKSEAT OF THE VIPER

Lesson Learned: I Can

We have all heard people say they can't do something. While many times they are correct, many times they aren't. "I can't" usually means "I won't" or "I don't want to" for a variety of reasons but attitude is generally the culprit. Laziness could be keeping them from the goal; creativity hinders many as well.

For example: "I can't afford the trip to Europe." Sure you can. Give up your cup of coffee every day for a year, figure out a way to get people to sponsor a trip by doing something truly unique during your experience that people would support financially. Don't stay at five star hotels the entire time. You can cheaply have a great international trip, trust me. When you hear someone else or yourself say "I can't," really consider if this is true and determine how important it is. They are usually saying, "I don't want to try." You can always find a way if it's worth it.

Week 1: Punks at 1,000 MPH

I got a couple more backseat flights and did some relaxing prior to class starting. I was able to ride along on a surface attack mission, a flight of two F-16s, going to drop real bombs and shoot the gun. Awesome. It was the first time in my life I had been on an airplane with live ammunition. Everyone says you are never fully prepared for the first time the gun goes off, especially if you are in the back seat as the gun is right next to your left hip. As it fired, the entire plane trembled in response to the amazing power. The intimidating part was actually the delivery of the shot. 450 knots, a 10-degree dive, and the minimum pull-off altitude was 75 feet. It may be hard for some of you to understand and appreciate how low 75 feet is, especially when you are descending that fast, but I nearly grabbed the stick to pull back for fear of being a flaming hole in the desert. It was as nervous as I had ever been in an airplane for half a second, and then just as quickly, it was one of those, "that was awesome!" moments.

The next story was from riding along on a "LFE" or Large Force Exercise. It was a simulated war, with thirty-two airplanes in the sky and we were red air (the bad guys). It was actually a really boring mission in comparison to the others, with two exceptions: after daydreaming a while, I looked back inside and noticed our speed. We were indicating 500 knots at 39,000 feet. Translated to normal terms, we were at Mach 1.5, or 1.5 times the speed of sound. Our true airspeed (speed correction for air density which is really low at high altitude) was 890 knots, or 1,024 mph, a milestone I had never considered.

There were 136 Vipers at Luke, a number significantly lower than its heyday, and 1,700 maintenance personnel kept the planes flying. The program was 148 training days long with 55 flights equating to about 75 hours of flight time. There were 54 simulator rides and 305 hours of academic instruction.

Week 2: Speed

Week two was a relatively boring week, especially to the outside observer. We had PT (physical training) before class during this academic phase and then attended class through the middle of the afternoon. The "death by PowerPoint" classes taught by retired fighter pilots were supplemented by self-run PowerPoint lessons. None of these lessons were very fun and, being not so mechanically inclined, none came naturally for me. Anytime I started complaining, I tried to remember I was learning the details of the F-16, one of the more advanced machines man has ever made, and the frustration was instantly relieved.

This was also drug-testing week with the idea being: take them now when you aren't flying so when we need to give them to you for performance in war, we know you won't experience any negative side effects. As I write this, I am taking a mild variant of speed. I took it today as we have three tests this upcoming week and I need to focus. There were a variety of sleeping pills, "go-pills" or the speed pills, malaria, anthrax and many more. Guys will often take these speed pills on long flights, often ocean crossings, to aid in alertness. We all loathe those long, eight-hour commercial flights across the oceans due to the confinement—I couldn't imagine doing one in the cockpit of an F-16, literally unable to move more than a few inches.

Week 3: Respect the Machine

If anyone knows me, or most kids and men for that matter, you know when we get a new toy the last thing we want to do is read the owner's manual. We want to go play with it. Welcome to week three of reading the owner's manual for the F-16. At over 1,000 pages in length, this is just how the plane operates. Nothing about using it as a machine of war.

Three tests this week: one on instruments, one on the hydraulic, fuel, environmental and electrical systems, and one on the glorious engine. Fill in the rest of our time with PowerPoints and the first simulator ride on Friday and you have a complete week. We had our flight control system test on Tuesday, which for most planes wouldn't exist, but it does for the F-16 and its fly-by-wire system. When we move (add pressure to) the nearly immobile stick, electric signals are sent through computers and then ultimately the control surfaces. They have programmed logic into the system which is very different from any other airplane and takes understanding and getting a feel for. For instance, in an effort to keep the plane from going out of control, there are limits to what the pilot can do. Depending on numerous factors, I can pull on the stick and the system can essentially say, "I hear you pilot but that's dumb, I am not going to let you do that so try something else."

I will leave you with an email from a Commander:

Gents,
F-16 pilots have killed way more F-16s than F-16s have killed pilots. I know it's cliché, but complacency kills. How many times have folks blown through altitudes or not handled an emergency quite by the book recently in this wing? We've been lucky...no one that blew through an altitude went beak to beak with some doctor out of LA in his private jet. Our luck will run out...it's inevitable. Only thing we can do is to make sure we eliminate the silly complacency errors before that luck runs out. Keep your nuggets in the game. We take flying F-16s for granted and often forget we are mere moments from disaster at multiple points during any given sortie. That's why those "on the outside" can't fathom what we do for a living.

Respect your machine. Respect the sky full of other machines within which you fly that machine. Respect the ground that will mercilessly break both you and your machine.

Week 4: The Tin Man

A short week with a simulator ride each day along with some classes, but the pace had slowed dramatically. The sims were going well and we were deep in emergency procedures. These were intense 1.5-hour events as the instructors crammed in as many problems as possible. In the 1.5 hours on Thursday afternoon, I had seven engine failures, two engine fires, alternator failures, oil system malfunctions, many takeoff emergencies and ejected three or four times. It was a lot for a mind to process and after each emergency, the instructor just reset the simulator and you started all over again. Overall, I enjoyed them as a fun challenge and as long as you knew your stuff, the instructors were really just trying to help you learn and possibly save your life one day.

We were fit for the Air Force's new G-suit this week and it was quite an experience in itself. After thirty minutes of getting it on and fitting it, I realized I could hardly move my legs or bend over. I walked like the Tin Man from *The Wizard of Oz*. I was sure it would stretch out some but there was no way I was getting into an airplane with the current fit. Working alongside your pressure breathing, [a system that activated above four Gs, forcing air into the mask and inflating a bladder in the back of the helmet to keep the mask on the face better], I had heard it improved G-force tolerance by a significant amount.

Not much else really went on except the realization I would be at the controls of an F-16 in nine days started to set in. Because this dream had seemed so far away, I had occasionally lost the giddy, childlike feeling of excitement. The feeling was starting to return.

Week 5: Xylophones and Bubbles

Another four-day week including two tests, two emergency sims, a flight riding in the backseat, a cheese incident and the most embarrassing moment of my Air Force career.

The sims continued to go well but the class was caught off-guard Friday afternoon when one of our guys failed his sim. We only heard his side of the story but there was this running joke that instructors should follow the "no-fail Friday" policy. This one really hurt because it was a simulator ride, and they are generally always passed. Further, we heard a kid from a different squadron washed out of the entire F-16 program this week, with only a month to go. I would estimate that one student washes out about every other F-16 class with 8 to 16 students in a class.

I had a free afternoon and jumped in the backseat of a 2v2 dogfighting ride. It was great. The student was a combat-ready F-16 pilot trying to qualify as an IP, an interesting dynamic to see in the brief and debrief. For F-16 student rides, there was a 1000-foot "bubble" we placed around the airplanes to avoid collision. Systems in our jet and the relative size of the other jet let us know when we were approaching 1000 feet and we stay outside of this distance for safety. Essentially, if you break the "bubble" you would be highlighted in the debrief and it is considered a training rule violation. After this course was over, the bubble would shrink to 500 feet. With all of these being qualified F-16 pilots, they were accustomed to 500-foot bubbles and I saw, or was involved in, five passes of less than 600 feet. I know 600 feet doesn't sound close, but with this jet being bigger than the last and being 50% closer than normal, doing the speeds we are, there were numerous expletives being excitedly thought or said from my mouth. As I saw these passes developing, the emotion tended to flow in the following order: this is awesome; that bastard is going to die; ok, this is going to be close; oh shit, I hope this works out; wow!; whew, that was crazy.

The brief for this flight started at 1:00 PM. The debrief ended at 10:20 PM and the flight had only lasted 1.1 hours. It was the longest event of my life. Fortunately the IPs, the ones who would be teaching and grading me starting next week, were impressed I was willing to stick around the entire time and I developed a nice rapport with them. However, at 10:30 as I was cleaning up the nachos our class made that day, I severely underestimated the amount of cheese remaining in the bag and as I picked up it, the plastic exploded under the weight. All over my new boots, all over the pool table, all over the floor. Knowing I had to wake up in seven hours, I spent the next thirty minutes furiously cleaning the Great Cheese Debacle of 2013, still leaving it in less-than-desirable conditions.

Unfortunately, I was sure this next story could create a call sign as well. The class we were replacing graduated last night. I, along with another guy in my class, volunteered to make the reception desk, take money and tell the guests where they were sitting. There was one additional detail to this job description that went unmentioned. After the social hour, leading into dinner, someone had to let everyone know it was time to take their seats by playing some ridiculous, quiet, horrible sounding, xylophone instrument. Let me point out, all of my future instructors were there, already making fun of everything we did, along with a few generals and other commanders on base. Basically, all of my superiors and some peers were lucky enough to observe me walk around this room of ~150 playing this xylophone. Knowing vaguely who I was, not a single one could pass up some jeering comment of humor about how much I sucked at it. My buddy who won the rock-paper-scissors against me was laughing so hard he forgot to document the scene. Imagine those scenes in movies were the one unpopular kid is walking through the dance and everyone is obnoxiously laughing at them and making comments. That was me, but they knew I had no choice, making it all the more fun. In hindsight, I am glad I lost and had to do it. One of the IPs who ridiculed me the most passed me as everyone was finally taking their seats so I stopped him, saying, "Sir, (with open arms pointing to the crowd) I did this."

Week 6: Viper Driver

If you have made it this far in the book, you know what went into getting me to this week. Maybe not all of the emotion, but you understand the work, stress and fun of getting to where I could say, "I fly F-16s for a living." The dream and goal to fly an F-16 had pervaded each thought and influenced every decision I made over the past four years. It had led me to temporarily quit marathon running, start lifting weights in specific manners, go out less on Saturday nights for fear it would mess up my sleep Sunday night and then my flight Monday morning and many other, sometimes neurotic, lifestyle choices. Many times I had said, "Just let me fly her once and I won't be so crazy anymore. I can die happy."

Thursday, June 6, 2013 was that day.

I was understandably having trouble sleeping the night before but ultimately had one of the most poetic dreams one could script. It was so real I must not have been fully asleep as nothing was fictional about it. It was a flashback of my flying career starting 10 years ago. There I was, soloing the Stearman at dusk, with the exact terrified feeling I remember so vividly; then, sitting at my grandparent's breakfast room table recounting each of my flights in the corporate jets with my grandpa; adding power to the Stearman in Galesburg, IL for the short field takeoff competition; and, ultimately, some of my military flying memories with Lt. Pal and dogfighting in IFF.

My grandpa wrote me the following note conveying how much the week meant:

"Tomorrow, June 6, brings your first flight in the F-16. All the preparation, testing, flight checks, etc have brought you to this big day. I know you will be locked in but take time to enjoy. I think I have had a fairly successful career, but it pales in comparison to what you will be doing tomorrow. To be able to say "my Grandson is an F-16 Pilot, and soon to be a F-16 Fighter Pilot, brings so much pride I cannot possibly express my feelings.
Love You, Pop"

As a class, we generally sent out a "lessons learned" email after flights and sims so the other guys in the class wouldn't make the same mistakes. A guy in my class wrote the following after his first flight, the day prior to mine. This, with some slight language editing on my part, is how he concluded his email:

"If you are not super pumped for this ride or B-Course or if you do not take 6.2 seconds on this ride to look at the AIM9's and AIM120's [heat-seeking and radar-guided missiles] on your wing and realize how badass you are...you are wrong!"

The first flight went as scripted and I had a great time. Naturally, I rode my motorcycle to work, fueling every fighter pilot fantasy I have ever had. Single ship, we flew to the MOA (military operating airspace) and did some aerobatic maneuvers to get a feel for the plane, pulled 8.6 Gs, went supersonic and just had some fun. After returning to Luke, we practiced landings and SFOs (simulated flameout landings). If our engine was to quit, we had to safely get the jet on the ground and we did so through SFOs.

1.1 hours of flying later, I was an F-16 pilot.

Highlights were the following: the visibility is incredible. From riding the backseat a few times, I had been really disappointed with the visibility from the cockpit compared to my expectations, but once I hopped in the front seat, I discovered it was better than expected. You sit so far forward in relation to the rest of the plane and so high up in relation to the cockpit, it felt like I could have tipped out when the canopy was open. Imagine the visibility if you were driving a convertible where the doors only came up to your waist, there was only one seat in the car and there are no support structures for the windshield. It was awesome. Hawk, the kid who had gone through all of this training in the same classes with me was coincidentally given the same takeoff time as mine. So there we were, each in our own F-16, with the maintenance guys arming missiles on our jet before takeoff. No words were necessary. We gave each other a couple of nods, acknowledging we had finally made it. We couldn't see each other's faces with the masks and helmets on but I had no doubt he had the same smile on his face as I did.

The lowlight of the flight was my organization. Picture some new assistant chasing around a politician. Imagine them awkwardly carrying multiple bags, dropping papers and pencils while trying to not disappoint anyone. This was me getting to the airplane. We had to carry a lot more stuff to the planes, some of which is secret so there are certain things you can and cannot do and I had none of it figured out. I looked like a fish out of water. I spent a significant amount of time rehearsing this in my mind today, in order to avoid this catastrophe tomorrow. Half of being a fighter pilot is looking and acting cool.

Witt had started the F-16 class ahead of me and along with his brother and dad, came out and parked short of the runway to videotape my first approaches. They had pizza and beer waiting for me after the debrief and proved to be a great celebratory audience for my war stories.

Lessons Learned: Reflect on Accomplishments

My first F-16 flight was a great experience and everything I wanted it to be. However, I will say it wasn't as magical as I had dreamed four years ago. The Air Force had trained us well so between flying the T-38 and getting F-16 simulator and sandbag rides, the flight wasn't this crazy leap that would blow someone away who hadn't gone through all of the training. However, after taking a step back and realizing what I had just done, partly thanks to my grandfather, I understood how special this day really was. The same can be said about getting a job, graduating college or owning a house. The lengthy process of reaching these goals makes the actual achievement slightly less exciting but if you can put yourself in your state of mind years prior, it can make the experience much sweeter.

Week 7: Sim Check

Another busy week with three flights, academics, a simulator ride and then a simulator check ride. Four flights in, and I still couldn't get over flying this jet. While they were infrequent, I took advantage of each quiet moment in the plane and reminded myself it was an F-16. When I took a step back and realized what I was doing I got truly excited, like I did when I was hired. I got a reply from my last post from Brian Hunter, a friend and former boss from civilian flying, who said,

"I read this post flying back from Spokane a couple of nights ago with another pilot. When I read this part I laughed out loud and had to read to it to him out loud: 'Single ship, we flew to the MOA (military operating airspace) and did some aerobatic maneuvers to get a feel for the plane, pulled 8.6 Gs, went supersonic and just had some fun.' You wrote this as such a mundane thing to do that I found it amazing. Do you know how bad-ass this is? And you were just having some fun."

Receiving notes like this are a great reminder, really helping keep things in perspective and the motivation to study up. During one flight, we flew over I-10 about 500 feet above the road at 450 knots and I couldn't help but remember the numerous times I had been willing to wreck my car trying to get a glimpse of these jets flying by.

As we approached the dogfighting stage, we had a brief from a flight doctor about our health and the things that could kill us in this jet. Part of the brief was about neck health. I had an eight-page document discussing possible workouts and expected neck injuries during our time flying the F-16. 50% of us would have a neck injury at some point. The rest was almost entirely about G-forces. I think seven have died as a result of G-LOC or blacking out in the ~30-year history of the Viper. G-LOC happens far more frequently but people usually wake up in time. So what can we do? Hopefully the new G-suit would help, as well as being well-rested, working out properly, being well-fed and hydrated, and most importantly, using the anti-G straining technique we practiced and were tested on in the centrifuge. The new G-suit covers most of our body from the abs down to the ankles and aggressively inflates and squeezes the legs when the jet senses G-forces. The squeezing keeps the blood from pooling in the legs and helps us keep the blood in our head.

The flights were relatively routine this week, practicing landings, engine out approaches and instrument flying. The simulator rides, however, were very important. The one on Friday, along with my flight check ride in the upcoming week, would go on my permanent record. With a higher-ranking pilot (not simulator instructor) observing the simulation, they gave us a series of emergencies and evaluated how we reacted to and ultimately concluded them. If this didn't go well, you started the program with a stigma and couldn't fly solo until it was remedied. This score would stay with me the rest of my Air Force career. You can get Q1, Q2 or Q3 and then any of those scores with "hits" (or strikes, basically) that don't look great. Everyone in our class got a Q1 but a couple of guys got hits. I came away clean. One of the guys who got a hit was told by his evaluator his performance showed a lack of motivation and was disappointed in his general knowledge of the plane. Knowing the student, I knew neither were accurate observations which reminded us that sometimes results have an element of luck.

Finally, I had a wedding in Sedona this weekend and Witt and I took motorcycles up around central Arizona from Payson to Flagstaff and then through Oak Creek Canyon to Sedona. It was probably the single best motorcycle ride I have been on and would recommend it to anyone.

Week 8: Deadly 31

As awesome as the first flight was, flying a fighter by myself was the true pinnacle for me. Eight years and three weeks ago my grandpa, dad, great uncle and I drove to Luke AFB, Arizona and parked in a no-parking area right under the approach end of the runway, outside of base. For an hour, we watched the jets blast off and land. Since then, and especially since I was hired to fly the F-16 three years and two months ago, I had visualized taking the runway for the first time solo in the F-16 no less than forty times. It was the exact same image every time. I would see the crystal clear blue sky, the bubble canopy allowing me to see everything, sitting on the tip of this spear we call an F-16 and the mountains off in the distance. I would turn to line up with the runway centerline, and in each recreation, I would pause a few seconds looking down the runway and take a deep breath. Oddly, I never took off in this fantasy but the deep breath was enough to leave me satisfied and motivated. In the last three years I couldn't even begin to count the number of times I had said, "I just need to fly it once by myself. One time."

Wednesday, June 19th was the day. I rode the motorcycle to work and I know I sounded excited about the first flight a few weeks ago—and I was—but this was on a whole different level. Flying a single seat fighter is something few get to do and I fully cherished it. Three days later, I still hadn't slept well due to the excitement. My dad and grandpa flew out for the big day and along with Witt and another friend, they came out to watch me start her and blast off. As callsign Deadly 31, I flew an hour and a half, burning over 1,000 gallons of jet fuel with another F-16 chasing me through various maneuvers, instrument approaches, simulated flameout landings and some formation work. We split at landing and I got to taxi back single ship, both arms on the edge of the canopy, mask down, soaking it all in. The three generations of Foxes had a celebratory dinner and my roommate and I had a celebratory cigar and beer by the pool, but with the important check ride the next day, the celebration had to be tempered.

The check ride essentially qualified you to fly the jet, without a chase airplane and in the weather. It was the first permanent record check ride of my Air Force career. It went exactly like the solo the day prior with the check pilot chasing me through all of the maneuvers. My IP and I hopped out of our F-16s parked next to each other and he walked over to greet me. After shaking my hand he mentioned I should meet him in the bar for the debrief. The debrief for a check ride could include a lot of questions and feedback, good and bad. When I sat down, there was a beer waiting for me and he said, "alright, for the debrief… hmmm… it was clean. Nice flight. Have a good weekend." It went as well as I could have hoped with a score of Q1 no hits. Cue the exhale and celebrations as we were legal F-16 pilots now. A nice salmon dinner and champagne from a cute girl awaited me Friday evening.

As I was taxiing back from that check ride I quickly humbled myself. It was the second day in a row flying a single seat fighter and I knew I had done well. So there I was, same scene as yesterday but today I was singing to "*Sail*" by AWOLNATION, maybe even bobbing my head a little to the beat and just enjoying the moment. I looked down at my lineup card and saw I should park in row 21. Perfect, back to my song and moment. The walk of shame in the fighter pilot world is when you miss the row you must turn down to park. Obviously unable to backup, you must go all the way around the awnings and do a large loop. Everyone in the area knows you screwed up because you are the only guy taxiing in this one particular area. Well, for whatever reason, I was fixated on my song, my moment and row 21. Unfortunately, row 19 was where I needed to be as they had switched my spot. So the the cocky kid singing in his F-16 got another two minutes of F-16 time doing the walk of shame. The maintenance guys found great humor in it and my crew chief and I shared a good laugh once I finally found my parking spot.

The one thing my forty mental recreations of the first flight over the past eight years failed to see was that I would actually be leading another jet for this takeoff. Being responsible for, and graded by the other jet, added just enough stress and required brainpower that I almost missed my moment. Fortunately, I made the other jet taxi around me to get lined up in formation on the runway so I had about six seconds to myself with nothing to do. I got to have the flashbacks and I got my deep breath. We ran up the power together holding brakes, I gave my IP a salute and finally threw in full power for the exhilarating rumble down the runway.

We would start fighting next week and as an IP briefing on Friday afternoon said, "It is as much fun as you can have with your pants on."

MY DAD AND GRANDFATHER BEFORE MY FIRST SOLO FLIGHT

Week 9: The Kissing Lieutenant

Even only flying once, it turned out to be an interesting week. The flight was an intro to BFM (dogfighting). I did my first formation takeoff and landing, shot missiles and gunned the other jet all in 50 minutes of flying. The gas gets used up quickly when in afterburner as much as we were during these flights. The number of switches and buttons on the throttle and stick were pretty amazing and this flight focused on getting the hands and mind comfortable using them. The pilot could do an amazing number of things without ever moving his hands off these two critical controls. This significant advantage the Viper has over many other jets can be crucial, especially when fighting under G-forces, as you are unable to move your arms to hit any buttons. As my last IP summarized our new phase of training, "We don't want to talk about formations and instruments any more. We are here to learn how to kill people and break their shit."

I was scheduled to fly again the next morning but another squadron here at Luke had an accident Wednesday evening around 7 PM. I had just left base a few minutes prior but most people heard the explosion as the jet went down. Rumors are spreading that he took off and a bird flew down the engine, shredding it. They were from the Duck squadron and since both pilots successfully ejected and walked away, the irony made for a nice laugh.

As you know by now, there are many traditions in this business. Most were pointed out to me throughout my experience the last couple of years, but I was unaware of the kissing lieutenant. It was his job, the lowest ranking officer, to present the departing pilot's spouse a gift of flowers from the squadron along with a kiss, which was as serious as the wife wanted to make it, in front of everyone. While I was higher-ranking than three or four other guys in our class, by the time it was time for the big moment, those bastards had fled the scene. So when the Squadron Commander walked up to our table and asked who the lowest-ranking Lt. was, I had no choice but to accept. I happened to have brought a date to this event and had the boss explaining to her that I had no choice. So I threw on some chapstick and awaited my moment. I had to give her these seductive looks as I approached, hand her the flowers, tip her back and go in for the kiss, twice. Apparently their four-year-old daughter watched the whole thing and was appalled by the act as the whole bar laughed. After my moment, the pilot gave a thank-you speech to us and then to his wife, concluding with a kiss. As they were kissing, someone from the back of the bar yelled, "hey Split, how does Fox taste?" The room broke into laughter.

Week 10: Tanking

The coolest part of my first air-to-air refueling was actually finding the tanker and efficiently getting into position to get the gas. There was a cloud deck 500 feet below our altitude which helped give our speed some perspective. I was in one F-16 and my flight lead, the instructor, in another. He put me in a formation position called fighting wing. Basically, I had to stay 500-3,000 feet behind his jet but could maneuver wherever I wanted, allowing him to freely maneuver as well. As we saw the tanker—an enormous plane compared to what I was used to seeing—off in the distance, it turned into us instead of the direction we were expecting. We were 500–1000 feet lower than him, with the clouds directly below us feeling like a floor, and had about 500 knots of closure when we flew directly beneath this enormous plane. I was close to and below my flight lead, looking through him to the tanker which felt like it was 100 feet away, while we did 400 knots and pulled 6 Gs trying to salvage this debauchery. Over the intercom you could hear me say an excited "oh shit!" as we passed under that enormous plane. Even the guy in my backseat, who had done hundreds of refueling, mentioned it was a little more intense than he had expected.

Now to the embarrassment. I moved in for my first refueling as the tanker rolled into a 30-degree bank turn which was just lovely. The tanker flew big rectangular racetracks through the sky and sometimes you get the unlucky bank. The whole process went fine and we disconnected and all was well. We decided to reconnect a couple of times for practice. I'll get into more detail on air-to-air refueling later but things started to go south. I blamed myself because I was screwing it up and not a stable jet but I also blamed the instructors for communication. The problem was too many coaches on the field. There were lights underneath the plane telling me what I needed to do with the plane. My instructor was in the backseat telling me what to do. My flight lead was in the plane next to us giving feedback and the boom operator in the tanker could talk and tell me what to do as well. So as you can imagine, when I started to screw things up, each one of those coaches had an opinion. With four opinions all communicating at once, I understood none. I still don't really know what happened because I couldn't hear anything but we disconnected from the boom and started sliding forward and up—closer to the refueler.

After fixing this impending problem, we stabilized 20 feet behind the tanker to try again, thinking nothing more of it. As we approached the boom again, a panel on the tanker opened and started venting red fluid. The panel would close and open again with what one would assume to be hydraulic fluid, streaming out of the plane, directly over the top of mine and off into the abyss. Two more F-16s had joined up with the tanker while I was getting gas and while I couldn't hear their frustration, their missions had just been cancelled as the refueler was now out of commission. So for the rest of the fortunately short week I was "Fox, the guy who broke the tanker."

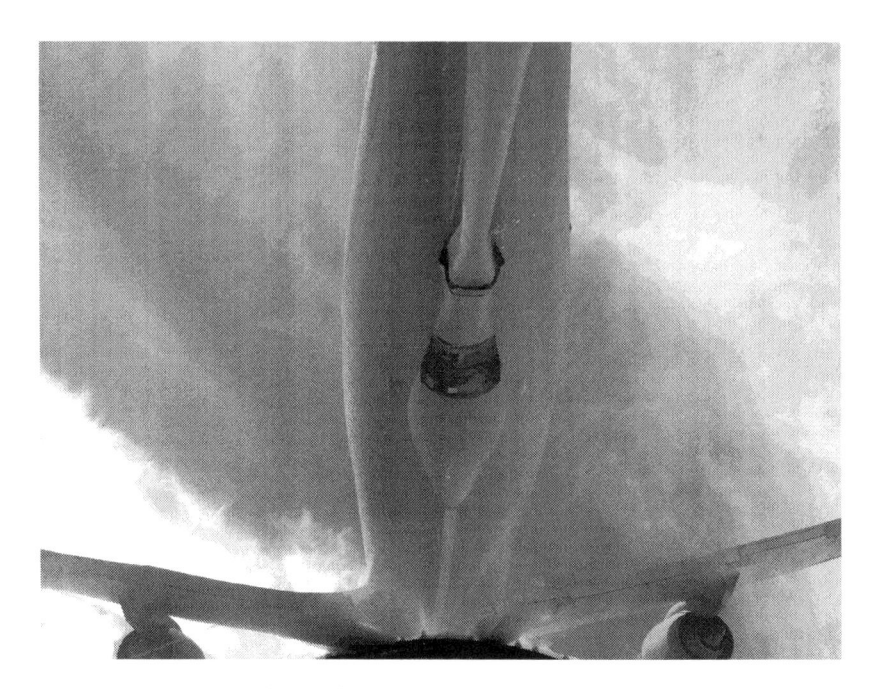

VIEW OF THE TANKER WHILE REFUELING

Week 11: Spike 2 Emergency

Three of the most intense flights I have had in my life happened this week.

Monday: The calmest of days with a tactical intercept simulator ride. We picked bogeys up on the radar and then calculated the angles, speeds and altitudes to intercept, identify and shoot down if necessary.

Tuesday: I had my last offensive air-to-air dogfighting ride and it included hitting the tanker for gas before the fighting began. This time I was solo and determined to get it right. My flight lead and I blasted off to find the tanker and when we did, there were already two Vipers getting gas. Unfortunately, it was one of my classmate's first attempts and he was having trouble connecting. In fact, in the time he spent trying to connect to the boom, my flight lead and I, and another F-16 and his wingman, all had joined the tanker, with more of us on the way. Unfortunately, there were no cameras to capture the beautiful sight of that many jets together. By the time I hit the boom, there were three Vipers on the right wing of the tanker, me in the middle and four on the left wing—eight F-16s all in this formation with the tanker over the Arizona desert.

Now rewind back to where I was watching my buddy continue to struggle on the boom. For five minutes he simply couldn't get hooked up. This started to make me nervous. Maybe air-to-air refueling actually was this difficult and after the previous week's festivities, I now had seven jets full of my closest friends ready to observe and judge. As with any exciting event, the more you think about and see someone in front of you panic before doing it, the worse it is for you.

So there I sat, solo, starting to realize I could soon be cementing my reputation as the guy who couldn't tank. Fortunately, when my turn arrived, I immediately connected, got my full tank of gas, disconnected, and got the hell out of there with one huge sigh of relief. We went on to fight for thirty minutes and had a great time, burning 1,300 gallons of gas each.

One of the more exciting moments to note was in a vertical fight. I started a mile behind the bandit and when the fight started, instead of turning laterally to get away, he rolled inverted (upside down) and pulled back on the stick. He continued the pull all the way around to point the other direction. I selected max afterburner, flew to the spot where he had aggressively descended, rolled inverted and pulled just as he did. As I did this, I pulled about 8.5 Gs the entire way around and realized that if I were to black out (G-LOC) while pointing straight down and doing 450 knots, it would only be a few seconds before I was a smoking hole in the ground. Fortunately, I recognized this and focused solely on my G-strain, flexing every muscle necessary to keep the blood in my head until I was no longer looking exclusively at earth. You can't kill the enemy if you kill yourself first. My mother wouldn't be excited to hear some of this but it is the nature of the work and we did our best to keep it safe.

Wednesday: My first defensive fighting ride. This is where the instructor starts the fights 1.5, 1 or a half-mile behind me and I try to survive. I spent the entire fight looking behind me, assessing his every move and trying to fly without looking forward. It was a really uncomfortable position as I had been twisting to look backward the entire time and under heavy G-forces. It could be comparable to driving down a four-lane road, only looking backwards, trying to drive forward, all while someone was shooting at you. In this jet however, real flares were shooting out at my command which was cool to see.

This flight also included another air-to-air refueling. This time, however, the tanker was in the clouds. In one of the most intense things I have done in an airplane, I radar-locked my flight lead and followed him in a one-mile trail. All completely in the clouds, he locked up the tanker and we maneuvered through the weather with ice to find the tanker. After finding it in a patch of clear air, we quickly rejoin before going back into the clouds. I got my gas but realized I needed another 500 lbs so I had to reconnect. I started to get spatially disorientated and the instructor I was with did as well. The tanker was in a 15-degree bank turn but it felt to me like we were spiraling into the ground in 90 degrees of bank and 40 degrees nose low. We end of breaking away and losing sight of the tanker in the cloud. So there we were, in the clouds with no radar lock because you turn the radar off for tanking. I knew there was this enormous plane less than 100 feet in front of me but I couldn't see it. It was an uncomfortable feeling to say the least. As my instructor said in the debrief, "That was about as much fun as I want to have in a training environment." I was glad we were on the same page as I was hoping that experience wasn't "normal."

Thursday: My second defensive BFM ride and my instructor was the Squadron Commander. It was the first day of puffy cumulus clouds we could fight around which was a rare blessing in the seemingly cloudless Arizona desert. As the last fight terminated, I told him I was out of gas and needed to head home. As we started flipping all of our switches to the safe position, I noticed one of the warning lights in my cockpit had illuminated. There were three or four lights we referred to as "no-shitters"—warning lights that mean, you need to find the nearest suitable piece of concrete and put the plane on the ground. The fire light is the classic example. However, this one was the hydraulic/oil light. It could mean a few things, but worst case, the engine could seize due to an oil problem.

I told flight lead and he responded with, "put Luke on the nose and get to a one-to-one," meaning I should point directly home and climb quickly so if the engine quits I can glide back and land. He chased me home, looking over my plane for any problems. I glided to 10,000 feet above the airport and started a spiral down to land, making sure I could always land if the engine quit. I landed uneventfully and the fire trucks and men in hazmat suits awaited me at the end of the runway. Other than the light, I never saw or felt any other abnormalities. It was a weird feeling to declare an emergency and have to tell them you only have ten minutes of fuel remaining and all of your weapons are safe. As a civilian flying, if I had ever had less than 45 minutes of fuel remaining, I was sweating and obviously had no weapons to worry about.

Week 12: Killing Nuns

Another fun and interesting week with a new phase of fighting and our first roll call. I finished up the defensive fighting phase and moved on to what we called "high aspect." It essentially meant we were pointing nose-to-nose at each other when the fight started, neither jet having an advantage. The jets would pass within 1000 feet and 900 knots of closure. Starting your first turn even just a half second late could ultimately cost you the fight.

While this fighting was incredible, it was painful as well. For two weeks both forearms felt like I had been taking a blood pressure test. Sometimes I just sat holding my arms straight up in the air, temporarily relieving the pain, as it felt like the blood was escaping. It was finally starting to go away as I assumed this pain was from the blood pooling in my arms during this high-G fighting. Further, these two phases were the worst on the neck and back. In defensive, I was always turned backward watching the adversary while pulling Gs, and in high aspect, they actually describe the passes as having "neck-snapping line of sight" as you snapped your head around to keep him in sight as we passed.

I really screwed up the other day during a fight as this "merge" of the two jets occurred. You had to time the turn just right and then pull as hard as you could, reaching 8-9 Gs. Unfortunately for me, I pulled as I was leaning slightly forward during this pass. Before I even knew what had happened, my neck snapped forward and my face was in my lap. I tried to sit back up but couldn't even budge. It was a moment where things slowed down and I remember deciding what to do, having the following conversation with myself. "Should I let off the stick and Gs and sit up? Hell no, this is the most important moment of this fight. If I can continue this for three more seconds I will have an opportunity to let off briefly, sit back up, and then reapply aft stick and the G forces." So I did that, got to stare at my crotch for a while, and ultimately killed him with two missile shots. Five days later I still didn't have full mobility in my neck.

On another flight this week, I started the jet and the crew chief found a problem so I had to shut down and get in a spare jet. It is not frequent but it happens. It required everyone to rush because we were behind the timeline for takeoff. As pilots, we inspected maintenance forms before we flew to make sure for accuracy but in this instance, they couldn't find the forms for my new jet. I told them it was fine, I would inspect the plane, get strapped in and when they find them, I'd inspect them in the cockpit.

Everything worked as planned and it really didn't delay me but as I was reviewing the forms in the cockpit I heard yelling. An idling F-16 is not quiet and there were four jets around me making a significant amount of noise. Further, I had earplugs in and a helmet on, so yelling I could actually hear would obviously grab my attention. I looked back and an older maintenance guy was throwing his arms and berating this kid in front of a decent number of people. It was the most unprofessional thing I have seen in the Air Force. I didn't know the exact subject of the yelling but I assumed it was about the misplaced forms. Even if his mistake was something that almost killed me, doing that in public, while the job was still going on, was unacceptable. I know I wouldn't be able to do my job as well if something like that happened to me right before I jumped in a plane and now this kid had to finish helping me get this jet ready to fly.

Regardless, I stopped reviewing the forms and just watched, making it obvious I was not approving. Numerous people saw the incident and me watching. This is not to say I was highly respected or had any weight to pull in a moment like this but I was, however, the only officer around and the pilot they were trying to get flying. The victim had been very nice to me as I preflighted both jets and had been helpful strapping me into the jet so unbeknownst to him, I considered him one of my favorites. The guy yelling didn't notice me so I had to give up my futile intimidation attempt as there was another F-16 waiting on me.

Usually you have the same maintenance team when you land but my buddy was nowhere to be found when I taxied back. I asked the crew chief about the situation and for names. He seemed relieved I was asking but he said the older guy ultimately apologized so I let it go. I was not sure if it was a drama, especially as a student pilot, I wanted to get in the middle of. Just as I got in the bus to drive back to the squadron I saw the kid walking around the side of a building so I asked the driver to stop and I jumped out and ran over to him. I could tell he was nervous with an officer quickly approaching and after his screw-up on my jet. He snapped to attention, acknowledging my presence.

I smiled, chuckled and said, "No, no, relax, I just want to say I appreciate the work. I am not sure what all that was about earlier but I am sorry it happened. You have a great attitude and wanted to say thanks for what you do and keep your head up."

I got a, "thank you, sir," we shook hands, and parted ways. He was probably 18 or 19 and I was hoping that made a bad day a little more tolerable—the older maintenance guys have told us they really look up to the pilots.

Finally, we had a roll call on Friday night. Another drunken storytelling, song-singing, history-educating event where students bear the brunt of the ridicule. This was no different but I was tasked with telling some form of squadron history, putting me square in the ridicule spotlight, by myself. I wasn't kidding when I told Hawk I was more nervous for this than for any flight I'd had in the last three years. Even worse, history was one of the first things up. So there I stood with probably forty people in the bar all surrounding me as I tried to hold and read my notes, a beer in each hand for effect. All in all, it went as well as I could have hoped—I didn't get booed off stage which happens most of the time—primarily due to one hilarious mistake. I won't fully describe what I said in this history but the idea is to take a little bit of the truth and run with it. Where I went comically awry was in a description of a former legendary Spike's hobbies (Spike was the mascot of our squadron). I was telling very tall tales and at one point I meant to say a hobby of his was killing Huns, one of the most feared enemies of the Roman Empire. Instead of saying "Huns," and this is an honest mistake, I said his hobby was killing "nuns." This made history far funnier and embarrassing than I could've dreamed.

Lesson Learned: Fortunate Accidents

I am a planner. I feel as though a decent amount of thought and effort can really help the quality of any project, trip or well, anything really. However, the beauty and surprise of the unexpected can truly make the most memorable moments.

Week 13: Hooks

It was early August and monsoon season here in Phoenix. Every day the afternoon clouds rolled in and there was the threat of a pop-up thunderstorm. While we still hadn't had any flights cancelled due to weather, it was speculated the weather was causing a lot of our maintenance issues. Airplanes are notorious for breaking when the weather changes. Cold to hot, hot to cold, dry to humid, the type of change hardly matters, just that change happened. The drop in temps to 105 were associated with a rise in humidity, leading to me fly only once this week after starting four different jets.

The most exciting of my maintenance issues occurred on a formation takeoff. In a formation takeoff, both jets line up together on the runway and release brakes at the exact same time for takeoff. There is about 10 feet of space between the two wing tips. These are hardly ever done any more for a variety of reasons but risk is high on the list. We had to know how to do them but I would probably do fewer than five more in my career. There are too many variables at this critical time of flight to risk putting these jets so close together for takeoff. If something goes wrong, 10 feet is not a lot of space to figure out what to do.

We ultimately accelerated together and began to take off at about 150 knots. This was the most exciting and dangerous point. After checking my engine after advancing power at the beginning of the takeoff, I hadn't taken my eyes off the other jet. I was constantly tweaking the throttle forward and back to keep my position right next to him. We spent a lot of time talking about emergencies during takeoff and what we would do, especially at higher speeds. The worst time for emergencies is right as you are rotating the plane into the air. You are very fast in relation to the ground and aborting the takeoff would be difficult and dangerous with limited runway remaining. However, you are very slow in relation to flying speed which doesn't leave you with many options. Just as we were approaching 140 knots or so, I heard "caution, caution" from the auditory warning system. We actually call her "Bitching Betty"—she never has anything good to say. I quickly took my eyes off of lead and glanced at my caution and warning panel. The leading edge flaps caution light was on.

What did this mean? Well, a few things could happen. Worst case, one of the flaps failed up or down and I would start rolling violently once airborne—not good if you are right next to the ground and another airplane. Best case, nothing would happen and after running the checklist you could reset the light and continue the flight. Regardless, I had about one second to decide whether to continue the takeoff or abort. I continued. I could probably save myself from a violent roll and the risk from aborting was too high at that speed with what could potentially be a very minor problem. I told flight lead after we were airborne and he gave me the lead so he could look me over. Turns out, it was the best case scenario and we had a great flight.

Our class had also reached a little bit of a rough patch. Hooks, or failed rides, had been creeping up on a few of us and a couple had been relatively dramatic. My roommate hooked his first ride for placing the switch that arms our weapons to "arm" versus "simulate." You don't ever want to put the switch in this position unless you are actually releasing ordinance from the jet. On training flights we used the simulate feature except when we dropped actual bombs or strafed.

The most intense hook was for a student getting low on fuel. We have a fuel state called Bingo, which is the minimum amount of fuel to get home from where you are fighting with a small reserve. He was in full afterburner and missed seeing he was at Bingo fuel. Further, their fight had moved farther away from Luke and they were lower in altitude—all factors potentially aggravating fuel shortage problems. By the time they realized what had happened, they almost diverted to Lake Havasu, Arizona. They chose to try and make it home. They declared an emergency and did everything they could to conserve fuel. They climbed as high as they could and then glided all the way home in idle power. I happened to be returning at the same time and gave way. To put it in perspective, we were supposed to land with a minimum of 950 lbs of gas. This kid was forty miles from the field with 750 lbs of gas. It was tense.

Hawk hooked his first ride for some poorly diagnosed avionics issues and a kid yesterday had to quit fighting because he lost all vision in a high G-pull, during the purely vertical down-maneuver. Scary. He bottomed out of the pull two thousand feet below the airspace, pulling 9.2 Gs the whole time. When he landed, he had to stay strapped in the jet, with his oxygen on, to meet doctors so they could determine whether the problem was him or something wrong with the jet's oxygen system or G-suit. It turned out he had done a big leg workout and his G-strain was not up to par.

I received in a reply to this post from a friend:
"Somewhere in all this the terms danger, adrenaline and addiction all come together. It can be compelling. Along with it comes alertness, courage and ego, all summed up in pride. Doing the right thing at the exact right time comes with practice, practice and the occasional almost mishap. You are in God's hands."

F-16 AFTERBURNER TAKEOFF

Photo Credit: Christian Culbertson

Lesson Learned: Emergencies

The Air Force is great about preparing us for emergencies. There are a countless number of things that can go wrong in the jet and while we can't practice them all, we practice a method of thinking applicable to all of them and always have a wingman to help. Having a plan when unforeseen circumstances don't go in your favor is critical. What do you do if the bank calls your note on the duplex you have been renting or a question completely stumps you in front of a large crowd? You can look like an idiot and freeze or you can have a generic answer buying you time. The Air Force doesn't expect me to have every step of every emergency memorized. It does, however, expect me to have a baseline level of knowledge of the jet and a formula to address problems, generally leading me to a successful conclusion to a problem.

Week 14: Furball

Two tactical intercept rides and an ACM (air combat maneuvering) ride highlighted the week. Every ride from here on out would be at least a three ship as I would have a flight lead and we would fight against at least one other jet as a team. Today, we actually fought against two jets and one was a Colonel on his last flight in the Viper.

The intercept rides relied extensively on using the radar and finding bogeys on it. They also taught responses when the bogeys were targeting you. There were many numbers running through our head: intercept geometry, enemy missile performance and our own jet's performance, all as we were closing at around 1,000 knots. At that speed, ten miles happens quickly. There was one maneuver, called a notch, which tries to defeat enemy radar lock on your jet. It is a high-G, high speed maneuver, for which I went supersonic on my first attempt and didn't realize it until the debrief. Fortunately, the enemy radar lock broke.

The ACM ride was my first 2v1 fight in the Viper and it was with the Squadron Commander as my instructor. It was one of my best rides and I wish I could convey through writing what occurred and what it felt like. Having to keep track of two planes in such a confined space, all trying to kill each other, was an intense experience. It was the feeling of fear and extreme fun all at once. If I screwed up the deconfliction between airplanes I would hook the ride, or even worse, hit another jet. If I shot my flight lead instead of the hostile, I'd hook the ride and owe a keg to the squadron. However, if I shot the hostile I'd be the hero of an epic scene involving three F-16s in a furball. We'd done this in the T-38 but the additional thrust in the Viper changed everything and jets were constantly going straight up and down, trying to gain various advantages. It is a wild scene.

At one point during the debrief, we saw that I accidentally locked onto my flight lead right when I was supposed to be shooting. He paused the tapes, looked back at me and said, "Fox, is this what I think it is?" (Meaning, are you about to shoot me?)

"I sure hope not, sir." Panic ran through my body as I couldn't recall exactly what happened next on the tape. He played the tape and I switched the lock from him to the hostile. Whew. $100, a hook and humiliation saved.

Week 15: Sasquatch

Well if there is one thing I can say, this job never seemed to have a boring week and week 15 was no exception. And yes, I was now called Sasquatch. I will get to the naming a bit later.

This week was one of the more exciting weeks due to the 2v1 type of fighting we were doing, and because our squadron arranged for Navy F-18s to be the adversary. Called dissimilar training, this was a big deal. Most students in the last five years at Luke had to fight F-5s, a modified T-38, and they never even got to see them during their fight. They just did radar work and attacked them from miles away. This fulfilled the training requirement saying we had to do dissimilar aircraft training. We, however, got to fight the Navy's best fighter in the most fun type of fighting you could do. The other squadron's jealousy was oppressive. Even the instructors were envious as this type of training was rare in this budget-constrained world.

My ride vs. the Hornets was Wednesday and I was flying with the second in command of our squadron for the first time. It was arguably the coolest flight of my life but was tempered by a near-disastrous mistake on my part. We took off as a two ship of Vipers and hit the tanker for air-to-air refueling (Pretty cool how normal this was now). Then, in a tactical formation a couple miles apart, we drove to the airspace and before we knew it, an F-18 was behind us and the fighting began. Flying against something different from your fighter was a great time. I relished the first time I got to say over the radio, "CUJO 2, kill Hornet, right hand turn, 15,000."

The flight went really well less one moment. Unfortunately occurring at the beginning of the second fight, it left me worrying the rest of the flight until debrief. The Hornet was in front of us and we were going to intercept it. Before we shot, we had to visually identify it was a Hornet to confirm it was a "hostile" aircraft per the fight rules. My flight lead flew straight towards him so he could quickly identify him and hopefully I would be in a position to shoot immediately after he did. So I moved a few miles away from my flight lead and had a radar lock on the Hornet. I turned to point at both jets as they merged when CUJO 1 called him hostile. I watched the two jets pass in front of me two miles away with over 900 knots of closure. They temporarily separated in opposite directions from my perspective and I, ensuring I was still locked to the Hornet, shot a radar guided missile. It went perfectly to plan. Almost too easy.

While my shot was good, my flight lead and instructor said over the radio it was a "PK miss." This just meant we pretended the missile missed him for whatever reason and we needed to continue fighting and shoot him again. Fine, except when I looked back inside the jet to shoot him again, I realized I was locked to my flight lead. My heart sank. When we watched our tapes after the flight you could hear me say to myself, "Hollllly shit."

Shooting your flight lead, or fratricide, is obviously a terrible thing. Not only would you have just killed a friend, husband and father, but you just did the Hornet's job for him and now it would be just you and him. In the training world it would mean I failed the ride and would have to show up to work in dress blues the next day, give a speech to the whole squadron and buy a keg. I was mortified. The radar guided missile goes where the radar tells it and unbeknownst to me, it had switched or I had done something to make it switch. From my perspective I had just failed my first ride of Air Force pilot training. I didn't say anything and continued fighting the next seven fights, trying to enjoy this rare flight but I was angry. Angry at myself for the oversight.

We were riding the bus back to the squadron and my IP excitedly got on the bus, "Fox, how was that?!"

I sheepishly replied it was pretty good, which offended him so he inquired further about why it was just "pretty good."

I confessed the potential problem and left it up to the tapes to determine what had happened. I rushed to setup our debriefing room and get the tapes cued up to try and get a glimpse of what happened before the debrief started. Watching my HUD tape real time revealed the lock randomly switched to my flight lead, right as I hit the pickle button to shoot. I echoed my reactive "holy shit" comment. I still had no idea what this would mean but I did notice I hit the pickle button ever so slightly before the lock switches. As the IP walked in the room, he asked if I had hooked any rides to see if this was going to affect me more than just my spirit. I hadn't but the depressing tone was now set and reminded me of what might be coming.

We end up watching this moment numerous times and ultimately frame by frame. I won't bore you and can't get into all of the details of what happened but it turned out I did not shoot my flight lead. I was safe by a mere .36 seconds. .36 seconds from my first hook in the Air Force and all of the other consequences previously stated. A .36-second difference from being the hero or killing my flight lead and ruining the most fun flight in the program. All of the stress of the day ended with him saying, "Fox, I know as instructors we don't compliment you guys very often and pretty much tell you that you suck all the time. Part of that is for fun but I also don't agree with it. I think it is important to tell someone when they are doing well and you are. That was an outstanding flight and it is known among all the IPs that you are doing a solid job. Keep it up." I had a couple drinks to celebrate this day.

In more somber news, one of the Hornets we were fighting G-LOCed while fighting us. Apparently he was unconscious for about 11 seconds and his plane went from 10 degrees nose low to 50 degrees nose low during that time. Scary—but all is well. I didn't really know what would happen next in a situation like this except that he would be observed closely and they would look into all of the physiological factors leading up to that flight.

Unfortunately, I went from great feedback from the boss to flying the same mission with a different IP the next day and getting an "average" overall grade. Frustrating, but there are days you don't fly quite as well and IPs you just don't gel with in the air. He did things differently from my expectations and left me at one point yelling, "What the F*&% is going on!" I still needed to remember even though I was in a single seat fighter, everything was recorded so we got to hear me say this in the debrief, to a chuckle.

Finally, the naming. It was my first fighter squadron naming and while the drinking and activities were optional, let's be honest, they are tradition and a lot more fun. This was, however, not my last call sign. The next time I got a call sign, at my operational squadron, would be my last. A majority of the time was spent as a class in the bar, waiting. All of the IPs were in a separate auditorium, conspiring and figuring out the names. We went out and stole things from another squadron, were asked to drink a variety of things, but mainly waited. We heard a few good speeches from IPs reminding us we were joining a brotherhood. A job not about hooking rides but about being a guy with whom they wanted to go to combat. A guy they could rely on and with whom they would be willing to put their life on the line.

At one point they called a kid into the auditorium by himself. We'd had to fill out a questionnaire before the evening, answering ridiculous questions they could make fun of us about, and he had mentioned he thought the wife of an IP was hot. All in good fun, apparently the IP of said wife came down to the front of the auditorium with said student, took a monster energy drink because his call sign was Beast, and bit the drink from the side of the can so it ripped it in half. Confiding with us later, the student couldn't believe what he had just seen.

They ultimately had us "fence-in," the term normally meant for crossing the boundary into war and the need to get all of your switches ready to fire. Here it meant, get your patches off, G-suit on, helmet on and visor down. We all did so and entered the auditorium. With the visor down in a dark room, you can hardly see anything. There is a roar of yelling, smoke machines going off and lights dancing around the room. Chaos. I couldn't remember or hear what the Mayor was even saying but ultimately I was handed a raw egg and a large dog treat, a Great Dane-sized dog treat. They requested we eat them both and we all knew we didn't want to be the last to finish. The egg, including the shell, was easy. I was surprised how smoothly it went down. The dog treat was a different animal. Besides being the driest thing in the world, the dog food aroma just doesn't sit well.

They handed us beers to help wash down the treat but it was simply too large and I resorted to cheating. I started breaking off chunks of it and putting it in my beer, hoping no one caught on. They didn't and I only ate about half of the treat and got out of there as quickly as I could. I returned to the auditorium alone to get my name. Because we were the Spikes, I kissed the ass of this Spike dog statue and was then told I was no longer FNG Fox, but Sasquatch. I received a squadron coin and was told to take a seat as a full member of the squadron.

Great night.

Week 16: Arriba

Not one of my finer weeks was this week 16.

The week started well with a great sim and flight. Lots of kills and little to debrief always put the instructor and me in a good mood but then things went downhill. We were a four ship with two students and two IPs and were flying to the airspace bordering Mexico. The instructors fought with the other student first so they basically told me to get lost. They wanted me to fly in the southern airspace and conserve gas. Sweet! It was really the first time I was in a Viper alone without a wingman watching me. So I start playing around and before I knew it, I looked down at my digital moving map in the plane and saw I had crossed an international boundary. You had to be kidding me.

I was visualizing the CNN headline: "Obama Administration answering questions about American fighter jet crossing into Mexico." I wasn't too far in but clearly had crossed the line according to my jet so I turned around as quickly as I could, using afterburner and 7 or 8 Gs. About that time, air traffic control called my flight lead telling us I needed to "work north" of my current position. Damnit! International consequences aside, I now had to worry about the ridicule and possible repercussions within the squadron as three other jets now knew what I had done.

Fortunately, the other jets ran too low on fuel before it was my turn to fight so my flight didn't count. Also fortunate because I flew mediocre at best after that. We get back and I vaguely played the, "I don't think I did anything wrong but it was close, the controller was just being cautious and I was avoiding weather" card. It ended up working like a charm and their cursory look at my tapes did not find guilt. Bullet dodged. Regardless, I may have accidentally flown an American fighter jet into a foreign country.

Bullet not really dodged on my simulator ride Friday. The instructors acknowledged this sim ride was a little advanced for where we were in training but I felt the brunt of an ugly debrief for the first time in my Air Force career. It was the first missionized ride of the program. All of the rides prior had been teaching individual skills like how to dogfight or launch a BVR (beyond visual range) missile. This ride put many of those skills together and now we actually had a mission we could be tasked with in war.

Today, it was defending a point from hordes of enemy aircraft. It was also my first time dying in a simulator due to a missile I took to the face, which was a little sobering. I had never been so frustrated and angry in a debrief. I went from the great comments last week of being well ahead of the game to being asked if I was focused. I only had two events, one flight and one sim, scheduled for next week. I would say this was probably the first time in my two years of AF flying that I needed to rebound a little.

Lesson Learned: Focus

We all have off days and it is almost impossible to prevent them. Even the best of any profession has a day where they aren't performing at their peak ability. Unfortunately for this profession, you can't afford an off day. Not only is it inherently risky in training, but a combat mission can't tolerate oversight or laziness. The best we can do is always try to give our endeavors 100%. Whether it is selling to a client or fighting at supersonic speeds, knowing you gave your all is fulfilling and others will notice, wanting to be around you.

Week 17: Sandbag

This was probably the quietest week of my Air Force career. I impatiently waited until Wednesday for my only flight of the week and Friday for my only sim. It was particularly painful as I felt the need to redeem myself for last week's missteps. Fortunately, it gave me time to prepare and both events went well. I was also able to ride in the backseat twice to take videos, pictures and try to learn something as well. Tuesday, I only had a one-hour class from 7:30–8:30 AM but somehow stayed at work until 11:00 PM after riding in the backseat and staying for the whole debrief. Some students thought it was crazy to wait around that long to just ride along for a flight but I always fell back on what we were actually getting to do for justification. I would have waited a week and done terrible things to get just one flight in this jet two years ago and was doing my best not to forget that.

The one flight went well and I was now left with just two air-to-air flights left before we started surface attacks.

Week 18: Spades

The only flight this week was the last tactical intercept ride during the day and the first with a four ship versus X number of opponents. It was one of the higher threat flights, an intense ride with actual air battle managers being utilized for the first time along with a couple of pilots on the ground to monitor our shots and call kills. There ended up being just two adversaries but in the briefing room, when you accounted for all of the pilots and controllers, there were six jets, eight airborne pilots and five controllers on the ground all for me and another student's training. On takeoff, the other student had to abort for a malfunction so there I was, the lone student with 14 other people taking seven hours out of their day for my training. While this should have made no difference, the thought, "don't blow it," crossed my mind several times.

The weather was awesome. These huge cumulus-to-cumulonimbus clouds pervaded throughout the airspace making the fighting around them, well, quite beautiful if I may. Sure, it added another variable to consider, making it more difficult but it all worked out and made for a great scene. Having to improvise often led to fun and instructor leniency on the grade sheet.

The flight went well, less one critical error on my part. There are different classifications of radar targets. To summarize in a simple manner, there were friendlies, unknowns (bogeys), guys that were most likely enemies but we needed more information to confirm (spades) and confirmed bad guys worthy of being shot (hostiles). Spades were a new concept introduced on this ride and I had a feeling I was going to struggle with it. There was a lot of pressure to acquire radar locks and shoot the hostile aircraft as early as you could and a lot of information was being communicated over the radio, making some subtle differences difficult to discern. So I had to listen to where the radar contacts were, find them on my scope and now determine whether or not I could shoot them, all while flying formation off another jet in my flight.

The controller updated us on the battlespace picture rather frequently and during one fight I heard her declare all of them hostile. Sweet! Now I didn't have to worry about the spades variable, I could shoot them all. So now I was scrambling to figure out which one I was supposed to shoot and get the missile off the jet. Turns out, over the next 30 seconds or so, she corrected herself twice and called my target a spades group. I heard none of this. Once I knew what I had to do, I tuned out the rest I assumed was not a factor for me. Classic student mistake.

So I got my lock, shot, and beaming with pride said, "Scold 2, Fox 3, South Group, crank left."

Next thing I heard was, "confirm that's the spades group?" Oh no. Considering I hadn't even thought there was a spades group, this was not good. Let's flash forward to the debrief. Those 14 participants were now all in a room together, watching this war unfold and everyone was listening to my tapes while watching the computer recreation of the fight. They listened to mine for no particular reason other than we had to listen to someone's tape so we could hear the radio calls. Unfortunately, they also got to hear my breathing and any other "talking to myself" that went on. I may have mentioned before this can be the source of some entertainment and this was no exception. I am paraphrasing here but after the question about the spades group I just shot, my tape sounded something like, "what!? She f$%&ing said they were hostile!" The room of people was now laughing and the controller, an 19 year old airman, was in the room as well. Did she screw up? Yes. Did I screw up? Yes, and it was far more my fault as she corrected herself and I ultimately took the shot. I looked back at her and gave her a sheepish, "sorry."

Week 19: Mom's House

This leads me to my first low level ride in the F-16. We flew low levels in the T-6 and it was cool to fly 210 knots at 500 feet. We had flown low levels in the T-38 at 360-390 knots and it was also a great time, but low level in the F-16 is a completely different experience, especially out in the Arizona desert. I assumed it would be a relatively unimpressive transition from the T-38 but the extra hundred knots made a considerable difference. At over 450 knots, or 520 mph, a ground rush seemed to begin. I compared the difference in speed to riding a motorcycle on the interstate at 70 mph versus 90 mph. At 70, it is very comfortable and I don't feel like I am going fast. Increase the speed to 90 and it feels almost unsafe and the tunnel vision sensation begins. The two other factors making low level in the F-16 a glorious thing were the lack of towers and the presence of mountains. In Texas, and basically everywhere except out here, towers peppered the landscape and we had to spend the entire low level flight looking for them. In the Arizona desert, they didn't exist and our attention could be spent on more fun and tactical tasks. I cannot express how much of a relief this was.

Finally, the glorious mountains. We were supposed to always be 500 feet above the ground and there was a great emphasis on being right at this number to stay below radar coverage and using the mountains to hide behind. So how did we maintain the 500 feet in a formation with another jet and on rugged terrain? The answer, beautifully, was the same as if you were trying to play around and just have fun. You could do one of two things. First, fly through canyons or gaps between peaks and use them to hide yourself, allowing you to stay low. Awesome. Now we were raging at 500+ mph with mountains on either side of us, less than a mile away and peaks well above our altitude. The second option was used when we came to a range where there was no choice but to go over the top and you 'got' to perform a ridge crossing. We waited as long as is legal to pull up, then as we were approaching the peak, rolled into 120-degree bank and pulled back down to hug the profile of the mountain. It was exactly the way I would do this in a video game just trying to have fun.

In the end, it was some of the most intense flying to date. Working the radar, flying in a formation, staying low and trying to avoid smacking into the side of mountains required a lot of attention but it sure was a great time. I was able to fly this ride with Hawk and as we got out of the jets, he called it the coolest thing he had ever done in an airplane.

I also had my last day, air-to-air only, ride the F-16 B-course on Thursday. It was the first real "missionized" ride. This means there was a fully briefed goal and desired outcome relating to a bigger picture war. In this case, we had to defend a point. We joked the point was someone's mom's house. The missionized aspect made it a lot of fun. We really felt like a team in the brief and I was legitimately fired up and ready to fight. It was another 4vX ride. In this case, there were two F-16s and two F-5s trying to get past us and bomb mom's house.

We were fighting in the airspace down by Mexico and a huge storm popped up right as we took off. There was a lot of lightning in one centralized cell in the airspace, which made for a cool scene. The opponents, even as we killed them, are allowed to regenerate so while there were only 4 enemy aircraft, we were fighting an infinite number, just four at a time.

In the end, it didn't go well. Three of the four of us died and mom's house was bombed. There was a controller on the ground who was a part of our team giving us the God's-eye view of the war. It was her "check ride," or final evaluation, before she was a mission-ready air battle manager and she did not do well.

I always hate to blame other people, but based on me and the other student passing the ride with complimentary comments from our IPs, you know they were blaming her as well. It would have honestly been better had she not spoken. For example, she would call a threat to me when it was for the other student. This was a huge problem as I would react defensively to a plane that wasn't there when I could be attacking or searching for new targets. Meanwhile, the other student was not reacting and getting shot. This happened numerous times. It was almost like she was on the enemy's side providing us false information as a tactic of theirs. It was horribly confusing for a pilot in an already chaotic environment.

My low point was flying out of the airspace while in a very dynamic moment not paying attention to where I was but just trying to survive.

Week 20: Andromeda

I had flown over 200 hours at night but it had been nothing like what I experienced during the past week. It was my first experience using NVGs (night vision goggles) and it was a wild experience. They gave the world this green tint and while they didn't turn night into day, when there was a decent moon and a clear night, they did an amazing job. However, you were essentially looking through binoculars so your field of view was small. Any time you wanted to look at anything, you had to turn your whole neck, which, when flying formation and the proper position is at your 3 or 9 o'clock (directly off your right or left wing; 6 o'clock would be directly behind you), becomes difficult. We put the goggles on about two minutes after takeoff and left them on until about five minutes prior to landing. In the first minute after I donned the goggles and had to rejoin on another F-

16, I felt like I was in a dream. They made your vision slightly blurry, looking at a green tint on the world in a small field of view. That, accompanied by perfectly smooth air with a lightning storm in the distance and the ability to see every star in creation, created this wild sensation and the thought that this must be a dream.

I had never seen so many stars in my life. My instructor let me relax for a bit and just enjoy the ride for a while so I experimented with taking the goggles on and off. Goggles on, in the small field of view, I estimated I could see 300+ stars. When I took the goggles off, at 20,000 feet over a dark desert, I could only see four stars. The goggles took any source of light and enhanced it. The moon looked like the sun, I saw a shooting star every couple of minutes and in probably the wildest surprise to me, my instructor showed me Andromeda, the next nearest galaxy. I know I sounded really "cool" with my giddy laughs of excitement but to see something I hardly knew existed or was even possible to see, really got me going. It looked like the pictures we have all seen of galaxies in textbooks, a fuzzy rotating mass of something. I pointed it out to the instructor I flew with the next night and he had an almost equal reaction. Because the goggles picked up on any light, we could see airplanes as far away as Vegas and L.A. making the entire sky a blinking mess. This made it difficult to determine who your wingman was. While they sound great and interesting, they have their significant limitations. After I had flown 200 night hours using the goggles, I was told I was eligible for disability, for an unknown reason.

We also air-to-air refueled the first night. The tanker had this bright light on the side so when you were waiting for other jets to finish refueling, it blinded you. It whited out the NVGs and ruined your night vision if you took the NVGs off, making it very difficult to see and avoid hitting the tanker. It was a classic example of some Air Force rule or idea making no sense. I think the light existed for the tanker pilots to see whether they had ice accumulating on the wings, but regardless, it was absurd. It was something so obscene that, had I been the first person in the history of the Air Force to air-to-air refuel and the tanker pilot had the light on, I would've been borderline angry with his stupidity. But here we were, refueling for decades and it was still an issue. Otherwise, night refueling wasn't that different. It was a little spooky rejoining on this massive dark object floating in space but it wasn't that bad.

The flights, performance wise, went well. The first flight was a night orientation ride and I had a fun instructor making it a great time. The second flight was our first night flight with some fighting going on. Unfortunately, most flights ended with me slightly frustrated at myself for my performance but this relatively easy flight was an exception, so I was in a very pleasant mood, enjoying the views on the flight back into Phoenix. It was about 10:50 PM when we landed and as soon as we shut down and raised the canopy, Taps began playing loudly over the base speakers creating a relatively sentimental moment.

There is a certain form of high you get flying these jets, especially afterward, when you know you have done a great job doing something pretty awesome. It is addicting and I was already concerned about the withdrawals I will feel one day.

Lesson Learned: Because We Always Have

Things being done a certain way for any extended period of time are comfortable. People don't love change. Further, change is difficult in large organizations, especially between separate entities within an organization requiring coordination. Regardless, "because we always have" is not a good reason to continue doing something. A bad idea could have been adopted from the beginning or the landscape has changed making the practice obsolete, requiring a change for optimum performance.

Week 21: Cleared Hot

Monday was my first actual air-to-ground attack flight. The flight marked the first time I moved the "master arm" switch to "arm" instead of "simulate." It turned all of the jet's weapon employment systems on and hitting the trigger or pickle button actually dropped and shot things from the jet. A considerable portion of the brief was spent discussing the importance of this as we could actually hurt people if mistakes were made.

We were strafing a panel measuring the number of hits we achieved. Being the low angle strafe event, we were doing about 450 knots and recovering a ten degree nose low dive about 100 feet above the ground. This was the same event that I sandbagged a few months ago where we got so low I thought we were crashing into the desert floor. But this time, in the front seat, I never got that sensation. The gun was amazingly loud and shook the jet. In two seconds of firing, I went through 210 rounds. At a 6000 rounds per minute firing rate, when the gun was full, the jet only had about five seconds of firing time before it ran out.

As my IP and I were walking back from the jet he looked over to me, smiled, stuck out his hand and said, "dude, you just dropped a bomb and shot the gun for the first time in your life. Is that not awesome?" He made a great flight even better. He happened to be in a band called the "Dos Gringos" and they were wildly famous and popular in the Air Force community, singing originally written fighter pilot songs. He was a really nice guy and a great instructor.

The other ride was a night 2v2 tactical intercepts ride—one of the most failed rides in the program. We flew in formation at night and it was relatively difficult to keep him in sight, maneuver tactically and employ weapons.

It was a really tough week for one the kids in our class. You could only fail so many rides in a phase and he had reached that number. He flew the defensive counter air (DCA) ride, the one where we were defending a target versus X number of enemy aircraft, with the Squadron Commander as his flight lead, and he hooked it. He then went to a progress check ride, a ride that begins to determine if you should continue flying the F-16. On Friday afternoon we found out he hadn't passed. No one knew what was happening but he was taken off the schedule for Monday and we feared the worst. As a class, two of us were struggling and one fully admitted it and was open to and encouraging help from the other classmates but this guy acted like he was doing fine, even after the rides he failed. It is difficult to help someone with that attitude.

Mom flew into town Thursday and was able to check out the jets up close, watch night afterburner takeoffs, try on my night vision goggles in a dark room and see a piano burning. Yes, it was my first piano burning as well.

Apparently, a fighter pilot from WWI who was famous for piano playing died on a mission and to mourn his loss they burned his piano. Ever since then, a piano is burned when a pilot dies or to remember those we have lost or who have "augured in" throughout the years.

Finally, a Turkish F-16 shot down a Syrian helicopter this week. I will confess this fired me up a little. Sure, you don't want to see someone die but it is the nature of our business when required and it was nice to see the F-16 being used.

Lesson Learned: Help

We all struggle with things. From relationships and happiness to work and school, life can be difficult. Fortunately, we don't have to do it alone and can make things much easier on ourselves. However, many are too prideful ask for help. Our culture may have created an image where it shows weakness to see a psychologist or marriage counselor. People avoid the use of tutors as it shows you may not be as intelligent. I encourage you to look at it differently. You are the CEO of your life and you have a lot to do. From creating a great family environment, establishing success at work or school, being a good friend or simply cleaning your house. There aren't enough hours in the day to be great at everything. To be successful, delegate your life whenever possible. If hiring a tutor helps you learn the same material in an hour that it would normally take three hours, it is probably worth it. If you don't have enough time to give to your marriage or relationship the attention it deserves, there are professionals who specialize in helping people figure these problems out. No one expects anyone to be perfect but those who are most successful utilize and rely on those around them for help.

Week 22: Terrain Masking

The week began with a great flight. My IP and I, each in our jets full of bombs and a hot gun, blasted off and flew a low level, ultimately dropping us off at the bombing range. It was another one of those flights I had dreamt about for quite a while. An afterburner takeoff followed by 20 straight minutes of 500 knots at 500 feet above the desert floor was a recipe to put me in a mood so pleasant I could be heard laughing with happiness on the HUD tape after the flight.

At one point, we were approaching this small range of mountains and I could have sworn a peak was on the far side of my flight lead, fully expecting to remain visual with him. I started to get excited for the ridge crossing and I saw him bank up to stay as low as possible as he disappeared behind the mountain. Wow, wasn't expecting that. I looked straight ahead at the approaching mountains and in front of me was what I would describe as a crevasse. While I'm probably exaggerating to some degree, it was a tight fit between these two peaks. Rules state I had to remain 500 feet above the ground and I had a strong debate with myself as to the wisdom of going through, instead of above, but of course my fun side won. It was tight but I definitely had a case for being 500 feet if you went straight below the jet and tactically, it was a great move. I rolled into 90 degrees of bank as I went through the pass with the side of the mountain and desert just a few hundred feet out the top of my canopy. At that speed, it truly was amazing. There is something about ripping across the desert mountains with two F-16s that gets the heart rate up, even as I write this.

The bombing and strafing went fine less one bomb. Bomb scores are measured in meters from the target during this "dumb bomb" phase. These bombs are hardly dropped anymore as we often use laser and GPS guided bombs, especially in the latest conflicts. The target area had a radius of 100 meters and if you were outside 50 meters, you had really screwed something up. Long technical story short, either I screwed up or the mechanical bomb release was slightly delayed which can happen. I dropped my bomb and initiated my pull away and then rolled 90 degrees so I could watch it hit. The main problem, regardless of whose fault, was the bomb coming off after I started pulling up. I was waiting to see it hit near the target when I saw the small explosion basically under me, in the middle of the desert, nowhere near anything. "Ohhhh shit" was the comment exclaimed on the HUD tape. No matter how ugly it was, it still couldn't ruin this flight.

Afterward, as I did with most exceptional flights, I called my Grandpa to tell him all about it. He sent the following email after our phone call Monday night:

"Wish I had kept track of all the excited calls we have received over the last couple of years exclaiming, 'Today was the greatest day of flying I have ever experienced.' Last evening was no exception. Thanks for sharing the bomb runs, strafing runs, and the low level flights through and around the desert. We are so glad you are loving the training and doing well. Thanks, Pop"

The other flight was a low altitude intercept ride. I have heard there are only three generals still flying in the Air Force and one of them was the enemy on this ride. My jet had all kinds of problems with the HUD and radar but it was a great 2v2 ride, carving around mountains because it tactically made sense to try and avoid the adversary's radar lock. The low point of the flight was the return to base. You never want anything to go wrong, but especially not with the General. I made the call while we were fighting that I had reached the fuel state to start heading home. I didn't determine this fuel state so I wasn't really at fault but because my jet had a lot of tanks and bomb racks, I used up a lot of gas on the way home. Enough that when I landed, I couldn't taxi back to my parking spot and had to shut down on the taxiway and get towed back. Embarrassing. It made me think about how little fuel we had compared to civilian flying. We normally landed with about 10-15 minutes of fuel until empty, which was far below normal civilian levels. The crazy part was that if we were to accidentally use the wrong power setting, we could be out of gas in forty seconds.

Week 23: Shack Two

Another week in the introduction to bomb dropping and strafing. We flew a set pattern to practice setting up for good approaches, and ultimately, dropping accurate bombs. Starting next week, the pattern would be gone and we would bomb and strafe random targets scattered throughout the desert and need to find the parameters for a good bomb on our own.

Through all of the congressional fighting, the U.S. government shut down this week in the fall of 2013. Fortunately for us here at Luke, we were one of few bases still flying. My friends in other fighter training programs and most Guard units, like mine in South Dakota, were grounded until this was sorted out. Tuesday, I got to have my 600 mph at 500 feet fun through the desert followed by dropping nine bombs and strafing. However, the cleaning staff was furloughed so I followed up the fighter pilot fun by having to clean the restroom. My grandpa thought it was a good trade.

My next ride included four jets ripping across the desert at 500 feet, all hugging the mountains as closely as we legally could and reacting to fictional SAMs and gun fire. My instructor was our squadron weapons officer. This means he had graduated from Fighter Weapons School, which was like the Top Gun of the Air Force, and he was the go-to guy for anything tactical. It was my first time flying with him and like the boss, he was a good guy to impress. As we started our passes, I began throwing strikes. At one point I got a shack, which means the bomb landed in the truck we were bombing. Later, after a series of good bombs, I got a no spot. A no spot was the ranger saying he didn't see it land or the bomb didn't come off the jet—not good. It was a 'no spot' when I slung that bomb way off into the desert in the previous week. On this ride, the ranger asked me if my system showed the bomb coming off the jet and it had. Then, in a classic case of the benefit of the doubt, the ranger said, "Well, I am not exactly sure what happened but I have to assume you flew it into the cab of the truck and that's why I can't see it. Shack, two."

I burst out laughing and we would never know the true fate of the bomb but I made money off of it.

With four rides of experience on the bombing range, things begin to slow down with respect to the task saturation and I started to notice more things. While setting up for the next pass, I started looking back and watching the jets after me making their passes. It was great. From the air, just after dropping a bomb on a target, I watched my wingmen roll into the same target on 10, 20, 30 or even 45-degree dives, drop their bomb, and then aggressively pull away from the ground. It was a beautiful sight. It was amazing to see how aggressively the jet could pull up with the ground providing a reference for my view.

Week 24: M-I-Z U-S-A

For the past few weeks we have been dropping training bombs. Wednesday, we dropped real bombs, the same size as those dropped every day in the wars we have been fighting. We were loaded up with six Mark-82 bombs.

There was crosswind on takeoff and I took off twenty seconds after my flight lead. As I was lining up for takeoff, I could see the afterburner plume from behind his jet but in a wild phenomenon I hadn't seen before, the flame was offset from the jet. All of the exhaust gas churning through the air wildly distorted the image, enough to the point I saw the afterburner plume hovering in the sky by itself, with the jet about 15 feet to the right.

We flew 80 miles south to one of a few areas designated for live bomb drops. This was an Air Force training course so after quadruple-checking I had the right mountain, I watched my instructor roll in and drop his bombs while I provided cover. I slewed my targeting pod—the latest gadget we had been trained on—to the target, just like you have seen on those CNN shots of bombs impacting targets in the war. Fortunately, at the last second, I remembered I was part of the TV and Internet generation and recognized I was about to watch the first bomb explosion of my life, in an F-16, over the target, through the tiny little camera screen in the jet. I ignored the pod to look out the window and watch the six bombs come off his jet, fall and impact the target, creating fireball and shockwave across the desert. Awesome.

Now it was my turn and I had significantly more adrenaline pumping than I expected. I rolled in, hit the pickle button and could feel the six bombs quickly come off one at a time with the plane shuddering at the release of each 500 lb bomb. I executed a 'safe escape maneuver' which was designed to keep us clear of the bomb fragmentation which can shoot up to 3,000 feet into the air with these bombs. As soon as I was safely away, I rolled into about 135 degrees of bank and started a turn back toward the target with my head turned all the way back around so I could watch the explosion.

The live drop was exciting but I actually had more fun strafing after the bombing. There were targets scattered around the desert and in this case, there was a mock airfield built for us to practice attacking. Unscripted, there was a bomber-sized aircraft on the runway as if it was about to take off and we each took two passes strafing it, I was able to see the dust fly up from the bullets as they hit from a 25 degree angle dive. It was a lot of fun. Finally, we practiced threat reactions, the maneuvers we learn to evade surface-to-air missiles and gun fire. Unfortunately, my instructor over-G'ed his plane during his reaction and we had to come home slightly early. I chased him through the landing to make sure his jet was fine the entire way home. I just practiced engine out landings in the pattern until I was out of gas. We celebrated the flight with a beer at 8:30 in the morning.

Let me rewind to the brief for this flight. I was feeling pretty badass going into this flight. I still hadn't gotten over flying a fighter jet and now I was dropping real bombs and shooting real bullets. The brief started at the ungodly hour of 5:00 AM. I usually showed up about an hour prior to a brief to get things in order but chose to try just 20 minutes for this flight, maximizing sleep time. I also decided to rush as much as possible at home for the same reason. 30 minutes into the brief before I realized why I had been so uncomfortable—my underwear was on backward. I also realized there would be no way to correct this unfortunate and uncomfortable situation before the flight. So what should have been this sweet strut out to this badass jet full of real bombs turned into an awkward shuffle—and it would get worse.

I had yet to use the restroom in the jet. Further, if you don't already know, the cockpit was beyond small. There really wasn't any way to move and we were strapped down with five straps, many in locations that would make this urination feat difficult at best. The harness had two straps that went between our crotch and we had a G-suit on. Finally, the F-16 had a seat that was reclined more than other jets which was the final challenge. As soon as I sat in the jet I realized I had to go. There was nowhere to go outside because they parked us a long way from any building when there were live bombs on board. I decided I was going to have to hold it. I started the jet and my instructor had a maintenance issue so he was going to be delayed about 10 minutes. After arming the bombs, I had time so I decided to give it a shot.

We basically got a plastic bag and no further guidance. I actually asked my instructor over the radio if he had any "racehorse" (the brevity word used to tell everyone you are peeing) tips. "Make sure your seat is safe, turn your HUD off when you disconnect things so you remember to reconnect all of the belts and good luck." So I began doing all of these things and got to the flight suit before I remembered my backward underwear problem. Now I was half-undressing in the cockpit with the arming crews on the ground wondering what the hell must be going on in there. The reclined seat proved to be the most difficult variable. Imagine sitting on a recliner with no space and all these belts. In the end I was about 90% successful and you can interpret that however you would like.

I wrote a couple of messages on the bombs. One read, "Go Mizzou, Beat Georgia." I posted it on Facebook and then sent a tweet to a Mizzou sports writer. For two hours, my phone didn't stop vibrating as people, 95% of whom I don't know, retweeted it over 100 times. Writers for the St. Louis Post Dispatch and a variety of other papers sent it out and it ultimately earned a thanks from the Mizzou head football coach Gary Pinkle. It made for a fun evening. Some of the comments included:

- *Sweeet! Those pointy nosed fighter geeks ARE good for something!*
- *M-I-Z U-S-A*
- *#Salute*
- *Thanks for sharing, GP (The head coach)*
- *And after Mizzou won: BDA looks good, target destroyed! (BDA stands for battle damage assessment.)*

205

Finally, an update on the two kids struggling as of late. There ride called an FPC (Functional Progression Check) was basically their last chance. It was flown with a commander and it was flight they used to determine whether they should continue with training. One kid failed it but they recommended him for reinstatement the next day and he returned to flying with us. The other kid failed it and was removed from our class last week. It is a tough deal almost three years into training and being as close as we are from graduating. No one really knew what the future held for him.

Week 25: Code Three

A relatively quiet week due to another disastrous week of maintenance issues. Our Squadron Commander called it the ugliest maintenance situation he had seen in his twenty-year career—all for an unknown reason. It was tough to mentally prepare for flights when the odds of actually flying were low due to jet availability.

I got to fly Monday but since it was an introduction ride to laser-guided bombs, I needed an operating targeting pod and laser. When mine broke, the flight didn't count for anything. It wasn't fun showing up at 5 AM to not accomplish anything on the syllabus but I was lucky enough to still fly and support the other student. In the end, I got to see how the ride went and a free F-16 ride with no stress. It made my flight the next day much easier. I had to wake up at 4 AM on Friday for a brief to find out there weren't any planes available. Not pleasant.

Everything up until this point had been a great time and as fighter pilots, we needed to know how to handle all of the various situations such as dogfighting, intercepts and dropping dumb bombs, but these laser and GPS-guided bombs, along with strafing, were the things we would have a high probability of doing at some point in combat.

Week 26: Precision Guided

My first three flight week in months has me in a fine mood. Monday was a solo ride practicing dropping JDAMS, or GPS-guided bombs. It was one of my best flights thus far and since we accomplished everything we needed to get done expeditiously, the instructor decided to bring us back with a little extra fuel remaining which was atypical. I was in a wonderful mood having not really screwed anything up and had about 20 minutes of extra fuel to play with.

Sounds like a great time but a theme from two weeks ago reemerged, as I had chosen not to use the piddle pack and relieve myself before takeoff. I was in serious pain. Do I just land to remedy the situation or do I practice engine out and normal landings and play in the Viper? I continued to fly, of course.

At this point you are probably wondering why I couldn't learn from previous mistakes considering most flights are 1-1.5 hours long. Well first, this flight was a 1.7-hour journey and when you consider we step to the jets about an hour prior to takeoff, 1.7 turns into 2.7 hours and that doesn't count time to taxi back and shutdown. Further, hydration is a critical factor for G tolerance so I couldn't afford to restrict drinking before flight. Regardless, I flew until I was out of gas and by the time I had landed, I was in serious trouble.

After I landed, I had to go to a de-arming area where a crew pinned up all of our weapons so they were safe. I considered using the piddle pack there but as you all know, it is quite a hassle and risk. I taxied back as quickly as possible before realizing I had the furthest parking spot from the building. Damn. Naturally, it all took longer than normal to shut down and the crew chief informed me he was training a new "B man" and it would take longer than normal. I was in so much pain I almost said no but unhappily agreed. Finally the time came to get out of the plane and it took four attempts. The cockpit was small and it hurt so bad to get out of that plane I considered using the piddle pack just a walk away from a bathroom. By the time I got out, I literally walked hunched over the hundred yards to the building with all of the crew chiefs laughing along the way, undoubtedly understanding my plight.

The flight Wednesday dropped an inert, no explosives, 500 lb concrete laser guided bomb and another GPS-guided concrete bomb. The bombs really have a jarring feeling coming off the wing as there are more connections to jet since they are "smart bombs." The flight went decently but we never saw the GPS-guided bomb hit with our eyes or the targeting pod. After realizing we had no idea what happened to the bomb, my instructor said, "I think the taxpayers deserve to know what happened to their $40,000." Yes, while each of those bombs were just concrete slabs, the kits and fins guiding them ran $40K a piece. Add together the cost of jet time, all of the bombs we dropped and bullets we shot, and we were looking at about $200K worth of fun on Wednesday. We examined our tapes extensively, making sure I had done all of the appropriate checks before dropping the bomb. They were relatively easy bombs to drop but just one mistyped number into the system could cause serious errors. Please rest assured knowing we did everything by the book. Most likely, the bomb was so accurate it went straight into the building and we just couldn't see the dust kick up.

Friday was a missionized surface attack ride. Of the 1.1 hours flying, probably 40 minutes of it was at 500 feet, 500 knots. As a two ship, we carved through the desert and mountains and would practice popping up at the last moment to identify the target, roll in to drop the bombs and get out of there. They even gave us six more 500 lb bombs. I flew this ride with the same IP I had on Monday. I almost called my ride Monday a perfect ride. I didn't mess anything up so when he told me it was "slightly above average overall," I was disappointed. Friday, I would describe as not pretty. Numerous things didn't go according to plan and he seemed unhappy in the backseat. At one point in the debrief he even mentioned he could have hooked me for one thing but since another IP had given me the technique, I was spared. So I was more than shocked when he said it was a strong ride, "above average."

Finally, the weekend. On Friday, the first F-35 squadron at Luke was created. Many of my instructors were moving on to be the first F-35 pilots with the first jet showing up in February. The new Squadron Commander had a party at his house after the ceremony and our Squadron Commander asked our class to show up. It was a nice party with all of the base leadership in attendance. My roommate and I were the only two students to show up and it turned out we were just being used to throw this new leadership in their own pool. Perfect. At least we got free beer and the right people in the pool.

Week 27: The Oscars

A couple of surface attack flights on a relatively interesting week. Tuesday was a flight practicing element pop attacks. As a two ship, we were a mile apart, 500 feet above the ground and at 500 knots. At around 5 miles away from a target we couldn't see because we were so low, we both checked about 25 degrees to the right and then started climbing. Flight lead climbed at 15 degrees nose high, military power, while I was in afterburner climbing 30 degrees nose high. So I am trying to find the target, looking at another jet making sure we didn't run into each other and on this day, avoiding a scattered cloud layer I flew through. It was a pretty sporty maneuver since as soon as we dropped the bombs, we got away from the bomb fragmentation and immediately descended back down to 500 feet in the mountains to avoid enemy radar and their associated surface-to-air missiles.

We'd had a couple incentive flyers the last few weeks in my formation. If flight lead was in a two seat jet, various airmen got to ride along in the backseat as a reward for their work in the Air Force. There is, however, a significant drawback to riding along on an actual mission: airsickness. One incentive flyer rode along in Hawk's flight and as they were reviewing the tapes in the debrief, you could hear the poor guy throwing up. It is an unfortunate reality of what we do, but the G-forces were usually a little too much for people. Thankfully, I was not given the airsickness gene.

We took significant precaution dropping even the inert concrete bombs in the middle of the desert. There were endangered Pronghorn Sheep that we had to check for every flight to see if they were near the targets. If they were, we wouldn't drop. Thursday's Pronghorn check yielded another interesting result as apparently there were illegal immigrants in the target area. Can you imagine? Risk your life crossing the border and walking through a desert for 30 miles to come across a few structures allowing you to find shelter from the elements only to find out you were practice targets for some of the world's most lethal machines.

My ride Wednesday was a lot of fun as we had entered the "missioned" phase of surface-to-air training. Previous flights were just about teaching us how to do certain tasks like drop a laser-guided bomb or how to strafe. Now we treated flights like combat missions. There were simulated SAM (Surface-to-Air Missile) threats, friendly forces on the ground and many other factors that go into a war. The coordination going into these exercises could be overwhelming. This was one of my first rides with those considerations and while none were real except our target and my flight lead, my instructor did his best to make them real and it was an Oscar-worthy performance. Over the radio he was impersonating about nine different 'characters' with differing accents. He pretended to be two different flights of F-16s, an Army guy on the ground trying to call in Air Support, the commanding entity of the war, AWACS, and many others I could hardly even keep up with. It was amazing to hear and I can only imagine what it's like in a real war scenario. It was a strong enough performance that I thanked him for all of the effort he had put into the flight, all while flying and keeping track of me.

As I have mentioned before, we landed with as little fuel as safely possible to maximize training. After this flight I was at that fuel level so when I put the landing gear handle down and only got two green lights instead of three, you can imagine my heart rate climbed slightly. It was one thing to have a landing gear problem, but when you had just a few minutes to resolve it or it would resolve itself, the excitement elevated quickly. I climbed up and left my gear down telling my instructor right before he touched down in front of me. He, having more gas, lit the afterburner and circled back around to look me over for any damage. I looked fine and after testing the lights in the cockpit, realized that it was simply a burned out light. We made one more check and decided it was safe and landed uneventfully. Even knowing it should be safe to land, I felt a little more tension upon touching down, hoping none of the gear would collapse. Exhale.

Finally, my grandparents informed me they were getting me a customized model F-16 for graduation next month and I was modeling it after the jet I soloed back in June. The crew chief's name usually went on the right side of the cockpit so I emailed him asking for permission to put his name on it. His reply was as follows:

"Good morning Sir, That would be AWESOME. Me and all the Crew Chiefs are here at Luke AFB, for you Sir. Thank you for thinking about me as your Crew Chief, it's an honor. Respectfully, Jose"

Lesson Learned: Recognition

So many nice things are done every day for each other and even the slightest recognition can go a long way. Even if I wasn't going to put his name on the side of the model, an email letting him know I appreciated his attitude and efforts as a crew chief would make him feel great and would take less than three minutes. This needs to be done more in all facets of life.

Week 28: Field Trip

Another wild week with two night flights and my first CAS (Close Air Support) ride.

My first couple night rides a few months ago were about getting used to the NVGs and an introduction to air-to-air fighting at night. The rides this week were about surface attack and they were wild. Monday night, the weather shop gave no indication of the weather being anything but the Phoenix standard, clear and warm. As we taxied out, the lightning show began and considering the Air Force's very conservative stance on storms, I was surprised they even let us get that far. A few minutes later we were airborne and the lightning seemed to get worse and was everywhere. It was my first night flight in a while and I was busy trying to get the NVGs on and all of the other things associated with flying a fighter in formation at 350 knots at night, so oddly enough, I remember being too busy to worry about the storm. All of the storms were exploding right as we took off so no one had any data on them until approach control alerted us to cells just a couple miles in front of us. Feeling task saturated, I rationalized the IP in the other jet wouldn't let anything bad happen, right?

The tactical airspace was cloudy but storm-free. We were able to shoot the gun for the first time at night and it was quite an experience. It was low illumination which meant the moon wasn't up and the clouds didn't help, making for a dark night. The NVGs still worked but not as well as they need some light to enhance to clearly see the ground. The darkness made rolling into a 25-degree dive into a black hole quite unnerving. You know the ground is quickly coming at you but you can't see it. Trust in the instruments was critical at this point and we have lost a number of pilots executing night strafe and not using the instruments effectively. Regardless, the gun was exciting in the day but nothing like it was at night. The barrel was behind our left shoulder and created a massive explosion of light, noise, and vibration at night. It got better as the heat coming off the bullets was picked up by the NVGs, displaying what looked like hundreds of small green lasers shooting out of our jet to the target. I had never seen anything more sci-fi in my life. Two seconds of fury followed by calm as my finger came off the trigger and I pulled away from the darkness toward the countless stars.

The daytime CAS (Close Air Support) ride was another great mission. Finally in a single seat jet again, I had a hilarious IPs as my flight lead with the flying callsign of Bikini. CAS has been the dominant mission of the last ten years in the Afghanistan and Iraq wars for the F-16. We set up in an orbit over a target area and got called in for airstrikes. On Thursday, the town of Sells, Arizona was the battleground. While its citizens were going about their day, we were targeting buildings and dropping simulated laser and GPS-guided bombs on them. It was a lot of fun to see structures, cars and people moving about through our targeting pod, more similar to a real war environment instead of the fake structures we normally bomb.

At one point I dropped a simulated laser guided bomb on the northeast corner of a building. I was zoomed in with the targeting pod, pulling the trigger to fire the safe laser and watching the bomb ftime-of-fall counter tick down to impact. About 15 seconds to go, a car pulled up in my thermal imagery screen and I watched this guy get out of his car, walk straight toward the door I was firing the laser at, and walk in. 2 seconds left, 1 second, "Bikini 2, splash." Timing is everything in this world and had this been real, it would have not been on his side.

I also executed my first moving target strafe on this ride. I had just dropped a bomb on what looked like a school in Sells that was holding the "insurgents." The guy pretending to be calling in the airstrikes got on the radio in a thick country accent for humor's sake, "Good hit! Good hit there, Bikini 2! Wait, it looks like we have some insurgents fleeing into buses and are driving to the east on the main road. Call contact two buses moving from west to east, just south of the building you just hit."

Me: "Bikini 2, contact."

Controller: "Alright Bikini, those are your targets. We need you to get them before they cross the bridge 3 miles to the east. Cleared hot, any direction."

It took every ounce of me to sarcastically respond, "Confirm you want me to shoot the two bright yellow buses that left the building, appearing to be full of schoolchildren on a field trip?" While I probably shouldn't make too much light of this, buses were an easier target for my first try at this strafe so it was better training. I can only imagine some ten-year-old kid daydreaming out the window with a couple of fighter jets rolling in and pointing his direction. Fortunately, and by design, we are pretty tough to see, especially at that height.

On another ride dropping a real laser-guided bomb, I happened to roll the wing up and watch it fall after releasing it. It was amazing how long I could keep the bomb in sight as it fell toward the target. It was a bit surreal as this chunk of steel raced toward earth relatively peacefully, before I began guiding it the last 10 seconds of its fall.

JETS LINED UP FOR TAKEOFF

PHOTO CREDIT: CHRISTIAN CULBERTSON

Lesson Learned: Disciplined Followership

From the moment a brief for a mission starts, there is silence from the other members of the team, regardless of their rank in relation to the flight leader unless he asks for questions. People aren't eating and there aren't phones or other distractions. In the air, wingman are also relatively quiet unless executing in accordance with the briefed game plan. There are times in the middle of battle the wingman can make a recommendation but they better be confident it is an appropriate course of action as every second of radio time is precious. Further, the flight lead always has the overall trump card and will be directive with the members of his flight when necessary. Imagine if shots are being fired in the fog of war and there is dissention among the team. Even if the leader's course isn't the most optimal, having the entire team on the same page is more important than a fractured unit with people acting individually.

Week 29: Sparkle

Another short week completed and it was all single seat rides from here on out which was a wonderful relief. It is hard to describe the annoyance of someone in the backseat watching and judging every action of every second. It was great to have them there teaching you but it was the same awkward feeling of having a video camera in your face, so it was nice to have that behind me.

The first ride this week was a four ship surface attack ride and I was in the #4 position. It was one of those rides coming off a three-day weekend where we all felt rusty. The IPs picked some tough targets within a city, which made everything more difficult. We were trying to hit small houses in neighborhoods full of similar looking houses. This meant we had to spend more time looking in the targeting pod trying to find the targets. It took time away from flying formation, calling up the right weapons, looking for enemy aircraft and other things we needed to get done. Ultimately, it was not a ride I was proud of. It wasn't terrible but I was feeling uncomfortable going into the debrief. From the other jet, my instructor was thinking it had been a solid ride. I'd always been in position and dropping bombs at the right time. But I was nervous for the debrief and tape review where he would see the details of where my bombs ended up and my actions, or lack thereof. As I was walking into the debrief, the guy at the front desk asked me to tell him how the video from my plane turned out and I jokingly said, "I hope the video didn't record cause that wasn't pretty."

Well wishes can come true as the targeting pod video failed to record. In many instances, this would mean I'd have to do the ride over again but the IP saw my last ride had gone well and he had no reason to believe this one went otherwise so I passed. Whew.

The second flight was awesome. It was a night CAS (close air support) ride and my first solo night flight since joining the Air Force. A pretty incredible statistic considering most our war fighting is at night. There was an actual JTAC (Joint Tactical Air Controller) on the ground calling in the air strikes. JTACs are guys embedded with army troops capable of speaking a pilot's language to get bombs and bullets on target in an efficient manner. My IP and I were in an orbit over the target area and they were using infrared laser pointers to identify targets on the ground. The moon was almost full and we could see the ground very well through the NVGs. The laser pointers were incredible to see. To the naked eye, it was as if nothing was going on, but through the NVGs, we could tell the JTAC to 'sparkle on' and we could see bright green lasers shooting miles into the desert at targets. We had a hot gun and in order to strafe the target the JTAC, perched on a hill, shot his laser onto a truck in the desert. Without actually seeing the truck, just the laser spot, we rolled in from 13,000 feet and put our gun sight on his laser spot and unloaded 200 rounds of 20 mm ammo, each bullet looking like a green laser shooting from the plane. It was interesting to get target descriptions from the ground, at night, versus a target description from an instructor in another jet. While looking at the same thing, the perspective is vastly different from the air creating an interesting challenge as we both try to describe what we are seeing.

Before every flight we established mission objectives and debriefed to them accordingly. Each flight had specific objectives for the type of mission but the lead objective was generally the same and had been for almost a year now. Kill and survive. It had taken me a year to realize what it was actually saying and that I had been training three years to simply kill and survive. Not many jobs quite like it and for being so technologically advanced, it is a primitive goal.

In more somber news, we lost the second student from our class on Friday. He was working his ass off but just couldn't get it together. It was a misinterpretation of a fuel-balancing problem on his last ride that did him in. It is a shame considering we were just a month away from graduation. Our class started with nine and was now down to seven—it was highly unusual to lose two from one small class.

Week 30: A Little Crazy

Week 30 was arguably the new best week of flying during my three year Air Force career.

My first four ship night ride was Monday and it was something to see that many jets in one piece of sky through the night vision goggles. The ride was all about dropping laser and GPS-guided bombs at night with more airplanes. It was a beautiful night with a full moon, making the NVGs work amazingly well.

The second ride of the week was quite an event. It was an opposed surface attack ride and my instructor was the base General. In other words, we had to fight through a wave of enemy aircraft, find our targets, drop the bombs, and then fight enemy aircraft that were scrambled in order to get home. It was easily the wildest ride I have been a part of.

The day prior we worked on the mission planning. We even had intelligence officers come over and brief us a scenario. The country of "Sells" is trying to invade the Phoenix metro area and they called upon us to drop bombs on a nuclear facility and weapons depot. We expected MIGs on the ingress and egress to the target with a few airfields on alert. Further, there was a surface-to-air missile threat, some of the SAMs we knew the location of, some we didn't. The amount of consideration given to all of these threats seemed almost infinite. It was the most dynamic hour of my life.

I wasted a simulated couple hundred grand on a missile when I shot chaff accidentally. Chaff, a cloud of thin pieces of aluminum, metallized glass fiber or plastic, appears as a cluster of targets on radar screens or swamps the screen with multiple returns. We dispense it to confuse radars and radar guided missiles. I locked up what I thought was a jet and even checked the speed to make sure it wasn't chaff. I saw 300 knots on the target so I took the shot and then looked back to find the General and get in formation. I never looked back to see the speed change but in the debrief we noticed the speed diminished to 70 knots, or the speed of the wind at that altitude. Damn.

At another point in the fight, our four ship had been separated into pairs. An enemy fighter, one we couldn't shoot until we visually identified him as an enemy, had spiked me, or locked me up with his radar as we were nearing. I was just supporting the general and didn't know exactly how far away we were from the enemy. Obviously his missile had a maximum range it could kill me but based on a gut feeling I assumed I was just outside of that range so I start a maneuver to break his lock. The General realized I was about a mile or two closer than I'd thought and told me to exit and run away instead of attempting this maneuver. Later in the debrief he made the comment, "You know my brother told me he thinks a lot of your mother and I have met your mother and I liked her as well. I decided I didn't want her to lose a son."

My jet also had a slight problem the entire flight. Not a big deal, but we had a fuel warning we could set to go off at whatever level of gas I inputted into the computer. On takeoff I had about 10,000 lbs of gas and had my warning set for 4,000 lbs. Right at the moment of liftoff, at about 160 knots, the warning went off. We spent a significant amount of time training for takeoff abort criteria and this, in my opinion, was clearly not worthy. I spent the next five minutes of departure deciding whether to tell the General. Some guys are very conservative and this entire flight, six jets and all of the preparation could be cancelled if he decided I should just land. I was less conservative and decided I would just monitor the fuel more closely than I would otherwise. Most of the time I was nervous about saying something over the radio for fear of showing ignorance. The flight went well and besides the warning randomly going off a few times, it was not a big deal.

Flash forward to the next evening when an instructor, who would be retiring in a couple weeks, was flying the same jet. On takeoff, he got the same warning I had but just a few knots slower at 130. He elected to abort. That's pretty high speed and we weigh a lot on takeoff due to the extra gas so stopping could be an issue. He put the hook down, mashed the brakes and blew both tires, closing down a runway for almost an hour. Just like watching football from your couch and criticizing the quarterback, many of our decisions and performance can be equally criticized. I rode the bus back to the squadron with him from the maintenance building and you could tell he was pretty disappointed with his choice. It probably didn't help when I tactfully mentioned I'd had the same 'annoyance' yesterday. Still learning when to keep my mouth shut.

During my flight Thursday night there were storms everywhere making for quite the epic battle. I was again #4 in a formation full of fun and relaxed instructors. It was my last night flight in the F-16 for a few months and I was feeling proficient so I really tried to enjoy any free second I had. On departure, I remembered I had this enormous 20-30-foot flame shooting out the back and twisted all around to see it from the cockpit. As we entered the clouds, I again wondered what that flame would do and lit the afterburner and this orange glow engulfed the small bubble that was my world at that moment.

I followed the three jets through the weather using my radar as we spiraled up in the airspace to get above the clouds so we could fight. We popped out at 24,000 feet to a beautiful shooting star-filled sky, a stark contrast to the rain and lightning below. It was normally difficult to feel the speed when we fought as we were so high but the clouds provided a floor we skimmed through as we intercepted and shot down these other jets before moving toward the target and dropping GPS-guided bombs. We even simulated dropping laser-guided bombs through the weather with a troop on the ground shooting the laser into the target. Once the bomb got through all of the weather, it would find the laser spot and guide toward the target.

My friend Eli, the same guy who had introduced me to the idea of the Guard but had decided to stay in consulting, came into town to check out the whole scene, flying the simulator, trying on night vision goggles and checking out the jets. After watching our night takeoffs on Thursday, I saw him about five hours later and he said his ears were still ringing from the noise and he wasn't prepared for the size of the flame. I would agree—it is one the most impressive things I have seen from the ground. If it doesn't make you feel a little patriotic, I am not sure what would.

Finally, at our pilot meeting, the leadership discussed the removal of the student last week. Knowing he was a very smart kid, they explained by saying, "we all have to be sharp, smart people to do this but we have to be a little crazy as well. Civilians have no idea how close we are to death at any given second when we are up there and it takes a certain person to do it. I didn't want to open the newspaper in a few years and see someone flew an F-16 into the side of a mountain and think to myself, 'I kind of saw that coming.'"

I'd never flown with the student they removed but I had to respect their judgement. Regardless, it was still a solemn time as we had lost one of the best guys in our class.

Week 31: Thank Gawd

A short week with a close air support flight and four ship simulator. I only had two more flights left in the B course.

The CAS (Close Air Support) ride was a wild time. We bounced around between various towns in the airspace getting calls from guys on the ground. Even though it was just training, the instructors really got into it, making gunfire noises and yelling in the radio as if they really were in distress. At one point the comm went something like this (we were Jasper 1 and 2):

Video 11 (Area Commander): Jasper snap heading 130, we have troops in contact, contact Cowboy on green 16 (a frequency) for talk-on.

Jasper 1: Push 16 [Change radio frequency to channel 16 as we are turning toward the heading].

Jasper 1: Cowboy, Jasper 1, two minutes out.

Cowboy: (Yelling and with static and sound of gunfire and heavy northeastern accent) Jasper! Thank gawd! We awe takin heavy fire ovva here. We have got multiple dudes down, we need 20 mike mike [20 millimeter strafe with the gun]!

He proceeded to tell us where he was by using landmarks and then where he wanted the bullets laid down. Further, he gave us restrictions for our attack heading, to lessen the chance of accidentally shooting a friendly. I will admit the intensity of the radio comm had my adrenaline pumping. It was amazing how badly I wanted to help and not let them down—and this was all made up. I can't even imagine if it had been real.

I got back to the landing pattern with a lot of extra gas and cruised around practicing patterns and simulated flame out landings until burning through the last drop of allowable fuel. I know when I am older and can no longer fly this jet I would be angry at myself for not taking full advantage of the time.

Two flights and a few more simulator rides left in the program. However, these were fun air-to-air sims where it was the four of us versus an unknown number of enemy airplanes. In one battle today, there were fourteen. I shot all of the missiles off my jet, twice. One thing the simulator can do better than the jet is actually seeing the missiles come off everyone's jet and aircraft exploding. My friends Eli and Nate each visited me during training and got to fly in these simulators. They are full 360-degree screens and the cockpits were identical to the jet except they didn't move. It was funny to hear their reactions after fighting for an hour. Nate had neck pain from twisting all around keeping jets in sight and Eli commented, "That was a lot more physical than I expected." And those were their reactions without experiencing the feeling of G-forces.

SHOT I TOOK ON A BACKSEAT RIDE DURING AN ECHELON TURN

Week 32: Vegas

Only one flight this week but it was a fun flashback to months prior when an IP and I had just fought each other 1v1. Anywhere from 1.5 miles down to 3000 feet behind each other when the "fights on" call was made, we did whatever it took to kill and not be killed, depending on who started behind who. All visual, this was the high G-force, trying-to-gun-each-other type fighting that is nothing but a good time. I found it less stressful as it was less about thinking strategically and more about feel and split second decisions. Sure, all the maneuvers were strategic to kill the other jet but a lot of instinct was required.

There were many mental images from this course I will never forget. One of these images occurred on this flight as I was the offensive fighter and while trying to evade me, the IP broke right and then climbed into a barrel roll. I essentially followed him and we ended up rolling around each other. The whole world was spinning wildly around us but relative to me, his F-16 was stationary. It was an amazing sight.

We continue to have these incredibly fun simulator rides. Two instructors and two students got into the four simulators and the person running the simulation threw all kinds of enemy jets at us to seek and destroy. I was always taught to say simulators suck and they usually do, compared to flying, but these were a good time.

Finally, this was the week of our squadron Vegas trip. Each class took a trip to Nellis AFB and checked out the "petting zoo." The petting zoo was a collection of all kinds of enemy weapons. Surface-to-air missiles, tanks, airplanes and other toys were available for us to learn about and play with. Further, we got briefings on the future of the F-16, the F-35 and aggressor squadrons at Nellis. An aggressor squadron's purpose is to fly only like the enemy does. It was an amazing world I had never even considered. They even had foreign-looking name tags all while studying, flying and employing only like potential enemies. The coolest part of the trip for me was seeing all of the various fighter jets flying around. There are typically only one or two jets stationed at each base. At Nellis there were F-16s, F-15s, F-22s, F-35s, A-10s and more. I could watch jets take off and land all day and this place was the best. Finally, we went out on the strip as a squadron and that was quite a scene. We had an honorary Squadron Commander who was a wealthy local businessman who came to most of our social functions. I am not sure of his past but he had private jets and was a very generous guy. We went to a steakhouse with $80 steaks and with all of the drinks included for 30 guys, he paid the bill along with flying some of the instructors up in his jet. Unreal how supportive the community can be.

RIDING A SAM AT THE PETTING ZOO

Week 33: Large Force Exercise

With one last event in the program being the large force exercise, I will give an in-depth look on what an F-16 training mission really is like. I hope you enjoy.

I walk up to jet and my crew chief approaches, carrying a black binder containing the jet's maintenance information. He snaps to attention and salutes, I return the gesture and we exchange pleasantries. I am wearing the conventional green flight suit along with the new G-suit, covering most of my lower body from the belly button down. I also have a harness that hooks into the ejection seat with a bag hanging from it, carrying three pieces of classified data I will put in the jet. When this data is outside our vault it is always either connected to us or in the jet. I am also carrying my helmet bag with all of my flight papers, including overall war information, target photos, area map and a GPS bomb attack card.

Normally, I try to have a decent conversation with the crew chief as I review the maintenance information to make sure it looks correct and up-to-date but I am behind schedule. I thumb through about ten pages worth of dates, problems, inspections and corrections the jet has gone through and it passes my passive evaluation. Maybe one in ten maintenance forms have a slight problem needing correction before I fly. I return the forms and start my preflight of the jet. I plug two recording devices into the exterior of the jet to monitor the jet and my actions. I do the rest of my walk-around, checking various hydraulic pressures, fluid levels, the security of missiles on the wing and overall condition. The crew chief has already done all of this in greater detail but ultimately, I am the one flying this machine so I have the final say. There are no actual bombs on the jet today but I will load two GBU-31s (2000 lb GPS-guided bombs) in the jet's computer so I can simulate dropping them.

Preflight looks good and I stand by the ladder, checking the engine start time and realize I am already a minute past. Shit. I quickly zip up the comfort zippers on the G-suit which makes it snug and take the two harness straps between my legs and up the front—very uncomfortable if not done properly, especially for men. If I forget this step and eject, I will fall rather quickly back to earth as my harness floats down under a parachute. I grab the helmet bag and carefully climb up the ladder. Sitting on the edge of the jet, I lay the helmet on the far side of the cockpit on the rail. I take the papers and checklist I am going to use and put them under elastic straps on the G-suit. Cockpit organization is critical as once you are strapped in, it is difficult to move around.

I carefully slide into the seat as the crew chief climbs the ladder to help me strap in. Some of the straps are pretty difficult to reach if you aren't freakishly flexible and I am in a hurry. Two seat kit clips by my waist: click. G-suit to the left: connected. Main seatbelt and shoulder clips for the parachute that the crew chief hands me: check. I already know I am going to pee before takeoff as this is supposed to be the longest flight, 2.5 hours, of the B course, so I keep some of the straps pretty loose. I thank the crew chief and he hops down, removing the ladder as I finish connecting the oxygen hoses to my harness. I run through pre-start checks and throw the helmet on, connecting the comm cords.

The crew chief plugs a cord into the jet and we are talking. I am in a hurry so I let him know I am already ready to start, five minutes late. Tardiness really matters today because of the Large Force Exercise (LFE). 16+ jets all needing to be in the same airspace at the same time and we need to get bombs on target on time. This tardiness just means I will have to expedite my checks on the ground to hopefully make time for a bathroom break. Flying fast jets is about "staying ahead of the jet," or getting things done before you need to because so much is going on. Little things like a bathroom break could really cause problems later when you can't afford to spend time thinking about them.

The chief clears me to start and I hit the switch. A separate motor spins the engine up for a minute before I add fuel and the main engine spools up. Three switches and the engine is running. I watch the engine temperature gauge to make sure the start is not overheating or a couple other anomalies I have seen only in simulation and this one is no exception. Once at idle power, I lower the canopy of the jet and begin a lot of switch flipping. Many of the preflight checks are done talking with the crew chief as he is looking over the jet as well.

After getting through all of the normal checks with the chief, we usually have about ten minutes to set up our avionics and weapons. Today, as soon as I clear him off, I hear on the radio, "Roar check"—pause—"three" and I reply with "four," indicating I am ready to go. Two didn't respond meaning something isn't right. The #2 guy is Hawk, going to the same unit as me after the B-course. 44 months ago to the day we were hired to fly the F-16 and here we are, on our last flight in the B-Course in the same flight. With all of the attrition, medically and from performance, it is unusual to have gone through every phase of training with someone. After not hearing from him, we delay a couple minutes and fortunately he checks in, saying his jet had a bad start and he is about five minutes behind. Lead tells him the three of us will taxi without him and he can join us in the arming area. I give the signal to the crew chief that I am ready to taxi and he begins marshalling me out of the sun shade. As I taxi by, he snaps to attention, saluting me and then giving me our squadron symbol, a boxer's standard fighting position with his fists. I return the salute and symbol and taxi by.

The taxi out to the runway for takeoff and back after landing is usually a pretty relaxed time where I get to remind myself what I am getting to do. I had an instructor in the T-6 who would always exclaim, "can you believe we are getting paid to do this?!" each flight as we taxied back. This thought stuck with me these last few years. Further, there is a high likelihood of doing something stupid or running into something so they encourage us to do nothing else but focus on taxiing. Today is a bit of an exception; I am behind on my checks and still have bladder concerns. I am checking the bomb settings, setting up what some of the switches do on the stick and throttle, fuel warnings, navigation instruments for departure, missile and gun settings, and a myriad of other settings and checks. I am following the two other jets in my flight as we pull into the arming area. A crew of about six guys marshal us in. I set the parking brake and they go around the jet, preparing it for flight and combat. I honestly don't know what really goes on but they check over the jet, pull pins arming the chaff and flares and if I have real bombs, get those ready to go.

Hawk finally calls for taxi, which means I have about five minutes. Perfect. I dig into my helmet bag stuffed behind my right arm and pull out the piddle pack. This will be attempt number three in the plane and I don't even need to go but know this might be my last chance. I turn down the heads up display and disconnect all of the straps. The dimmed HUD is a reminder that I need to connect everything back up. Sparing you the details here, the relief goes uneventfully and I secure the bag as much as possible for obvious reasons and hide it in the back of the helmet bag. I strap back in and put my gloves on with a new wave of confidence and give a thumbs up to #3 which he passes down the line, indicating we are all ready to go. Lead checks us in on the tower frequency and they clear us for takeoff on runway 03R.

I quickly run through my final checks including a note of the time, turning the landing light, transponder, and pitot heat on and arm the ejection seat. The rubber handle between my legs is now ready to launch me out of the jet with just a ~25 lb tug. It was an unnerving feeling the first few flights with your hands always so close to something so dangerous. We change to departure frequency before taking off and lead checks us in before he blasts, "Roar check, 2, 3, 4." Check-ins are generally said as quickly and coolly as possible because well, we are fighter pilots, and we are always supposed to sound cool on the radio.

Flight lead starts his takeoff roll and you can faintly see the flame coming out the back of the jet as the afterburner lights. Twenty seconds go by and Hawk's afterburner lights. We are doing a twenty second interval takeoff and rejoining to a formation that, from above, looks like a rhombus with a jet in each of the corners. As three starts his roll I take a glance at the clock, 18:32:45. Cool—I'll blast at :05 after. Being #4, I have to catch up to everyone and must waste more gas so I choose to cheat by a couple seconds. I note my rotation speed of 155 knots and briskly move the throttle all the way forward, glance at the oil pressure to check for at least a 15 psi rise and then twist the throttle toward the outside of the plane, pushing it even further into full afterburner. There is slight pause before a nice kick in the butt as the burner lights. Our first simulator instructor told us that if we don't yell "Yeeehaw!" on every afterburner takeoff, we are wrong.

Quickly accelerating through 100 knots, I give the engine instruments one last glance before choosing to take it airborne. This is probably the most dangerous moment of the flight because in relation to the ground you are going fast, but in relation to the air, very slow, both the opposite of what you want if you have a problem, especially in a jet with one engine and wings so small. The rumble of the runway's imperfections under the gear add to the feeling of speed and stress of the takeoff. 145 knots. As I approach 150, I gently ease back on the stick to put the nose 10 degrees high above the horizon. The stick in the F-16 only moves a quarter of an inch in any direction and you really just need to think about what you want to do to make the jet do it. It is more about pounds of pressure to make the jet respond to your inputs. Takeoff is a relatively light pull-back and then ease back forward to capture ten degrees. Before you know it, the rumble and tension of takeoff turns to a smooth peaceful glide and the jet is rapidly accelerating.

By about 190 knots, I reach forward and lift the gear handle. I wait from about 160 to 190 knots just in case the engine happens to eat a bird or have another problem. I could possibly still land it back down on the runway, put the hook down, and catch the cable laying across the runway like they do on carriers. The flaps automatically come up and I anxiously watch to make sure the gear is up by 300 knots. It takes it about six seconds to retract and extend the gear fully and on a cool day like today, 300 knots comes quickly. The light in the gear handle goes out to indicate the gear is up and I cancel afterburner at 300 knots. My fuel flow immediately goes from 50,000 lbs of gas per hour to 10,000. Five times as much fuel for 40% more performance.

The jet is purring along now and you can really feel the speed as I am accelerating to about 375-400 knots, just a thousand feet above the subdivisions of Phoenix. I glance down, remembering this is my last flight for a couple months and the last of the B course I had dreamed and read about for years. I look out and identify the three other jets in our formation, all now wildly moving about the sky as we are making turns for the departure procedure. I no longer can tell who is one or two but three is my element lead and I just need to rejoin on him. I could lock him up with my radar but then he would have an annoying indication in his cockpit and it would tell him I "needed" the assistance to rejoin so I abstain and do it just by feel.

We all form into this rhombus-like formation, one mile apart from each other and I set the autopilot. A lot of guys don't use it but I do as much as I can. It allows me to get things done without having to worry about my altitude. Every few seconds I still must glance at the other jets. One mile sounds like a long distance but at those speeds it can disappear quickly and our biggest threat is running into each other. I look inside the cockpit and check the fuel quantities of the various tanks in the jet to make sure fuel isn't getting stuck somewhere. I also open the targeting pod and look around at various houses and buildings to focus the camera. Air traffic control keeps changing our altitudes by small increments which is frustrating as I have to keep turning the autopilot on and off as I do various other checks.

Hawk is directly in front of me and I lock him up with the radar. My AIM-9 missile is making a growl noise, meaning it sees a heat source that it's ready to guide on. I uncage the missile with a button on the throttle and, just like in *Top Gun*, I get good tone. I hit the pickle button and simulate a launch. A few seconds later Hawk is simulated dead. Flip another switch and I call up the AMRAMM, a radar guided missile and shoot him again. Sweet, all of my weapons seem to be working just fine. Just as I finish these checks I feel my feet buzzing a little from some form of a vibration. This is more vibration than I have ever experienced and as I glance at the oil pressure, it is fluctuating about 7 psi which is just within the 10-psi limit but the most I have ever seen. I move the throttle around a little and it continues to do the same thing. I make a note to keep a close eye on it.

About this time the weather starts getting worse and since we are heading to a tanker before the fight, we are definitely going to be climbing through these clouds. Flight lead elects to have #2 rejoin in close, to within a few feet of him. He has #3 lock him up on the radar and fly in one-mile trail, basically just following him as he climbs through the clouds while I rejoin on #3 to within a few feet. Close enough that even flying through clouds I can still see him. It is challenging and fun for a while but it is also very tiresome. You are reacting by the millisecond to everything that happens in relation to his jet. Get too close and hitting him is obviously a problem but if I get too far away and can't see him through the clouds I cause a lot of problems for everyone, especially myself. Clouds often make it turbulent which makes it even more wild flying so close. This goes on for quite some time as we climb all the way through 26,000 feet in fingertip formation. While this is physically tiresome, I will never grow tired of the opportunity to fly next to a fighter. From my perspective, I have a face full of F-16 and a purely white background. I can see nothing except the pure white of cloud. I honestly can't even tell which way is up. For some reason we go to this refueling track well south of Tucson and it takes quite a while to get there. Now I am flowing at my discretion between fingertip and route position which is out to 500 feet away from the other jet to give myself some rest. Looks like clouds are approaching? I move in close. Clear skies ahead? I widen it out.

Finally we enter the tanker airspace. Coder 11 is the tanker callsign and there is a four ship of Vipers already getting gas ahead of us so he clears us to a trail position behind for a half-mile. Two tankers are being used for this large exercise—the other is about 8,000 feet below us at 18,000 feet. As we are cleared up to the left wing, Claw 4 is getting his gas and all of a sudden, a relatively large amount of gas comes streaming out of his left wing. This white cloud is constant, thick and at 310 knots, quickly moving aft. No one says anything. Talking with the other students after the flight, each of us desperately wanted to let him know but realized there were six instructors in their own jet also choosing not to say anything so I guess this is normal?

For a couple of minutes there are eight F-16s around this tanker before Claw flight departs for the fight. Flight lead gets on the boom and actually struggles, disconnecting three or four times. Then it's Hawk's turn and he is struggling as well, disconnecting four or five times. Meanwhile I am last just hanging out watching all of this off the wing of number three. Three slides down once Hawk is done and gets all of his gas. Once an offload of fuel is complete the boom retracts, the jet slides back and then onto the right wing of the tanker. When the boom re-extends, they are telling me they are ready for me to get gas. I silently slide down from the wing of the tanker to about 20 feet behind the boom extending from the refueler. In an unnerving maneuver, I put the boom right in front of my windshield and drive straight ahead at it. At the last moment before my canopy hits it, the boom operator swings it to the side and I, by feel, decide when I think it's at the right spot and crack the power back to stop the forward momentum. You can feel it plug into the hole and once it does, lights underneath the tanker turn on to give me information about my position and I am able to freely talk to the boomer without having to key the mic.

THE ACTUAL SHOT OF US TANKING ON THIS FLIGHT. HAWK IS GETTING GAS AND I AM AT THE TOP OF THE SHOT AS #4

After getting my gas, I pull back from the tanker and rejoin with my flight on the right wing as the tanker clears us off. We have a 20-minute drive to the airspace for the big fight and having already flown an hour, I am in need of that second piddle pack. I pull it out of my bag in eager anticipation for this relaxing 20 minutes when I realize the weather is getting worse again. If they would let me lock them up with my radar and fly a couple miles behind this would be no problem but they elect to keep me in close just as they had on departure. There is no chance for a restroom break when I am that close to another jet. Talking with Hawk after the flight, he wasn't able to use the restroom in the arming area before takeoff or at any other point in the flight and described it as the worst pain he has ever experienced.

We make the 20-minute drive in and out of fingertip position, approaching the largest and most complex battlefield I will have experienced in my career thus far. I have a couple target maps and airspace depiction on my left leg and I am beginning to study them in my free time. #1 and #2 are a mile in front of us and are producing the contrails you often see from airliners overhead. Flying directly behind them, we are flying in and out of them which was a cool sensation. The clouds were forming about halfway between us and them, and you could see them expanding as we flew around them. I look forward and see my HUD randomly flicker and disappear.

Three seconds later it reappears. Odd and potentially a serious problem for weapon employment but I won't say anything yet. These jets are old and we just get used to knowing when something is worth mentioning and not. The one I am flying today was built in 1984, two years my senior.

We are just a few miles from entering the airspace and air traffic control switches us to the tactical frequency. Callsign Snakeye, he gives us an overview of the different flights in the airspace and any civilian traffic that might be a factor. He passes us along to the fight frequency where I truly learn the importance of brevity and why we have an entirely different language to describe things. On this one frequency there are twelve aircraft, the air battle managers on the ground observing the fight from the God's eye view, and a couple of other guys on the ground pretending to be various other assets that would be present in a war.

Using the United States as a reference for the airspace again, our target is Salt Lake City and we entered from the east coast. Bad guy country starts around Alabama, running north to south. We have a specific window of time to drop our bombs so we begin capping, or holding a position over, Washington D.C., Atlanta and Miami. My flight held over D.C.; Claw flight, also dropping bombs, held over Miami; and Spike flight, an offensive counter air escort, over Atlanta. Spike flight will push five minutes before the other two flights loaded with more missiles and no bombs to defeat the air threat. I have four missiles as well, but my main job is to put bombs on target. A few minutes before the push we get the 'lowdown.' They give us an overview of the airspace, highlighting locations of surface-to-air missiles that are active. I mark down on the map where they are located to the best of my ability but am flying relatively close to #3 as we orbit, making it difficult to do anything other than deconflict from him. We have SAM sites, an SA-2 and SA-3 in the target area and an SA-6 actively radiating over Albuquerque. This was the type of SAM responsible for shooting down the F-16 in Bosnia. Just before the fight starts we do a G exercise, turning the jet 90 and then 180 degrees under progressively higher Gs to essentially warm us up and make sure we are feeling ok to be aggressively maneuvering. We also check our flares, dispensing one each to make sure the system is working.

The battle starts and Spike flight pushes west. Claw and Roar (me) will spin one or two more times to give them a head start. About this time, the radios start going crazy as the air war begins. Initial call sounds something like this:

"Venom, Spike, picture."

"Venom picture. 3 group champagne 10 wide, 25 deep, South Lead group bullseye 180/50, 2 contacts, 25,000, hostile. North lead group, 2 contacts, 23,000, hostile. Trail group range 20, 24,000, hostile."

This initial call describes the enemy formation and ultimately determines the game plan we use to target and attack them. Today the weather is causing some significant issues. There are layered clouds from 15,000 up to 25,000 feet and we can't fight or legally go in the clouds in this airspace. All of the air-to-air fighting is going on above the weather and we, the strikers, are flying below the weather.

The radio is a constant chatter of shots and picture/threat calls from Venom, the air battle manager. Even if I wanted to say something, it would be difficult at this point. As strikers, we keep pressing west into bad guy territory. My flight lead told #2 and me if either of us ever go blind, or lose sight of our element lead at this critical time as we press toward the target with all of the radio chatter, he would probably just tell us to go home. It would be too difficult and detrimental to spend time on the radio to locate the wingman who couldn't do his primary job of staying visual when guys are getting shot at by other jets and SAMs. I chuckled at the thought in the brief but it is serious. As a wingman, we aren't making strategic-level decisions, we are basically a weapon and they need us to be there, ready to employ when called upon. Fortunately, the clouds are making it easier to see him with the white backdrop.

We continue to press west, listening to Spike flight, our offensive counter air, seriously do great work above us. I am anxiously waiting for any opportunity to shoot but they are cleaning up. At 15 miles from the target with a clean radar picture, we switch to an air-to-ground mentality. About that moment, I get a terrible metal grinding/radio static noise in my headset followed by alarming beeps. I glance down at the gauge to see an indication that an SA-2 is engaging me. We have actual devices on the ground capable of simulating a shot at us and make our plane think we are getting engaged for training just as it would in real life. I exclaim, "Roar 4, Singer 2, 270, defending north!" I light the afterburner and begin a maneuver to defeat the radar lock and missile. For almost a minute I am performing this 5G maneuver involving a decent amount of turning, rolling and dispensing chaff. Finally the indication goes away and later, in the debrief, I discover a missile was shot at me. Fortunately, my maneuver defeated it. Alright! The adrenaline is pumping now and I get back in formation and we press toward the target.

I have two GBU-31s which are 2000 lb GPS-guided bombs. We are going in to destroy the same SAM site that just engaged me. I am about a mile and a half away from #3 and we have lost #1 and #2. It's fine—they will run in first and we will follow a few miles behind with our bombs. I start running through my checks to make sure the bomb will hit the target. I have already triple-checked the coordinates and now I am checking that the bombs are ready to drop and I have a good GPS signal. All is going well as my HUD flickers off again for the same three seconds and reappears. Weird, but there is no time to do anything about it now. We hear Roar one and two get their bombs off and I start to get a little nervous. If I do everything right the entire flight but screw this up, we fail the mission. About 10 miles away I start to pick up the target area in the targeting pod. We enter the window to drop the bombs and I hit the red pickle button. I get the indication of the first bomb away and quickly change to another target, having only about four seconds to get the second bomb off because we are forced lower due to weather. The second bomb is now away and I don't think I have screwed anything up. We light the afterburner, roll into about 120 degrees of bank and perform a 5G, 180-degree U-turn to get the hell out of there. It is not advisable to hang around an area you just bombed. We use terms like stirring the hornets' nest as you, too, would be pretty pissed off if 8,000 lbs of American steel just destroyed a lot of your toys.

I move a switch, called the dogfight switch, from the air-to-ground position to the air-to-air position and all of the symbology changes in the HUD and I now have a radar-guided missile ready to go. There is an enemy airfield over Denver and chances are high they are going launch aircraft in retaliation and we need to be ready to take them out. I frantically move my cursors around on the radar hoping to see hits and be the hero with a shot. We fly northeast and start circling over Minneapolis, always having someone pointing their radar at the Denver airfield to watch for enemy jets taking off.

Both Roar 3 and I get targeted by the SA-6 and we both start reacting together as I did for the previous missile attack. This time, it doesn't launch. Roar 1 and 2 are low on gas and start heading east to find friendly airspace. We have numerous predetermined fuel levels to ensure we can execute the various aspects of the mission. Let's say with 7,000 lbs, I can fly from D.C. to Utah and back while assuming I have to use the afterburner for a while to get away from a SAM. If I am below the predetermined push fuel before we push west from D.C., I don't get to fight. As we are now orbiting Minneapolis, I still have about 800 lbs until my Bingo fuel, the fuel I need to start heading back to Luke.

All of a sudden, an enemy jet launches off Denver, simulating a Mig-21. Venom, the air battle manager, notifies us. "Roar 3, Venom, pop-up group bullseye 160 36, 25,000, hostile." I am fired up. We turn the formation to look for him. I start slewing my radar, tilting it up. One of the most difficult things about this large exercise is there are jets everywhere and it is difficult to tell the good guys from the bad guys. We must do it by correlating the location Venom calls with the location our radar is indicating hits. If they don't match, you would probably be shooting another allied force. Just as I find the match and am waiting to hear whether I am supposed to shoot or whether #3 will, we hear that damn Spike flight, Spike #2, take a shot on the Mig. He gets the kill and the enemy is suppressed. Good news—but yours truly wants to be the guy taking that shot.

Just after that, the last bombing package releases their bomb and the mission commander calls "Millertime," meaning it's time for everyone to get the hell out of there. All of the assets flow east and we discover Roar 1 and 2 are just across the border and have enough gas to wait for us so we can return as a four ship. We find them, and again, get in one-mile trail and do a battle damage check as we head toward Luke. During a battle damage check, we simply get close to the other jet and fly around and underneath him to see if he sustained any damage during the battle or has anything that doesn't look right. There are hundreds of things that could be wrong with the jet even in a peacetime battle like this and occasionally you will notice something requiring attention.

After the battle damage check, they position the formation just like they did on departure in the rhombus-looking shape. It is pretty quiet overall, especially compared to what we just encountered with air traffic control giving us the occasional traffic point-out. A small propeller plane flies pretty close to our formation and I lock him up on the radar. I display the target pod on the screen over my right knee and it slews to where the targeting pod is looking and I can see the Bonanza through the infrared image. I have autopilot on and am relaxing and taking it all in. As my last flight here, I know I did a solid job and have nothing really to fear at this point with regards to failing the ride. We call ahead to our squadron and tell them the maintenance conditions of our jets. I am code one, which means no problems, but Roar 1 is code two with a radar issue.

As we approach Luke, lead rejoins all four jets to a close formation, echelon left. Being #4, they say it's like being on the end of a whip. Flight lead flies as steady as possible but #2 is constantly tweaking to stay in the perfect formation you would see the Thunderbirds in, with 3-feet wingtip clearance. #3 is adjusting off both of those jets and then I have to adjust off all three. So if #2 bobbles, #3 will probably bobble a little more and then I am on the end having to deal with the aggregate error. #2 does a great job and I'm sure we looked good from the ground. Lead gives the signal to take five-second spacing and then either waves, salutes, or jokingly flips us off and aggressively banks his jet up and pulls away from the formation in a circle to land. Five seconds gives us enough spacing on the runway, 3,000 feet, to safely make our own landing and not have to worry about the other jets too much. Five seconds later, #3 breaks away from me and I continue driving straight head. Being last, I add another second or two as I had an extra 1,000 lbs of gas and want to light the afterburner in celebration and really G it up for the turn. That low, at an altitude I have never fought at due to safety, the jet is still accelerating under six Gs. It is awesome. I snap the throttle back to idle on downwind, throw the speed brakes out and put the gear down at 290 knots so I don't close on #3. Turns out, we all did the same celebratory break.

ACTUAL SHOT OF US COMING UP INITIAL ON THIS LAST FLIGHT OF THE F-16 B-COURSE

For the last time, I make my, "Roar 4, base, gear down, stop, left" call and tower clears me to land. I fan the speed brakes after checking three green lights for a safe gear indication and check the hydraulic pressure indication. It is about a 45-degree bank turn at 190 knots the entire way around the final turn to line up with the runway. I know about what speed, based on my weight, I should fly on the final approach but I mainly fly off an instrument called the angle-of-attack indicator. Touching down 500 feet down the runway at 150 knots, I hold the nose off, like a wheelie, for as long as I can until the nose falls aerodynamically at about 85 knots. After testing to make sure the brakes work, I coast until needing to pull off the taxiway. After clearing the runway, I run the after-landing checks. I disarm the ejection seat so I don't accidentally launch myself out of the jet, close the speed brakes and turn the light and transponder off. The traffic pattern is very busy now as all the jets are returning. We taxi to the de-arming area and they pin our landing gear, flares and everything else. Hawk and I are parked next to each other and it only takes a simple nod of approval to say what we are both thinking after three years of training together and doing what we just did in our own F-16s.

The taxi back is uneventful and the crew chief marshals me back into my spot. We go through the shutdown procedure and I climb out, taking a little more time as I walk around the jet, looking it over and pulling out the recording devices. I am stiff, having been secured in the same position for the last three hours. I am also sweaty after the Gs and adrenaline rush during the fight. I have never tired of the post flight walk around of this jet, especially after a good flight. The crew chief approaches me, hands me the maintenance logs, shakes my hand, snaps to attention and renders the salute. I return the salute, thank him, and my final mission is over.

The debrief had multiple layers due to the scale of the battle. At first we were in an auditorium with about 30 of us to watch the events unfold and determine when jets were shot down and if the targets were bombed. The mission commander brought in a cooler full of beer as the mission seemed very successful. Ultimately, we lost three of fourteen jets to SAMs but all the targets were successfully bombed. Finally, we split off and had our own flight debrief with just the four members of Roar flight, going over what went well and what we could have improved on. Ultimately, #3, my instructor, pulled me aside to say he pleased with my performance and that I would make a great wingman.

Passing this ride marked the end of three years of flying and passing every flight and simulator mission I was assigned. At each phase of training they said we would all hook rides and it was a great feeling to continually prove them wrong. There was no recognition for this as it would be hard to know about prior training courses but the personal satisfaction was more than enough. It is not that I was better than the rest—I would say I was of similar capability to three or four guys in my class—I just managed to never do the critically dumb thing necessary to fail a ride.

Lesson Learned: Mission Planning Cycle

Missions can be important, wildly complex and dangerous. Being effective can save your life and the ideals we fight for. Because of this, properly planning, executing and debriefing is critically important and the foundation of being a lethal fighter pilot.

Mission planning involves setting objectives, gathering intelligence and then formulating a strategy or game plan for a mission. What type and how many enemy fighters are we expecting? Where are the surface-to-air missiles located? What type of tactics do we expect from them? What is the political situation and when can we attack? Any time you walk into a meeting, asking as many questions beforehand to gain an advantage over the person across the table and thinking through contingencies can be the difference in success and failure. If the objective is to sell something you would need to determine the entire competitive landscape. What is more important to this specific client? What are the assets you can bring to the negotiating table? The list is endless but must be thoroughly thought through. We have extensive checklists to make sure we cover all of the details.

In the hour before getting suited up to go fly, the flight leader briefs the mission, our game plan and tactics to meet our objectives. He talks about the basics of all starting on time and taxiing together as a formation to giving examples of enemy maneuvers and how we will fight them. Getting your team on the same page with showing up on time, dressed appropriately, with the projector working all creates an image of your brand. When briefing, consider giving examples of client reactions to various parts of the presentation and how that will be addressed. What if they start looking uninterested? What if price is keeping them from saying yes? If your entire team can seamlessly respond with confidence because the orchestration was talked through beforehand, the results will undoubtedly be more positive. You should also talk through contingencies such as a projector not working or other potential administrative issues. The brief always concludes with a reminder of the objectives, the reason to fight.

Effective execution comes from acting in accordance with the brief. You must recognize the changing battlefield and react based on the brief, the training and experience you have previously acquired. The wingmen, or other members of your team, need to know their time and place to step in and fight from what you briefed and know their material. The nerves disappear if you prepared properly.

The debrief is a sacred learning environment where pilots of all ranks and experience levels meet as equals with the sole purpose of improving themselves and their team. Arguably the most important part of the mission, the debrief can last over six hours for a fight of just thirty minutes. It is a thorough evaluation of the successes and failures of mission planning, the brief, the leader's tactical game plan and each member's execution. It is led by the flight leader and a tone of owning up to personal mistakes is crucial to removing other team member's defensive guards. No one likes to publicly admit mistakes but when the leader begins by pointing at himself, the environment will be more conducive to openness.

Week 34: Fighter Pilot

Week 34 was possibly the last week of a formal flying training course I would ever enjoy in the Air Force. Poetically similar to the first week, it was all academics and two sims as we began a transition to our next jets. While they are all F-16s, they had different avionics and more powerful engines so we were taught the differences, most notably, the helmet-mounted-cuing system. The heads-up display (HUD) normally presented on a glass pane in front of us could be displayed on the visor attached to our helmet. Without getting too technical or divulging the actual capability, imagine just looking at the target and shooting a missile instead of having to point the entire jet at him. It is an amazing and lethal technology.

The rest of the week was preparing for and enjoying graduation. My family arrived on Thursday night and the festivities began Friday morning. The seven students and their families all joined at the squadron as our commander gave a small presentation, outlining the course we just went through. They gave out the first awards and I came away with Air-to-Air Top Gun. Basically, this was saying that through all of the dogfighting and air-to-air combat beyond visual range, I had scored the best throughout the class. There was also one for Top Air-to-Ground that my roommate won. This brief was also the first time I was called a fighter pilot by an active fighter pilot. To a civilian, it would be difficult to tell the difference. Previously, I was a qualified F-16 pilot. As of today, I am a qualified American F-16 fighter pilot. It was the most rewarding moment of the day for me and I doubt anyone even noticed.

The families walked out to look at the jets and were even able to climb around on the wings which made for a cool family picture. They also got into a simulator which was an actual cockpit set inside a full 360-degree image. While it didn't move, the screen did, enough to make some people sick. Before getting in, I demonstrated with a mock stick and throttle to explain the basics. With hundreds of switch combinations in that cockpit, we focused on five as they only had fifteen minutes to figure out how to fly a machine that had taken me seven months: more power, less power, shooting the gun, shooting missiles and talking on the radio.

Leela, my seven-year-old cousin was the only one with questions after my brief and they were of genuine concern. "So what if we don't shoot the bad guys and they shoot us? Will we die? So if we eject, where will we land? Could we land on a cactus? How will they know how to find us?" While the simulator did a decent job of simulating flight, I was obviously not clear enough on its limitations.

Following the sims, we got a tour of air traffic control and the tower and watched eight jets blast from a unique angle. This was after watching the afterburner takeoffs Thursday night, which I argue is the most impressive thing you can see from the ground. The flame extends out the back of the jet 20 to 30 feet which looks, sounds and feels incredible.

Throughout the day my family, and the family of others, would ask us how we feel to be graduating. My natural response was of pride but also not overly excited. This day had been planned for months and my learning would continue, starting next month. This was just a part of the journey, not a jarring change in life like getting hired had been. Getting hired had evoked a wild, "can't sleep," excitement, but this graduation was the culmination of three years of hard work. While a whole lot of awesome was still ahead, a lot was behind me. However, I will sheepishly admit if you gave me a few minutes to think about where I was, I would still get pretty excited. Not one year ago I was dying to be in this position. Not four years ago, fighter pilots were gods to me and were in a position that seemed unreachable. After the difficulty of getting hired, the months of waiting, the hundreds of flights, tests and sims where everything was critiqued and evaluated, it was a pretty sweet feeling to be on the other end of that dream. I shall stop there before I make anyone nauseous.

Finally, graduation arrived. It included the standard cocktail hour, toasts, dinner and speeches with the highlight being our squadron commander introducing us as America's newest fighter pilots. My roommate and I essentially split the awards for the class. In addition to the Air-to-Air Top

Gun, I came away with the Top Academic award and The Red River Rats, a fighter pilot heritage organization, gave me the Jinxx Mitchell Wingman Warrior Award. Voted on by our instructors, the award recipient was the student they would choose to be on their wing if we went to war tomorrow. At the end of the day, that was what this business was all about. Of anything I had ever received in my life, I was most proud of this award.

So after three years and 2–4 million dollars' worth of fun later, my initial qualification as a fighter pilot was over. I would now move to Sioux Falls, SD and the operational fighter squadron.

THE FAMILY ON THE WING DURING GRADUATION DAY

PART 6: MISSION QUALIFICATION TRAINING

Soda Straws

I stopped my weekly writing after I returned to Sioux Falls and this was my first update in three months, now April of 2014. I was ten flights in and three away from being mission qualified for combat in the F-16. Overall, the flying and experience had continued the trend of improvement as I moved along in my Air Force career. Hawk and I were treated with far more respect and our performance in training the last three years had not gone unnoticed which made life easier as they knew they could trust us to get things done.

This jet had significantly more power than the one I flew in Phoenix. Based on engine specs it had only around 16% more power, but combined with the colder air up here, the results continued to amaze me. From takeoffs in afterburner to more Gs while fighting, I could really feel the difference and it could cause quite the grin. My fourth ride was a high aspect dogfight which meant we started the fight pointing at each other, passing within 1,000 feet and 1,000 knots of closure. It is the highest G-force type of fighting we do. They always said this was the most dangerous type of fighting with respect to blacking out from the Gs, especially if you fought, got low on gas, air-to-air refueled, and fought some more. Well this was exactly what we did and on my 7th fighting set (we normally did 3 or 4), I started the fight a little fast and pulled 9.1 Gs at the initial turn, the highest I had seen in the actual plane. Already exhausted from the previous fights, I saw the light in my vision start to disappear and was down to a soda straw of vision left before I eased off the G a little to bring it back. I felt fine all the way home through landing but once I shut the engine down, my body shut down as well. I felt drunk trying to get out of the plane and walking back to the squadron after eight fights of that intensity. There was a security line on the pavement we weren't to cross except at certain spots and I just walked right over it without any idea, due to my daze. After describing this over the phone, my mom reminded me how amazing adrenaline can be.

After six flights, my new helmet came in. $120,000 of American taxpayer kindness now fitted on my head each flight. It was an amazing piece of technology but I would probably go without it and take the $120K instead. I sat through a two-hour fitting last weekend in preparation for the flight. It was made specifically for me. The helmet connected to the jet's avionics systems and projected an image onto the visor, for me to see pertinent information. I could guide missile-cuing with the swing of my head or see targets around the ground with a superimposed triangle over the spot in my visor. The technology was truly amazing.

Two weeks ago, I fulfilled a lifelong dream of dropping bombs on the state of Kansas. Our primary bomb-dropping range was near Salina, KS and it made me so happy, thinking about my collegiate past going to the University of Missouri and the tremendous rivalry between the two schools.

I also had my first low level in eight months. 500 feet above the sand hills of Nebraska at 500 knots was a wonderful time until my flight lead took a bird to the nose of the plane and blood splattered all over his windshield. It wasn't a big deal but a foot or two lower and it would have gone down the engine, possibly creating an ejection situation. A foot or two higher and it would break through the canopy, an even worse situation. On this same flight a farmer called our squadron complaining about how low we were. He claimed we were so low he could see the whites of our eyes. Knowing we hadn't broken any rules, this made me chuckle with happiness.

Finally, I signed up for the Big Brothers, Big Sisters Program and took my little brother, Tom, out one Saturday night to watch the jets take off. I was able to get us about 50 feet from the runway as the ~30-foot flame of freedom roared by. We watched six jets blast by and Tom, 13, made the following comment, "I thought this was going to be cool but I wasn't prepared for this. This was the coolest thing I have ever done in my life." I think Tom and I are off to good start.

THE SOUTH DAKOTA TAILS LINED UP

Mission Qualified

I was sworn into the military a little over four years ago. For four years, I had essentially been a liability. The Air Force threw millions of dollars into my training, yielding nothing until now. On Friday, June 13th 2014 I passed my mission qualification check ride, which meant they could send me into combat. It was arguably the most fun and fulfilling flight of my life, considering its meaning and how well it went.

The flight prior, a warm-up for the check ride, had not gone well. I had missed the target with one of my bombs and was shot down. I didn't have a lot of momentum going in to the check ride with our Squadron Commander, but off we went. I was #2 and Hawk, my counterpart throughout the journey was #4, flying on a beautiful Friday the 13th afternoon. I bought cigars the night before and handed one to Hawk as we were putting our gear on. It was a ride we called opposed surface attack. There would be red air—hostile airplanes—trying to keep us from moving forward and dropping bombs on targets we had specifically planned to attack. The jets in South Dakota also had the ability to see surface-to-air missile sites radiating their radar energy and we expected to see numerous

SA-2, SA-3 and SA-6s in the battlefield on this day. We each had two 2,000 lb GPS-guided bombs along with radar and heat-seeking missiles. Even after we had killed the red air, there were simulated airfields they could scramble from and keep re-attacking, causing us more problems. After we began our run to the target, the hostile jets began their attacks and after a while, we killed them all.

Our four ship was now running to the target when a surface-to-air missile (SAM) came online and began targeting #1, the Squadron Commander. Since I was his wingman, it was my job to support and I began frantically searching for this missile site. (For training we used grain silos as simulated missile sites.) One sensor on my jet was telling my camera the approximate location and then I began guiding the camera around with a button on the throttle, looking for a grain silo. I found it and enthusiastically let him know, lit the afterburner and pointed towards the silo, accelerating and climbing so I could lob a bomb toward it and get the hell away. Even though it was not targeting me, there was nothing saying it wouldn't stop looking at #1 and shoot at me instead. I throttled back at .97 Mach as I couldn't go supersonic in this airspace due to noise restrictions, and at almost 30,000 feet, released the bomb, lobbing it miles from the target. The G-limit on the plane with bombs was 5.5 so I pulled 5 during my turn to get away from the SAMs reach and find #1, who was maneuvering to defeat the SAM heading his way. We got back together as #3 and #4 dropped their bombs on targets in this small town in Iowa. I ran in and dropped my other bomb on an additional target, just as #1 was targeted again by another SAM. He started evading as I climbed to get out of his way and get a great view of the action. I watched as this F-16 was rolling around and turning back and forth, supporting in any way I could.

Eventually he simulated getting hit and having to fly very slowly to make it back to "good guy land." I now had to protect him and enemy fighters were taking off from enemy airfields. #3 and #4 were busy attacking one of them when I picked up a low radar contact. The controlling agency wasn't talking about him because he was below their coverage but I couldn't shoot him until I saw him—per the rules of engagement. I used my targeting pod, the high-powered camera on the jet, to see him from miles away and shot, just as he shot at my flight lead. Fortunately, due to the type of missiles being used, mine hit him first, rendering his missile useless. We continued to run home and moments later the Squadron Commander announced the fight was over. Knowing it had gone well, I pulled my nose up twenty degrees and performed a couple aileron rolls in celebration.

The debrief went well and the Commander concluded with his congratulations. He extended his right hand, saying, "You are ready for war."

AFTERWORD

CHOP

It is now October of 2014 and barring some unforeseen "hostile renaming," I shall forever be known as CHOP, my new and permanent callsign. It was a great evening at our Squadron Commander's hangar, which was the ultimate fighter pilot man-cave. Hawk and I provided gifts of piñatas of a Fox and a Hawk, cigars, food, alcohol and a cell phone-holding device with F-16 parts for the squadron. They told stories of things we'd messed up while flying and tried to make fun of our personal lives, all to create ideas for a potential name. It was hilarious. As I have written, relieving thyself (peeing) in the jet is not easy and it is in reference to one of these attempts gone awry on a longer flight down to the bombing range. For perspective, I walked straight from the jet to my car after the flight so I could shower at home before returning to debrief the mission. The C, H, and O stand for Can't Handle Own….

Just this past week we had a trip to fight the F-16s up in Duluth, MN. It was the first time I had ever landed the F-16 at a place different from the one I took off. We flew there as a five ship and dropped into a low level around the northern Minnesota countryside near Lake Superior. It was lucky timing as the fall color was in full force. At 600 mph and 500 feet, it was a glorious thirty minutes flying over the lakes and trees. We flew each day in a 12-jet war which was more than we normally got to train with. The airspace was half over land and half over Lake Superior, which was a refreshing change of landscape. While the lake is beautiful and enticing, they warned us not to fly too far out over the water—an ejection would be fatal if you ended up landing in the cold water.

Back home, the flying was so great I was afraid my life had peaked one week. It was a three-day week and I flew five times. Thursday, I flew with the newest flight lead in the squadron, a guy who I hung out with some on the weekends. It was the first time I really felt like it was just me and a buddy going out to play in F-16s. Further, we got a tanker to refuel in the morning and flew again in the afternoon so we managed three dogfighting flights in one day. I got my first inverted guns kill, as, in one of his maneuvers to defend himself, he went straight up into a loop and I was able to attack while we were both upside down. It was one of the wildest things I have done, shooting a plane just a thousand feet away, each very slow, upside down. We also fought a couple times with no restrictions, just F-16 v. F-16. In one of those, after he had become slow and couldn't do much, I applied full afterburner and went straight up. After getting 5000 feet above him, I rolled back over and attacked pointing straight down at him and the ground. If I missed the shot, I would accelerate out in front of him and end up getting shot. It was too much fun.

Red Flag

I spent three weeks in Las Vegas for the largest air combat training exercise in the world, Red Flag. I was one of the lucky eight to fly a jet out from South Dakota. We air-to-air refueled twice as a six ship and got an aerial tour of the airspace we would fight in the next three weeks. The airspace surrounded Area 51 which had a runway. However, even if my engine flamed out, I would have to ask permission to try and land there. They might essentially say "we would rather lose a $40 million jet" because they didn't want a person, even with a top secret clearance, to see what was going on there. Wild.

Besides combat, Red Flag is the Super Bowl of the fighter pilot world. It is generally a warm-up before a deployment and they make it difficult. As we landed in Vegas fighter jets of all kinds, including foreign jets, were all over the sky. During my landing rollout, I looked up and saw the entire Thunderbird formation fly over me and break to land. It was ten degrees outside in South Dakota when I took off and a pleasant 75 degrees when I raised the canopy in Vegas, with a buddy climbing the ladder to hand me a beer while still sitting in the cockpit. Not bad.

I flew the night shift for the first two weeks. I would go to work at 6 PM and leave work around 6 AM. There were typically over 100 jets in the sky for each fight and we had 29 fights. That's a lot of jet fuel.
Our squadron hadn't flown much lately due to weather in South Dakota and I had not flown a night flight in over four months so I was a little

anxious about the first flight. It happened to be raining and as our four ship launched, we quickly climbed into the clouds. With rain pouring down, I entered the clouds, my first time flying in a mountain environment in over a year and I immediately got a flashing X on all my screens with Bitching Betty telling me to "Pull up! Pull up." It honestly scared the hell out of me. I have always heard guys die in moments like this because they didn't see it coming. I remember thinking, is this how it ends? Plowing into the side of a mountain for no reason. I gave everything a quick scan so I knew which way was up, threw more power in and pulled back on the stick. Turned out that the warning altitude, which is normally set for just 100 feet, was set at 9,000 feet so I needed to pull up to get above 9,000 feet instead of 100 feet. Regardless, my heart lost three years off its life.

During the same flight, I got an engine malfunction notice and we had to return, quickly. It was not too serious but in a single engine plane, you must be overly cautious. The rain had intensified and I was the fourth to land of our four ship, with all of the fire trucks waiting and eighty aircraft landing behind us. On a runway with that much activity in a desert where it hardly rains, water on rubber is not a great combination. #1 landed and radios back that it's really slick. #2 said, "Holy shit, it's like landing on an ice skating rink" #3 told us afterward he almost put his hook down to grab the cable at the end of the runway to prevent him from sliding off. I heard all of this and for the third time this flight, I was nervous. I touched down as slowly as I could without hitting my tail on the runway and within the first 200 feet of the 10k-foot runway. I slid for 7,000 feet before finally getting to a taxi speed. We all had a drink after that flight.

Every day there were different missions and I could write for days about some of the stuff that went on but we dropped live bombs, dumb bombs and GPS-guided bombs multiple times. We were shot at by surface-to-air missiles (SAMs) every flight and were assessed on whether we had died or not. They even shot smoke trails up at us so it appeared as though we were being shot at.

The highlights of the trip were my two low level flights, the first of which I described to open the book. The second low level was during the day. Night was awesome but very intense. The daylight made things a lot easier for obvious reasons and I was paired with one of my better buddies so we had a great time. I remember playing video games as a kid and being less aggressive than I was on this day. At one point we were a little behind schedule so we pushed it up to over 700 mph just 500 feet off the desert floor, going through mountain passes. We did this in Phoenix but the mountains were bigger out here and I didn't have a grade sheet to worry about. We raged for 20 minutes and 4 miles from the target, lit the afterburner, popped up 6,000 feet, rolled in and dropped our bombs on a building and then hit the deck again, hiding amongst the mountains to get home. We were never targeted on this flight. I said afterward if my final flight in the F-16 could be like that I would be pretty happy.

On the flight where we dropped GPS-guided bombs, we got attacked by numerous SAMs so we were trying to avoid getting shot while I used the targeting pod to identify the building I was supposed to hit—I needed to tell the bomb where to go. I found it, shot the laser and dropped the bomb. I felt the jet shudder as it was now 500 lbs lighter on one wing, and rolled my wing up to watch it fall away from my jet. That sight didn't get old. I then looked forward to my flight lead and saw his bomb fall away from his jet. My bomb missed the spot I wanted by 6 feet. Not bad.

As the F-16, our main role in this exercise was dropping bombs. There were other jets like the F-15, F-22 and Eurofighter specializing in air-to-air fighting. We could do it all too but they had better radars, making them more capable. Leading up to the last day of Red Flag, yesterday, I had shot around six missiles at other jets but all had either already been killed by the time mine got there or the enemy turned away and defeated it. I was frustrated. Again, it didn't really matter but it was fun to get air-to-air kills. Poetically, I finally got my chance in the last five minutes of the entire Red Flag exercise and shot down three jets. A great way to end a fun, but tiring, exercise.

ABOUT TO TAXI OUT FOR MY LAST RED FLAG SORTIE

Transition

Even through Red Flag, I was still torn about whether to try and stay full time with the South Dakota Air National Guard or go part time and get a job in the local area. Naturally, life happens and it appeared neither of those were going to happen.

With three days left in Red Flag, I got an email asking if anyone had interest in applying for a job flying the F-22 at Tyndall AFB in Panama City, Florida in the Reserves. Being a person always looking for opportunities, of course I was interested. I asked one of my South Dakota bosses if this was even ok to explore and he agreed—in my shoes, he would look into it.

I traveled down to Panama City during spring break as a newly promoted Captain. There was a get-together in the squadron bar on Friday night, a tour of the facility and I watched a fight debrief on Saturday. Saturday night was a party at the Squadron Commander's house and then a simulator ride Sunday morning followed by the formal interview. The F-22 is the world's premier air-to-air fighter jet and the simulator was almost overwhelming for me to experience. As a stealth fighter, its capabilities compared to the F-16 are staggering. Thrust vectoring, more power, stealth and vastly superior avionics puts this jet in a class of its own. While it can also drop bombs, those capabilities are limited.

The interview seemed to go well and I left for the spring break beach of Panama City to enjoy some sun and libations. About eight hours later, I happened to walk back in the beach house to my phone ringing with a Florida area code. "*Hey Chop, we want to know if you want to be a Raptor driver with the Kats?*" Carefully choosing my words, I excitedly accepted and spent the evening celebrating on the beach.

I would still go on a deployment to Korea with South Dakota the summer of 2015 but that would be the end of my Viper career. I would miss many things about the F-16. Close Air Support with troops on the ground, low levels and all of the various bomb-dropping we did, but this should be a great move. The F-22 provides not only amazing flying, it is a far more select group of pilots flying these jets since, at $170 million a pop, we simply didn't make that many. It's the only jet solely flown by Americans and not exported to any other country. It's the premier air-to-air fighter jet the world has ever built and I was humbled to have the opportunity to take her for a spin.

OUR FOUR SHIP OF LOBO F-16S AFTER GETTING GAS FROM THE TANKER ON THE WAY TO KOREA

The Raptor

At 8:04 AM on December 21st, 2015, I pushed up the throttles on an F-22, commanding 70,000 lbs of thrust and roared down the runway. As the world's most advanced air to air fighter jet, the avionics and performance upgrade from the F-16 in the aerial combat world is eye watering. Imagine walking down the street with people on both sides of the road trying to shoot at you. In the F-16, they know you're coming, you have 20/400 vision and you can only jog. In the F-22, they don't know you're coming and might not know you're there until you standing right behind them, you have 20/20 vision and you can sprint.

It is the only jet in the American arsenal with thrust vectoring and it is a wild sensation. It defies some basic rules of flying most of us expect. It is a dramatic decrease in G, a slipping from under a skateboard type feeling and the cockpit gets loud as the air separates from around the canopy. In the F-16, we had almost no control of the jet at 120-130 knots while we were fighting. In this jet, I can move the nose around at 50 or 60 knots and it weighs twice as much. It's also a jet I can cruise above the Mach without using afterburner and climb high enough to see the curvature of the earth and black of the sky looking up.

As I finalize this book in the fall of 2016, it has been a whirlwind first eleven months in the Raptor. I finished the transition course in February and was mission qualified the next month. Sean Schiess, the guy who had to become an instructor out of UPT, has poetically moved onto the F-22 and realized his dream. Just six months later I was starting the flight lead upgrade program and in my first ride, I led a 2 ship of Raptors, with four F-16s led by Jeff Witt, just a month after being in his wedding. We have come a long way as the two of us lead our 6 fighter jets against 20+ enemy bandits.

We deployed to England in the spring to "reassure and train with our NATO allies" and "deter Russian aggression." Britain has a large population of plane spotters and were obsessed with our trip. One guy climbed a mountain every day for two weeks in hopes an F-22 would fly down this valley. We did only once but he got his picture. He called it the greatest day in his life.

The flying in England was awesome and I was able to share an office with Derek Olivares for a month, my good buddy from UPT flying the F-15E. I was able to dogfight the British Typhoon fighter and the F-15E along with the F-22. There were also large exercises everyday with often more than 30 jets in the fight over the North Sea.

One day I was scheduled to be the bad guy, red air, in a two versus one visual dogfight with two F-15Es. Often regarded as the best job in the Air Force, being the bad guy is even better in an F-22. The two of them would try to kill me and, since my stealth advantage is gone in this type of fight, they should be able to since there are two of them. While I am picking on one of them, the other can shoot me. It was one of those epic days over the English countryside in the sunlight but with towering cumulus clouds to fight around. We would pass at over 900 knots of closure and then violently turn toward each other in an attempt to get behind the other to shoot with a missile, or even more preferred, the gun. Twice, I was able to guns kill both of them before they could kill me. I am genuinely not very good or experienced at dogfighting in the F-22 so this is meant to be a brag on the jet and not me. Being in the F-22 felt like I was playing a video game with a cheat code. At one point, I was gunning one of the F-15Es at 1200' (feels really close) in front of me when I noticed his buddy sneaking up behind me to gun me. I call the first one dead over the radio and then execute a turn only the F-22 can that basically spins it in place and puts me behind him. He went from almost killing me to being shot with my gun in 15 seconds. My entire jet was covered in a vapor cloud and we were only about 700' apart, staring at each other through our canopies as I spun around his jet. It is a moment I will remember decades from now.

The other great memory was my last flight in England. It was supposed to be an 8 versus 10 and the bad guys can regenerate three times after they die. Four of our jets broke so it was just me and another F-22 escorting F-15Es to bomb the target against all of those jets. It was another beautiful day and at times I was above 50,000' doing Mach 1.5, while at others, I was skimming the ocean at 1,000' during the fight. I shot all eight of my missiles and 400 bullets. My last radio call of the trip was calling a guns kill on an F-15 in this large battle, something I never did in two years in the F-16. There were streaks of contrails like we see from commercial jets flying over wrapped up in fights all over the sky. I had never seen anything like it. As my wingman and I were flying back to base talking about how awesome that was, the English coast came into sight. I couldn't help but think how refreshing that site must have been seventy years ago to the P-51 coming home from a similarly intense fight…with real bullets.

TAKEOFF OF MY FIRST FLIGHT IN THE F-22A RAPTOR

PHOTO CREDIT: BILL FAUTH

Final Thoughts

The journey from civilian to fighter pilot will undoubtedly be the best years of my life. I was able to experience things most can only dream about. Getting to fly these jets is actually better than expected, and I set my expectations high. Flying at 600 mph through the mountains of Nevada or Korea in the day or night, dogfighting just 500 feet away from another one of these amazing machines, seeing the curvature of the earth at 60,000', I could reminisce for hours but that is what this book was for. While the stories are great, the guys I flew, trained and partied with will be a part of the rest of my life. It is an exceptionally talented, intelligent and fun group of people to get to work with every day. There was stress and a lot of hard work but I would recommend the journey to anyone who asks.

LESSONS LEARNED AND LOCATION IN BOOK

IFS
The Power Curve

UPT
Week 1: Tradition and Heritage
Week 6: Enjoy the Ride
Week 7: Luck
Week 9: Critical Self Evaluation
Week 10: Habit Patterns
Week 11: Ignorance is Bliss?
Week 12: Proficiency Advance
Week 13: Do What You Love
Week 14: Setbacks
Week 20: Camaraderie
Week 22: Trust
Week 23: Spice
Week 27: Being a Bro
Week 28: Stand Up for Your People
Week 29: Always be Personable
Week 30: Popularity
Week 34: Consistency
Week 35: Respectfully Object
Week 38: Never Blame Others for Your Mistakes
Week 41: Instructing
Week 48: Push the Envelope
Week 49: The Little Things
Week 54: Life is Not Fair
Week 55: Celebrate

IFF
Week 5: Man up
Week 6: Lose Sight, Lose Fight
Gradation: Different perspective

Post IFF
It is about who

B course
Viper Mecca: I can
Week 6: Reflect on Accomplishments
Week 12: Fortunate accidents
Week 13: Emergencies
Week 16: Focus
Week20: Because we always have
Week 21: Help
Week 27: Recognition
Week 28: Disciplined Followership
Week 33: Mission Planning Cycle

GLOSSARY

AB – Afterburner

ACM – Air or Advanced Combat Maneuvering. A complex fight involving multiple aircraft at close ranges.

AF – Air Force

AFB – Air Force Base

AETC – Air Education and Training Command. The Air Force Command in charge of most training.

Aileron Roll – a maneuver where a plane does a full 360° revolution around its longitudinal axis. There is little change in altitude and the aircraft ends the maneuver on the same heading as it entered.

Afterburner – a component on some jet engines, mostly military supersonic aircraft. Its purpose is to provide an increase in thrust, usually for supersonic flight, takeoff and for combat situations. Afterburning is achieved by injecting additional fuel into the jet pipe downstream of (i.e. *after*) the turbine.

ANG – Air National Guard

AWACS – airborne warning and control. Derived from the Boeing 707, it provides all-weather surveillance, command, control, and communications, and is used by the United States Air Force, NATO, the Royal Air Force, the French Air Force, and the Royal Saudi Air Force.

Barrel Roll – a maneuver in which an airplane makes a complete rotation on both its longitudinal and lateral axes. It can be described as a combination of a loop and a roll.

B-Course – Basic Course. The basic course to learn to fly a fighter jet, in this case, the F-16.

BFM – Basic Fighter Maneuvers. Often associated with dogfighting.

Bingo Fuel – Bingo fuel is the predetermined fuel level at which the pilot will terminate the mission and return to base with normal reserves.

Bogeys – unidentified aircraft

BVR – Beyond Visual Range. Usually associated with a longer-range missile.

Call Sign – A nickname given to a pilot or the various name Air Traffic Control uses to identify a military aircraft formations.

CAP – Commander's Awareness Program. Program designed for struggling students to fly with certain IPs and with more consistency.

CAS – Close Air Support. Air attack against hostile targets that are in close proximity to friendly forces.

Cuban Eight – an aerobatic maneuver with multiple loops and course reversals. From the side, grandstand view, it should look as though the airplane is drawing a horizontal eight in the sky.

DCA – Defensive Counter Air

Double turn – Fly or go on a simulator mission twice in one day

ENJJPT – Euro-Nato Joint Jet Pilot Training. An international presence of students and IPs learning to fly the T-6 and T-38 over 13 months.

FAIP – First Assignment Instructor Pilot

Fingertip formation – A formation position you often see at airshows where jets are very close together, often with just a few feet of wingtip clearance.

FOD – Foreign Object Damage. Anything on the flight line, such as a rock or pencil, that could damage an airplane.

Fuge – Slang for centrifuge, the device designed for G-strain training.

Furball – A hectic situation including many dogfights or multiple airplanes, occurring at the same time within the same relatively small airspace.

G – G-Force. One G is the acceleration due to gravity at the Earth's surface.

G-LOC – Loss of consciousness due to G-forces.

HABFM – High Aspect Basic Fighter Maneuver. We start the fight with a high-speed pass pointing at each other, just as you might pass someone on the highway.

Hook – To fail a training ride

Hot Gun – A gun capable of firing actual ammunition. As opposed to a cold gun, one that can't fire and has no actual rounds.

HUD – Heads up Display. A transparent glass display presenting information regarding aircraft performance, navigation and weapons cueing.

IFF – Introduction to Fighter Fundamentals. The initial 12-16 rides learning combat maneuvering in the T-38 before moving on to an actual fighter jet.

IFS – Initial Flight Screening

ILS – Instrument Landing system. Using radio signals to precisely navigate through clouds and weather to arrive at a runway.

Immelmann – a maneuver with an ascending half-loop followed by a half-roll, resulting in level flight in the exact opposite direction at a higher altitude.

IP – Instructor Pilot

JDAM – Joint Direct Attach Munition or GPS-guided bomb

JTAC – Joint Tactical Air Controller. Qualified troop on the ground capable of calling in airstrikes.

LFE – Large Force Exercise. A large aerial event.

MOA – Military Operating Airspace

NVGs – Night vision goggles. A device allowing images to be produced in levels of light approaching total darkness. The image may be a conversion to visible light of both visible light and infrared.

OG – Operations Group

Piddle pack – Plastic bag containing a coagulating substance, which pilots use to urinate in while in the cockpit.

ROTC – Reserve Officers' Training Corps. Often associated with universities around the country to teach cadets to become officers while going non-military university.

SAMs – Surface-to-air missiles

SFO – Simulated flameout. Something single engine pilots practice in case their engine quits.

Strafe – Attacking ground targets at low altitude using the machine gun on the airplane.

Two ship – two airplanes in formation

UPT – Undergraduate Pilot Training. 13-month program to learn to fly the T-6 and T-38.

USAF – United States Air Force

About the Author

Captain Taylor Fox grew up in Springfield, Missouri before graduating with a Master's degree in Business from the University of Missouri. He went on to graduate in the top of his pilot training classes and flew the F-16 for the Air National Guard before transitioning to fly the F-22 in the Air Force Reserves.

For more information about the book visit www.combatreadypilot.com.

Acknowledgements

Putting this book together may have been more difficult than pilot training. The decisions of what to include, my mediocre ability to write and the intricacies of publishing, were at times, overwhelming. A special thanks to the following people for making it easier.

Christina Fox
Emily Fox
Eli Bozeman
Sara Jackson
Derek Olivares
Aneta Zarubova
Mackenzie Myhre
Bill Fauth

This page is for fighter pilots.

Made in the USA
Lexington, KY
13 January 2019